Karsten Harries
The Antinomy of Being

Karsten Harries

The Antinomy of Being

—

DE GRUYTER

ISBN 978-3-11-062622-3
e-ISBN (PDF) 978-3-11-062932-3
e-ISBN (EPUB) 978-3-11-062591-2

Library of Congress Control Number: 2019939354

Bibliographic information published by the Deutsche Nationalbibliothek
The Deutsche Nationalbibliothek lists this publication in the Deutsche Nationalbibliografie; detailed bibliographic data are available on the Internet at http://dnb.dnb.de.

© 2021 Walter de Gruyter GmbH, Berlin/Boston
This volume is text- and page-identical with the hardback published in 2019.
Cover image: Die wandernde Frau von Kaliningrad (mit drei Bildern) – Drew Walker (2018)
Typesetting: 3w+p GmbH, Rimpar
Printing and binding: CPI books GmbH, Leck

www.degruyter.com

For My Students

Foreword

It is an honor and a privilege to write these prefatory words to Karsten Harries's *The Antinomy of Being*. Harries is an expert in the philosophy of art and aesthetics, on the philosophy of architecture, on the work of Martin Heidegger, and also on the emergence of modernity (following on from the great historians of ideas, Ernst Cassirer, Alexandre Koyré and Hans Blumenberg). Harries has been extremely influential in American philosophy but is perhaps not as well known internationally as he should be, although many of his books have been translated into languages such as Japanese, Chinese, Korean and German. The welcome publication of his latest book, *The Antinomy of Being*, based on his graduate seminars, gives the reader a very vibrant sense of what it is like to participate in one of Harries' renowned seminars given at Yale, giving a direct experience of his unique style of questioning and interrogating a classical text for its still living significance and relevance.

Karsten Harries was Howard H. Newman Professor of Philosophy at Yale University until his retirement in 2017. He was born in Jena, Germany, in 1937, and, as a seven-year-old boy in Berlin, witnessed at first hand the catastrophic end of the Second World War. His father–a physicist –emigrated with the family to the USA, where Karsten studied at Yale University with such leading figures as Charles Hendel and Wilfrid Sellars, receiving his B.A. in 1958. He remained on at Yale University as a graduate student, receiving his Ph.D in 1962, with a dissertation entitled *In a Strange Land: An Exploration of Nihilism*, directed by George A. Schrader, a leading Kant scholar and one of the founders of the Society for Phenomenology and Existential Philosophy (SPEP).[1] Upon completion of his doctorate, Harries was appointed Assistant Professor of Philosophy at the University of Texas at Austin (1963–1965), but he returned to Yale in 1966 as Associate Professor and remained there for the rest of his teaching career. Harries was promoted to full Professor of Philosophy at Yale in 1970. He then held the Brooks and Suzanne Ragen Professor of Philosophy and, most recently, until retirement, the Howard H. Newman Professor of Philosophy. Karsten Harries has held many visiting professorships, including the University of Bonn (1965–1966; 1968–1969) and a Guggenheim fellowship (1971–1972). His publications include *The Meaning of Modern Art* (1967); *The Bavarian Rococo Church: Between Faith and Aestheti-*

---

[1] This dissertation (Yale 1962) was microfilmed by University Microfilms, Ann Arbor, Michigan in 1967 (no. 67–9640) and can be found online at https://cpb-us-w2.wpmucdn.com/campuspress.yale.edu/dist/8/1250/files/2011/10/in-a-strange-land_an-exploration-of-nihilism-1zusd5v.pdf.

cism (1983); *The Broken Frame* (1989); *The Ethical Function of Architecture* (1996); *Infinity and Perspective* (2001); *Art Matters. A Critical Commentary on Heidegger's "Origin of the Work of Art"* (2009), and *Wahrheit: Die Architektur der Welt* (2012). With Christoph Jamme, he edited *Martin Heidegger: Kunst, Politik, Technik* (1992), published in English as *Martin Heidegger: Politics, Art, and Technology* (1994).

A native German speaker, Prof. Harries is particularly known as an original interpreter of the work of Martin Heidegger, especially his later writings on art, poetry, language, and technology. Indeed, Harries was one of the select few invited by the publisher Vittorio Klostermann to contribute to Heidegger's 80th birthday *Festschrift*.[2] Professor Harries was also one of the first philosophers in the USA to challenge Martin Heidegger's intellectual relationship with National Socialism, something that became a matter of controversy in the 1970s.[3] He translated and commented critically on Heidegger's notorious Rectoral Address (*Rektoratsrede*) of 1933, where Heidegger aligned Freiburg university with the National Socialist cause.[4] Harries was also one of the first to compare critically Heidegger's and Wittgenstein's conceptions of language as providing the canopy of our world,[5] something later taken up by Richard Rorty. In opposition to Wittgenstein, Harries shows that Heidegger is a proponent of the inadequacy of everyday language and of the necessity for poetry to keep up a space for meaning. But Harries has always been inspired by Wittgenstein's concern that philosophy assist us in finding our rightful place in the world.

Harries' first monograph, *The Meaning of Modern Art* (Northwestern, 1968)[6] grappled with the question of nihilism. Nihilism is the view that the entire world has no sense, our existence has no point. It is essentially futile. Harries points out that nihilism is first named as such by Jacobi, and, for him, it arose from a certain direction in Kant and was marked by an "intoxication with self" as the poet Jean Paul Richter put it. Interestingly, Harries sees nihilism as emerging from a relentless rationalism – from the philosophy of Spinoza, for instance. A philosophy that attempts to bring everything under reason ends up in absurdity.

---

[2] Karsten Harries, "Das befreite Nichts," in *Durchblicke: Martin Heidegger zum 80. Geburtstag*, ed. Vittorio Klostermann (Frankfurt am Main: Klostermann, 1970), pp. 39–62.
[3] Karsten Harries, "Heidegger as a Political Thinker," *The Review of Metaphysics*, vol. 29, no. 4 (1976), pp. 644–669.
[4] Karsten Harries, Translation with Notes and Introduction of Martin Heidegger, The Self-Assertion of the German University and The Rectorate1933/34: Facts and Thoughts, *The Review of Metaphysics*, (March 1985), pp. 467–502.
[5] Karsten Harries, "Wittgenstein and Heidegger: The Relationship of the Philosopher to Language," *The Journal of Value Inquiry*, vol. 2, no. 4 (1968), pp. 281–291.
[6] Karsten Harries, *The Meaning of Modern Art: A Philosophical Interpretation* (Evanston: Northwestern University Press, 1968).

Harries returned to the theme of nihilism in his essay, *Between Nihilism and Faith: A Commentary on Kierkegaard's Either/Or* (2010).[7] Since his very first book, *The Meaning of Modern Art*, Harries has been particularly interested in Heidegger's reflections on the meaning and status of art in modern times and especially in the current age dominated by technology. His central question is: does art still speak to us today? Or, has art, as Hegel put it, lost its highest function? Are we truly in an age of nihilism? Is it a medium for truth or merely for pleasure or distraction? If art still functions meaningfully for us as more than mere distraction or ornamentation—how does it do so?

Since the 1980s, Harries has been one of the leading figures in the emerging discipline of the philosophy of architecture. Harries has always been deeply interested in the relation between the sacred and profane, between the religious and the secular world view, the tension between mortals and gods, to invoke the terms of Heidegger's "fourfold". For thousands of years since the Greeks, Western culture has lived in a sacred space but now, as Hölderlin put it, the gods have fled. Nietzsche exclaimed that no new god had appeared in the last two thousand years. Our culture – especially with the dominance of scientific knowledge and technology – seems resolutely secular. Does this secular culture still leave room for a relationship with the transcendent – with what Kant called "the starry heavens above me"? Harries addresses these issues in his collection of essays, *The Broken Frame*.[8] Heidegger's reflections on the Greek temple in his magisterial essays "The Origin of the Work of Art", and "Building, Dwelling, Thinking", on the nature of "dwelling" (*Wohnen*) have inspired Harries' own excursus into the philosophy of architecture. His second book, *The Bavarian Rococo Church*, published in 1983 (and, more recently, in 2009 published in German as *Die Bayerische Rokokokirche. Das Irrationale und das Sakrale*),[9] quickly led to Harries being recognized as a leading expert on German regional Church architecture, specifically in the age of Rococo. Here his question was – what separates the age of Baroque and Rococo, an age of faith from the age of Enlightenment, with its obsessive commitment to rationalism? He is now recognized as one of the world's foremost theorists of contemporary architectural theory, especially since the publication of his ground-breaking third monograph, *The Ethical Func-*

---

[7] Karsten Harries, *Between Nihilism and Faith: A Commentary on Either/Or* (Berlin and New York: DeGruyter, 2010).

[8] Karsten Harries, *The Broken Frame. Three Lectures* (Washington: Catholic University Press, 1989).

[9] Karsten Harries, *The Bavarian Rococo Church: Between Faith and Aestheticism* (New Haven: Yale University Press, 1983). The reworked and expanded German edition is Karsten Harries, *Die Bayerische Rokokokirche. Das Irrationale und das Sakrale* (Dorfen: Hawel, 2009).

tion of Architecture, in 1997.¹⁰ For Harries, the central and profound question is: what separates architecture from mere building? For Harries, as for Heidegger, architecture is opposed to ornamental representation. Professor Harries has close intellectual collaborations with internationally renowned architects including Kevin Roche. In 2007, the School of Architecture of Yale University recognized Harries' work in this area by awarding him the degree of Master of Environmental Design. He has a dedicated *Festschrift* in his honor, *Himmel und Erde: Festschrift für Karsten Harries*, "Heaven and Earth: Festschrift to Honor Karsten Harries," a special issue of *International Journal of Architectural Theory* in 2007.¹¹ In 2013 he was awarded an honorary Doctorate of Literature by University College Dublin.

Harries' fourth monograph, *Infinity and Perspective*,¹² is a sustained reflection on the limits of human existence in the modern world through an exploration of the tension between finitude and infinity, immanence and transcendence. It is inspired by the early modern philosopher and theologian Nicholas of Cusa's meditations on the unspeakable transcendence of the infinite deity which is nevertheless reflected and refracted in the various perspectives one can take on the deity, just as there are infinite radii in a circle. For Harries, one could just as well mark the emergence of modernity with the work of Nicholas of Cusa (or Renaissance scholar of art and perspective, Alberti) instead of the more customary figure of René Descartes.¹³

Karsten Harries lectured for many decades at Yale University – 54 years in total. He has the distinction of directing the most doctoral students in Philosophy in the USA – a grand total of 63 dissertations (the present author's included!). On April 28th and Saturday, April 29th, 2017, the Philosophy Department of Yale University held a two-day seminar, *Truth and Beauty: A Conference in Honor of Karsten Harries*, attended by his colleagues and by many of his former students. Besides being a renowned philosopher and expert in architectural

---

10 Karsten Harries, *The Ethical Function of Architecture* (Cambridge, Mass.: MIT Press, 1997). The Chinese translation appeared in 2001 (Beijing: Hua Xia Publishing House, 2001).
11 See Special issue, "Heaven and Earth: Festschrift to Honor Karsten Harries," *International Journal of Architectural Theory* 12 no. 1 (August 2007).
12 Karsten Harries, *Infinity and Perspective* (Cambridge, Mass.: MIT Press, 2001). Susan E. Schreiner, *Are You Alone Wise? The Search for Certainty in the Modern Era* (Oxford: OUP, 2011) is appreciative of Harries' analysis of the discovery of perspective in early modernity for its impact on the theological understanding of infinity and the finitude of the human place in the world.
13 Karsten, Harries, "Problems of the Infinite: Cusanus and Descartes," *American Catholic Philosophical Quarterly* (Winter 1989), pp. 89–110.

theory, he is an accomplished artist working with pastels and oil paintings and recently had an exhibition of his work at the Yale Whitney Humanities Center. For Karsten, art is the concrete complement to the abstractness of philosophy.

Karsten Harries' lectures and seminars have enthralled and challenged generations of students at Yale. His lectures and seminars have been appreciared by his students as models of the rigorous interrogation of classical texts for their enduring relevance. Harries regards philosophy as an essentially ethical reflection – it demands that all forms of knowledge, including contemporary scientific knowledge, give an account of their own meaningfulness. What is the human place in this amazing non-human world? Kant and Heidegger asked this profound question in their own unique ways.

The current book is one such lecture course. In *The Antinomy of Being* Harries meditates on the central problematic of Kant but through the lens of Martin Heidegger. The central dilemma or antinomy of the human condition is that humans have a sense of a transcendence that they can never articulate coherently; they are somehow in touch with reality as it is in itself, while at the same time they dwell in a world of appearances. The objective world is what is experienced by us, but we are condemned to experience it in our conditioned human way. Yet, as soon as we come to the realization that what we experience is precisely the world as constituted by our embodied and embedded human existence, then somehow we have already transcended this limitation and grasp the way things really are. To see a perspective and to be able to identify it *as a perspective* is already to occupy an a-perspectival stance or a transcendent position above that perspective itself.[14] Or, as Kant and Hegel knew, to identify a limit is already to have transgressed that limit. Our experience of living a life, then, already puts us in touch with a transcendence that is at the very ground of our being. This is the nub of Karsten Harries' argument. The very recognition of the antinomy of being, of the ambiguity of our human knowledge that straddles finitude and transcendence, puts in question the very idea of an entirely objective body of scientific knowledge. Harries claims we can experience a genuine 'window' which invites us to leave our own limited view behind when we truly encounter another person as a person, as a unique source of value.

Kant, of course, is responsible for the theme of antinomy. But Harries claims that the notion of antinomy – this time under the name "the ontological difference" also permeates the work of Martin Heidegger. The very title of Heidegger's

---

14 See Karsten Harries, "On the Power and Poverty of Perspective: Cusanus and Alberti," *Cusanus: The Legacy of Learned Ignorance*, ed. Peter Casarella (Washington, DC: Catholic University of America Press, 2006), pp. 105–126.

main work, *Being and Time*, calls attention to the fact that being has always been in an inextricable relation with time and temporality. Despite the efforts of Plato and others to posit the idea of an eternal, timeless realm of true being, human existence is intrinsically temporal, historical, conditioned, limited, finite, fragmentary and fragile. From the outset of his philosophical reflections, Harries has grappled with the idea that humans seek to impose meaning on their existential situation and to exert control over their lives, and at the same time live in conditions they do not control and can never surmount. Heidegger himself is struggling with this issue in relation to the disclosure of Being. On the one hand, Being is disclosed and in and through human Dasein, as Heidegger affirms; and, even in the *Letter of Humanism*, Heidegger states that Being is only as long as Dasein is. On the other hand, Being's truth and meaning cannot be solely dependent on human Dasein; and Being, as the condition of all beings, is other than those beings. In short, Being transcends beings; it is the 'there' (*Da*) of beings; but, as such, it also transcends language, even though, as Heidegger maintains, language expresses the intelligibility both of the world and of *Dasein*'s being-in-the-world. Beings, moreover, are independent of *Dasein*. There were beings in the world before *Dasein* existed.

Harries sees Heidegger as recognizing the same challenge as Wittgenstein – how do we escape the language which forms our world? How do we avoid being imprisoned in language? Wittgenstein in the *Tractatus* recognized the limits of both logic and language. For Wittgenstein, the sense of the world has to lie outside the world, in transcendence. Language, for Heidegger, is the house of Being, but it can also be the prison-house of human being. Harries explores this architectural metaphor – language as home, as house, but also language as the conceptual frame, even a prison.

Harries' meditation on the antinomy of being and of language is rich and many-sided and also fascinating and compelling. Harries forces us to rethink our intuitions about contemporary scientific culture, with its commitment to rationalism and explanatory closure. He is showing that the drive for metaphysics and for scientific objectivity, for a complete theory of everything always exposes the antinomy that there is another side to this rationality, an unarticulable transcendent ground. Philosophers since Kant have grappled with these antinomies. But the tension has a deeper source in modernity. On the one hand, Harries is inspired by the Christian Neoplatonic mystical tradition of Eckhart and Cusanus to enter into and engage more deeply with this dialectic – between what can be said and what resists all saying. He is deeply aware that Heidegger too was inspired by Eckhart, and even, at one stage, planned to write a book on him. On the other hand, Harries recognizes that a very special shift took place in modernity – a conceptual shift that was noticed by everyone from Nietzsche and Husserl to Ernst Cassirer,[15] Alexandre Koyré,[16] and Hans Blumenberg.[17] Somehow, the project to liberate human beings from the grip of a limiting anthropocentric worldview led to the opposite extreme, dislocating human beings entirely from their home in the world. Is the price of technological culture that human beings will be permanently adrift and alienated from their home?

In the *Antinomy of Being* Harries offers us a rich meditation on the question of the home and homelessness of human being in its embodied and embedded historically conditioned existence. Harries is aware that the Kantian bifurcation of appearance and reality led to a 'thing-in-itself' which is both necessary and impossible to grasp. This tension is equally present in Husserlian phenomenology's attempt to ground all "sense and being" (*Sinn und Sein*). In fact, all science, as Schopenhauer and Nietzsche both knew, is an attempt to inscribe reality within some kind of closed and complete order of concepts, principles and rules.

Harries' book is a work of original philosophizing. It is a work of deep and serious questioning yet it is written in a conversational style without heavy technical jargon. Harries' range of reference is also extraordinarily wide – from Plato to Aquinas to Nietzsche, and ranging across poets from Hölderlin to Hugo von Hofmannsthal and Trakl, to the mystics, such as Meister Eckhart and Nicholas of Cusa. Harries is forcing the reader to think about the nature of modernity. Where do we stand today? He is following on from the great thinkers – including Nietzsche and Heidegger – who have questioned our modern culture seeking its significance and its truth. Harries is struck deeply by the deep human desire for truth – especially as it manifests itself in the desire for control and mastery over the universe and everything. As Harries writes: "The philosopher, possessed by the pathos of truth, does indeed look a lot like Goethe's Mephistopheles." This book has a very deep meditation on the nature of truth, working primarily with Heidegger's notion of truth as disclosure against the more traditional known of truth as adequacy to reality. Harries discusses not just Heidegger and his critic Ernst Tugendhat, but also Nietzsche's challenging assertion that

---

15 Ernst Cassirer, *Individuum und Kosmos in der Philosophie der Renaissance* (1927), trans. *The Individual and the Cosmos in Renaissance Philosophy* (Oxford: Basil Blackwell, 1963).
16 Alexandre Koyré, *From the Closed World to the Infinite Universe* (Baltimore, MD: Johns Hopkins Press, 1957).
17 Hans Blumenberg, *The Legitimacy of the Modern Age*, trans. Robert M. Wallace Cambridge, MA: MIT Press, 1985); and his *The Genesis of the Copernican World*, trans. Robert M. Wallace (Cambridge, MA: MIT Press, 1987). See Karsten Harries, "Copernican Reflections," review of Hans Blumenberg, *Die Genesis der kopernikanischen Welt*, Inquiry, vol. 23, 1980, pp. 253–269. See also Elizabeth Brient, *The Immanence of the Infinite: Hans Blumenberg and the Threshold to Modernity* (Washington, DC: Catholic University of America Press, 2002).

truth is really a series of metaphors and illusions that have been forgotten as such, coins that have been effaced. For Nietzsche, humans have an irrepressible drive to generate metaphors but they end up living within them as prisons impeding their ability to see beyond the scope of these dead metaphors. Humans live in a "columbarium of concepts" (*Kolumbarium der Begriffe*). To break out of the prisonhouse of language and of concepts, one has to go beyond everyday language. One has to experience transcendence in art and most especially in the human person. The person is always more than the subject who is contrasted with the objective order. Harries' discussion on the transcendent nature of persons and his return to the personalistic language (found in Kant, Scheler and Stein) is an interesting contrast to the post-personalist language of Heidegger in his discussion of Dasein. But it is in the notion of the person that Harries' work comes together.[18] Harries boldly challenges the modern technological outlook. He writes: "science cannot know anything of persons as persons." The person (and the loss of the person) is the focal point for his engagement with art, architecture, poetry, modernity, and indeed part of his struggle with Kant. Kant demands we treat persons as ends in themselves but does not give a theoretical account of how we recognize persons as persons. Persons function in a different space from that of the material universe. As Harries puts it, with reference to Wittgenstein, "The subject, the person, has always already fallen out of this picture." Harries turns to Kierkegaard for the recognition of the person in his or her pure subjectivity. Persons occupy first-personal stances or perspectives on the world. These perspectives are ineliminable even as one tries for an a-perspectival 'objective' view of things. In a way, Harries' claim is that art and architecture as well as philosophy have to make space for persons. This is surely a thought worth pursuing.

Dermot Moran (Boston College and University College Dublin)

---

[18] See, for instance, Karsten Harries, "The Ethical Significance of Environmental Beauty," *Architecture, Ethics, and the Personhood of Place*, ed. Gregory Caicco (Hanover and London: University Press of New England, 2007), pp. 134–150.

Contents

Abbreviations —— XIX

Preface —— XXI

Introduction —— 1

I	**The Antinomy of Being** —— 13	
1	The Antinomy of Being —— 13	
2	Word and Thing —— 17	
II	**The Antinomy of Truth** —— 24	
1	The Ill Will Against Language —— 24	
2	Truth and Thing in Itself —— 27	
3	The Truth of Phenomena —— 30	
4	Truth as Disclosure —— 35	
5	The Antinomy of Truth —— 46	
III	**The Architecture of Reason** —— 48	
1	Spider and Bee —— 48	
2	A Social Contract Theory of Truth —— 49	
3	Mother and Father of Our Concepts —— 55	
4	Nietzsche and Kant —— 59	
5	The Tower of Babel —— 60	
IV	**The Devil as Philosopher** —— 64	
1	Knowing Knowledge —— 64	
2	Idealism and Nihilism —— 66	
3	The Man Without a Shadow —— 72	
4	The Devil as Philosopher —— 73	
5	Science and Faith —— 75	
6	Fichte's Faith —— 77	
7	The Loss of the Shadow —— 78	
V	**The Shipwreck of Metaphysics** —— 81	
1	Introduction —— 81	
2	Time as the Ground of Being —— 81	
3	Sackgassen and Holzwege —— 85	

4		Theories of Double Truth —— 88
5		Neurath's Principle —— 90
VI	**Limits and Legitimacy of Science —— 96**	
1		The Meaninglessness of the World —— 96
2		"Only Lawful Connections are Thinkable" —— 97
3		Pictures and Models —— 100
4		Kant's Metaphysical Foundations of Natural Science —— 103
VII	**Learning from Laputa —— 110**	
1		Metaphysics and Thinking —— 110
2		The Age of God's Decomposition —— 114
3		The Goddess of Reason —— 117
4		The Whore of Babylon —— 123
5		The Two Faces of Curiosity —— 124
VIII	**Abysmal Freedom and the Antinomy of Space —— 128**	
1		Freedom and the Infinite Cosmos —— 128
2		The Freedom of Thought —— 134
3		The Antinomy of Space —— 140
4		Place and Space —— 142
5		Elusive Space —— 144
IX	**The Antinomy of Freedom —— 148**	
1		Introduction —— 148
2		Fichte: Freedom and Necessity —— 149
3		Kant: The Third Antinomy – The Thesis —— 154
4		Kant: The Third Antinomy – The Antithesis —— 157
5		The Objective Reality of Freedom —— 158
6		The Condemnation of 1277: Divine Freedom —— 160
7		The Condemnation of 1277: Human Freedom —— 162
X	**The Antinomy of Time —— 164**	
1		Kant's First Antinomy Reconsidered —— 164
2		The Sublime —— 167
3		The Time of the Everyday —— 172
4		Saving and Spending Time —— 178
XI	**The Rediscovery of the Earth —— 181**	
1		The Terror of Time and Space —— 181

2	July 20, 1969 —— **182**	
3	"The Spirit Loves Colony and Brave Forgetting" —— **187**	
4	Looking at the Stars —— **190**	
5	The Disenchanted World —— **194**	
XII	**Astronoetics —— 199**	
1	What is Astronoetics? —— **199**	
2	Loss of the Center —— **200**	
3	Postmodern Levity —— **203**	
4	Icarus —— **207**	
5	Our Unique Earth —— **208**	
6	Post-postmodern Geocentrism —— **212**	
XIII	**Conclusion: The Snake's Promise —— 216**	
1	An Old Story —— **216**	
2	Return to Myth in the Age of Technology? —— **217**	
3	Our Discontent with Technology —— **219**	
4	The Objectification of Reality —— **222**	
5	"We Have Art So We May Not Perish From The Truth" —— **226**	
6	The Art-Work of the Future —— **229**	
7	The Artist as Leader? —— **231**	
8	The Snake's Promise —— **233**	

Bibliography —— 235

Index —— 243

Abbreviations

A/B refers to the first and second editions of:
Kritik der reinen Vernunft; *The Critique of Pure Reason*, Paul Guyer, Allen W. Wood (Eds. and Trans.), (Cambridge: Cambridge University Press, 1999);
Kritik der Praktischen Vernunft; *Critique of Practical Reason*, Werner Pluhar (Trans.), (Indianapolis: Hackett, 2002);
Kritik der Urteilskraft; *Critique of Judgment*, Werner Pluhar (Trans.), (Indianapolis: Hackett, 1987).

GA Martin Heidegger *Gesamtausgabe* (Frankfurt am Main: published by Vittorio Klostermann, 1977–). When I use a translation, the page reference follows that to the volume of the *Gesamtausgabe*. I refer to the following volumes:

GA2 *Sein und Zeit* (1927); *Being and Time*, John Macquarrie and Edward Robinson (Trans.), (New York and Evanston: Harper, 1962). Since the translation includes the pagination of the 7th edition (Tübingen: Niemeyer, 1953), I also refer to that edition, abbreviated as SZ.

GA3 *Kant und das Problem der Metaphysik* (1929).

GA4 *Erläuterungen zu Hölderlins Dichtung* (1936–1973).

GA5 *Holzwege* (1935–46).

GA7 *Vorträge und Aufsätze* (1936–1953).

GA9 *Wegmarken* (1919–1958).
"Letter on Humanism," Frank A. Capuzzi and J. Glenn Gray (Trans.), *Basic Writings*, David Farrell Krell (Ed.), (New York: Harper and Row, 1977).

GA12 *Unterwegs zur Sprache* (1950–59)
On the Way to Language, Peter D. Hertz (Trans.) (New York: Harper & Row, 1971).

GA13 *Aus der Erfahrung des Denkens* (1910–1976).

GA14 *Zur Saches des Denkens* (1962–1964).
On Time and Being, Joan Stambaugh (Trans.), (New York: Harper and Row, 1972)
"The End of Philosophy and the Task of Thinking" in D. F. Krell, (Ed.), *Basic Writings* (New York: Harper Collins, 1993).

GA16 *Reden und Zeugnisse eines Lebensweges* (1910–1976).

GA24 *Die Grundprobleme der Phänomenologie* (1927).
The Basic Problems of Phenomenology, revised edition, Albert Hofstadter (Trans.), (Bloomington: University of Indiana Press, 1988).

GA52 *Hölderlins Hymne "Andenken"* (1943).

GA53 *Hölderlins Hymne "Der Ister"* (1942).

GA65 *Beiträge zur Philosophie (Vom Ereignis)* (1936–1938).

TL Friedrich Nietzsche, "On Truth and Lie in a Nonmoral Sense," in *Philosophy and Truth: Selections From Nietzsche's Notebooks of the Early 1970's*, Daniel Breazeale (Ed. and Trans.), (Atlantic Highlands: Humanities Press, 1979).

VM Johann Gottlieb Fichte, *Die Bestimmmung des Menschen* (1800). References in the text are to *The Vocation of Man*, Roderick M., Chisholm (Ed. and Intro), (New York, Liberal Arts Press, 1956).

Preface

After more than fifty years of teaching I feel a bit like an old gardener whose labors over the years have been rewarded. I am thinking of what I have written and of its reception; but even more of my students, especially of the 63 dissertations I have directed: they helped me find my own way. Directing dissertations is a bit like pruning: keep the good growth, get rid of what is not wanted. So is philosophical reflection.

I have experienced no significant tension between teaching and my own work. Interaction with students has been indispensable. With only a few exceptions my articles and books have all grown out of my teaching. That is especially true of the present book, in substance the notes for what I knew would be my final seminar, given in the spring of 2017. A dissertation by Omri Boehm, "Kant's Critique of Spinoza" (2009)[19] deserves special mention. The discussions I had with Boehm and the dissertation's co-adviser Michael della Rocca, a well-known Spinoza scholar, helped me to sharpen my understanding of what I had already come to call the Antinomy of Being, which calls into question the architecture of reason, exemplified by Spinoza's *Ethics*, and more importantly by our science. Both deserve my heartfelt thanks.

I first presented this antinomy in a seminar "Kant's Concepts of Nature" that I co-taught with Boehm in the fall of 2009. I developed it further in ten lectures I gave at the Leuphana University in Lüneburg in June 2010, subsequently published as *Wahrheit: Die Architektur der Welt*. I thank Christoph Jamme for the opportunity to present my thoughts in my native German.[20] A number of articles explored aspects of that antinomy further.[21] This book, in substance my final seminar, gathers and deepens these reflections.

---

19 See Omri Boehm, *Kant's Critique of Spinoza* (New York: Oxford University Press, 2014).
20 See Karsten Harries, *Wahrheit: Die Architektur der Welt* (Paderborn: Wilhelm Fink, 2012).
21 Karsten Harries, "Architecture and Anarchitecture: The Antinomy of Building," *Aesthetic Pathways*, Vol. 1, Nr. 1, December 2010, pp. 59–78.
Karsten Harries, "Vom Widerwillen gegen Architektur oder die Antinomie des Seins"/ "On the Ill Will Against Architecture or The Antinomy of Being." *Displaced Fractures. Über die Bruchlinien in Architekturen und ihren Körpern*, Thomas Trummer und Heike Munder (Eds.), Migros Museum für Gegenwartskunst, Zürich, 2011.
Karsten Harries, "The Antinomy of Being and the End of Philosophy," *Division III of Being and Time: Heidegger's Unanswered Question of Being*, Lee Braver (Ed.), (Cambridge, MA: MIT), pp. 133–148.
Karsten Harries, "The Antinomy of Being: Heidegger's Critique of Humanism," *The Cambridge Companion to Existentialism*, Steven Crowell (Ed.), (Cambridge: Cambridge University Press, 2012), pp. 178–198.

Dermot Moran deserves special thanks for convincing me to publish these reworked seminar notes. Given the long prehistory of these thoughts I find it impossible to name and thank all the many people who have helped me find my way. Some are mentioned in the following pages. But, as mentioned, especially my many students have been essential. To them I dedicate this book.

Introduction

That, after 56 years of teaching, I chose to entitle my final seminar "The Antinomy of Being" calls for an explanation. What did I have in mind when I chose this title for a course meant to explore what I had come to think of as the unifying thread of my philosophical musings? Why did this antinomy matter to me? And why should it concern us?

As the word, which joins the Greek *anti*, (opposed to) and *nomos* (law), suggests, "antinomy" refers to an incompatibility of what appear to be two well-founded positions. When a philosopher uses the word "antinomy" he is likely to think first of all of Kant and his four antinomies, which were meant to prove that the being of things has to be understood in two senses: what we experience are first of all phenomena, appearances, and as such their being is essentially a being for the knowing subject. Science investigates these phenomena. But the things we experience are also things in themselves, and as such they possess a transcendent being that eludes our comprehension. The identification of phenomena, of what science can know, with reality is shown to mire us in contradiction.

In the ninth and tenth chapters of this book I take a closer look at Kant's antinomies, especially the first and the third. I show that they open the only way towards an overcoming of that nihilism that is a corollary of the understanding of reality that presides over our science and technology. And it is the problem of nihilism that has preoccupied me ever since my dissertation.[22] It seems only fitting that I should have returned to this problem in what I knew would be my final seminar.

But when I am speaking of the Antinomy of Being I am thinking not only of Kant and his insistence that the being of things be understood in two quite distinct senses, but also of Heidegger. Not that Heidegger spoke of such an antinomy; but his questioning of Being led him and will lead those who attempt to follow him on his path of thinking into that antinomy. As I show elsewhere, it is in this antinomy that Heidegger's much-discussed *Kehre* or reversal of the direction of his thinking has its foundation.[23]

---

[22] Karsten Harries, *In a Strange Land. An Exploration of Nihilism*, PhD dissertation, Yale University, 1961.

[23] See Karsten Harries, "The Antinomy of Being and the End of Philosophy," *Division III of Being and Time: Heidegger's Unanswered Question of Being,* Lee Braver (Ed.), (Cambridge, MA: MIT Press, 2015), pp. 133–148. See also Karsten Harries, "The Antinomy of Being: Heidegger's

What I am concerned with in this book, however, is at bottom neither Kant's nor Heidegger's thought. I shall try to show that our thinking inevitably leads us into some version of this antinomy whenever it attempts to comprehend reality *in toto*, without loss, and that a consequence of that attempt is a loss of reality. All such attempts will fall short of their goal. What science can know and what reality is are in the end incommensurable. Such incommensurability however, is not something to be grudgingly accepted, but embraced as a necessary condition of living a meaningful life. That is why the Antinomy of Being matters and should concern us.

As suggested by the decision to name my final seminar in which I sought to address once more what I had come to consider the unifying theme of the arc of my still evolving philosophical reflections "The Antinomy of Being," my concern with what is at issue antedates my use of the expression by a great many years. I can indeed trace its origin back to a time when I had not yet read a single philosophical text.

I became seriously interested in philosophy only as an undergraduate at Yale University. That time—I arrived as a freshman in 1954—now seems both close and distant. Less than three years had passed since my family left then still war-torn Germany. Memories of all too frequent air raids, images of the burning Berlin, which we children could watch night after night from the attic of our house in Eichkamp, of the bunker my father had built in our garden, of glittering sharp bomb splinters that we children found beautiful and collected, but that tore the pockets of our pants much to my mother's chagrin, of a neighbor forced to wear the Jewish-star, of strafing planes, of a prison camp on which my brother and I stumbled, having lost our way in the fog on the Große Gleichberg, horrified by the look of the prisoners; and then, after the war, of war-torn Munich, of hunger and living in the last, barely inhabitable story of an apartment house that had lost its roof, these and countless other memories were still fresh in my mind then and remain very much with me; also much more positive images of a land still beautiful, despite all that had ravaged it, of rococo churches that have retained their magic, of Munich's Maximiliansgymnasium, which even though I attended it only for four short years, laid a firm foundation on which I could build. That school and its teachers were one reason why I did not want to leave Germany when my father, a physicist, accepted a generous offer to come to the United States.

Critique of Humanism," *The Cambridge Companion to Existentialism*, Steven Crowell (Ed.), (Cambridge: Cambridge University Press, 2012), pp. 178–198.

What made me turn to philosophy? Aristotle's account of what lets human beings turn to philosophy seems to fit my own case: "For it is owing to their wonder that men both now begin and at first began to philosophize; they wondered originally at the obvious difficulties, then advanced little by little and stated difficulties about the greater matters, e.g., about the phenomena of the moon and those of the sun and the stars, and about the genesis of the universe."[24] As a boy I was interested in how things worked; watermills especially fascinated me; so did animals and trees. I dreamed of becoming a forester. As a young teenager I became interested in astronomy. Still in Germany, I got hold of a volume I still own that included an essay by Pascual Jordan on the expanding universe.[25] Like that book, one of only a handful of books I brought with me to the United States, the questions about the genesis of the universe Jordan's essay raised have stayed with me: How are we to think a beginning of both space and time? At the time I had not heard of Kant's antinomies; but such questions led me to wonder even then about the legitimacy and limits of the reason that, presiding over our science and technology, is shaping our life-world ever more decisively. That has remained a central concern. Five years later, now an undergraduate at Yale, I thus drifted, after considering mathematics and history as possible majors, towards philosophy.

In this connection a course in freehand drawing I took with Josef Albers in my sophomore year deserves special mention. Going back to my childhood, an interest in art and architecture has remained a central part of my life. I have always loved to draw and paint. I saved nothing of what I produced in that class, but some of my work, as I recently learned, has survived in the Archive of the Albers Foundation.[26] What I remember about the class are first of all some of the exercises. On large sheets of cheap newsprint paper that soon turned yellow and became very brittle, we were asked, e.g., to recreate with our pencil the texture of some newspaper just with vertical lines parallel to the paper edge. We were then asked to paste what we had come up with into that newspaper to judge how well we had succeeded. There were exercises, where just with bands of differently spaced parallel lines we were to create a vibrating surface; we were asked to rotate some geometric figure; or to capture the texture of a certain kind of wood, say of beech as opposed to oak. And once Albers asked us to

---

24 Aristotle, *Metaphysics*, I, 982b12–22, W. D. Ross (Trans.).
25 Pascual Jordan, "Kosmogonische Anschauungen der modernen Physik," *Naturwissenschaft – Religion – Weltanschauung. Clausthaler Gespräch 1948* (Clausthal-Zellerfeld, 1949), pp. 25–33.
26 See Anoka Faruqee, *Search Versus Re-Search: Recollections of Josef Albers at Yale, a film by Anoka Faruqee*, Published July 1, 2016, https://www.youtube.com/watch?v=cC7671N76_Q

draw the essence of daffodils, daffodility if you want, without drawing even one clearly recognizable daffodil. I found this a particularly memorable exercise.

Only after that course did I decide to turn to philosophy. Is there a connection between what I learned from Albers and my later work in philosophy? It seems to me that there is. Studying with Albers opened one's eyes. In that class Albers did not burden us students with theory. No doubt his *Interaction of Color* owes a debt to Johannes Itten, with whom he studied at the Bauhaus, before beginning to teach there; also to Kandinsky. Itten in turn would seem to have owed a debt to Adolf Hoelzel, who looked back to Schopenhauer's and especially to Goethe's color theory.

But if Albers did not seem especially interested in developing a theory about color, his explorations, especially in the *Homage to the Square* series, offer material for such a theory. Albers made one aware of how impoverished our color vocabulary is when compared to the infinite shades of color we experience. That insight into the incommensurability of what we perceive and what we are able to put into words has remained with me. Without being named as yet, the Antinomy of Being here announced itself. My interest in the visual, in the primacy of perception, has taught me not to overestimate the power of language, taught me to question the claim that our concepts give us a more adequate access to reality than our eyes or, more generally, than our senses. What here is the measure of adequacy? Thus this course raised the question: how are we to understand reality? Related is Heidegger's question of Being that later came to preoccupy me and with which my final seminar was still wrestling. It is a question that I believe has no good answer. Albers helped me to appreciate the wisdom of Nietzsche's words:

> Oh, those Greeks! They understood how to *live*. What you need for that is to be brave and stop at the surface, the fold, the skin, to worship appearance, to believe in tones, words, the whole Olympus of appearance. Those Greeks were superficial – out of profundity.[27]

The key to what makes life meaningful, I am convinced, is to be found in what Nietzsche here calls superficiality. My exploration of the Antinomy of Being is intended to support that claim.

Although a poet, Albers was suspicious of words. I share that suspicion. I have thus long been interested in, but also suspicious of the linguistic turn taken by philosophy in the 20th century. I also question the claim that science gives us the most adequate access to reality. Not that we should call its legitima-

---

[27] Friedrich Nietzsche, *The Gay Science*, Walter Kaufmann (Trans.), (Random House, 1974). Second Preface, p. 38. Cf. *Nietzsche contra Wagner*, Conclusion.

cy into question: to deny the legitimacy of science, to fail to recognize its achievements, is to lose one's place in the modern world. But, as this book shows, science is inescapably shadowed by nihilism. To do justice to the legitimacy of science, but also to exhibit its limits has thus been a central concern of much of my work. In this enterprise I found a kindred spirit in Hans Blumenberg,[28] whom I once attempted to lure, in the end without success, to Yale.

Plato taught us to distinguish the subjective appearance of things from their objective reality. Galileo and Descartes and the science they set on its course tell us that roses are not really red, grass not really green. They have properties that dispose us, having the kind of bodies and brains we happen to have, to see them that way. In principle, should physics not be able to explain all that needs explaining? But can science so understood really provide us with a fully adequate explanation even of color, e. g., of how color functions in nature? Albers invited one to raise such questions. His work with color opens windows in the house of language. Heidegger called language the house of Being (GA9, 333). Albers made one wonder whether Being is ever really at home in that house. That thought has remained with me.

As a child I wondered why we speak of high and low tones while the color spectrum can be arranged in a circle: there is no gap that separates the last visible red before we get to infra-red from the last visible violet before we get to ultra-violet. Artists have thus long made use of the color wheel. Why should there be this difference between the way we hear and the way we see? After all, both, the tones we hear and the colors we see, depend on wavelength.

The apparent discrepancy between the physical and physiological, and between the perceptual and psychological fascinated me, as it would seem to have fascinated Wittgenstein, who asks, "Why should there not be a psychological regularity to which *no* physiological regularity corresponds?" And comments: "If this upsets our concepts of causality then it is high time they were upset."[29]

I have always been a boundary-crosser. As an undergraduate I thus ended up not really majoring in any one subject. Yale's Scholar of the House program freed me in my senior year from the normal course requirements. It required instead a dissertation-length essay. I gave mine the title *Change and Permanence. A*

---

28 See especially Hans Blumenberg, *Die Legitimität der Neuzeit* (Frankfurt am Main: Suhrkamp, 1966). Trans. Robert M. Wallace, *The Legitimacy of the Modern Age* (Cambridge, MA.: MIT Press, 1983), and *Die Genesis der kopernikanischen Welt* (Frankfurt am Main: Suhrkamp, 1975). Robert M. Wallace (Trans.), *The Genesis of the Copernican World* (Cambridge, MA: MIT Press, 1987).
29 Ludwig Wittgenstein, *Zettel, 40th Anniversary Edition*, G. E. M. Anscombe, G. H. von Wright (Eds.), (Oakland: University of California Press, 2007), p. 610.

Study of Structure, Symbol, and Idea in Eight Major Prose Works by Hermann Hesse. It was indeed quite a bit longer than my dissertation was going to be. In the Plato scholar Robert S. Brumbaugh I had found a caring adviser. He introduced me to Zeno's paradoxes and to Plato's late dialogues, especially the *Parmenides*, anticipations of what I came to call the Antinomy of Being.

In its groping way my Scholar of the House essay already attempted to address that nihilism which inescapably shadows the progress of reason. Three years later my dissertation, *Stranger In a Strange Land: An Exploration of Nihilism*, confronted that shadow more directly.

Continuing my studies at Yale, two teachers especially helped shape my thinking; Wilfrid Sellars, who introduced me to Wittgenstein, and George A. Schrader, with whom I studied Kant, Husserl, and Heidegger. He became the adviser of my dissertation and for the rest of his life—he died in 1998—continued to be my most important discussion partner.

The dissertation itself was written, after quite a bit of preliminary work, mostly in the course of one cold March in Florence in 1961. I thought it only a draft, respectable enough to show my department that I had not frittered away my year abroad, visiting churches and climbing mountains. But Yale had offered me an instructorship, my wife and I were expecting a child, and the draft was thought sufficient. So I submitted the dissertation in the fall of 1961, when I began teaching.

Looking back at that all too quickly written dissertation, I am struck by how many of the themes and thinkers that have continued to occupy me are addressed or at least touched on in those 170 pages. In a nutshell it already included what was to become my first book, *The Meaning of Modern Art*; and for hints of an answer to the problem of nihilism I looked even then to Nicolaus Cusanus, especially to his dialogue *On Not-other* (*De li non aliud*). Much later Cusanus was to become the central figure of my book *Infinity and Perspective*.[30] What holds the different themes, addressed already in the dissertation, together is a concern with what I came to call the Antinomy of Being. Not that I then called it that. Then it was not yet Heidegger's *Being and Time* or Kant's *Critique of Pure Reason* that informed my discussion. Of Heidegger's works I had studied closely at the time only the essays collected in *Holzwege* and the essay *Zur Seinsfrage*. The texts that most significantly shaped my reflections included Descartes' *Meditations*, Husserl's *Ideas*, and Wittgenstein's *Tractatus*. These works provided me with a needed foil. The first volume of Kierkegaard's *Either/Or* offered me a key to understanding the aesthetic approach to art and life that I, too, wanted

---

30 Karsten Harries, *Infinity and Perspective* (Cambridge, MA: MIT Press, 2001).

to criticize.³¹ I found essentially the same key in Sartre's *Being and Nothingness*. Drawing on both, I located the origin of nihilism in the inability of freedom to bind itself. Nothing in experience, Sartre insists, provides a transcendent guarantee of values, other than the subject itself. "Human nature, cannot receive its ends … either from the outside or from a so-called 'inner' nature. It chooses them and by this very choice confers upon them a transcendent existence as the external limit of its projects. From this point of view … human reality in and through its very upsurge decides to define its own being by its ends. It is therefore the positing of my ultimate ends which characterizes my being which is identical with the sudden thrust of freedom which is mine."³² But, as Sartre knew all too well, life becomes precarious when values are determined by the choice with which the individual determines him- or herself. If I am truly free, what lets me fix value to this rather than to that? My inescapable embeddedness in some particular situation may limit my freedom, but it does not provide the necessary orientation. So understood, freedom has to lead to an understanding of the world as it is in itself as a mute, meaningless desert that is transformed into a meaningful world only by the upsurge of freedom. But just that upsurge, that embodiment of freedom or its descent into an inevitably particular situation, remains unintelligible.

In the dissertation I began my reflections in good phenomenological fashion with an experience: "Just a few minutes ago, my attention was suddenly caught by a piece of music. For a moment I forgot what I was doing and listened. Then I recognized the melody and almost at the same time noticed that I had stopped working. I became conscious of listening and soon went back to work, while the song receded into the background. The magical moment had passed."³³ I linked such auratic experience, be it of a work of art, a person, or an object to an experience of transcendence. What I call the Antinomy of Being opens windows to such transcendence.

I can trace my love of art and architecture to my childhood. My book *The Bavarian Rococo Church: Between Faith and Aestheticism*,³⁴ which was first pub-

---

31 That work continued to inform much of my subsequent work. See Karsten Harries *Between Nihilism and Faith: A Commentary on Either/Or* (Berlin and New York: DeGruyter, March 2010).
32 Jean-Paul Sartre, *Being and Nothingness*, Hazel E. Barnes (Trans. and Intro.), (New York: Philosophical Library, 1956), pp. 440–443. See Karsten Harries, *In a Strange Land. An Exploration of Nihilism*, PhD dissertation, Yale University, 1961, pp, 16–17.
33 Karsten Harries, *In a Strange Land. An Exploration of Nihilism*, PhD dissertation, Yale University, 1961, p. 7.
34 Karsten Harries, *The Bavarian Rococo Church: Between Faith and Aestheticism* (New Haven: Yale University Press, 1983).

lished in 1983 and has now appeared also in a considerably revised German version,[35] was born of that love. The very fact that I wrote such a book suggests a certain impatience with academic philosophy, although I do not see a profound break between this book and my more obviously philosophical work. *The Bavarian Rococo Church* touches on many, perhaps all the themes that matter to me as a philosopher and to which I first gave expression in my dissertation. Let me mention here just three of the themes addressed in this book, themes that have continued to matter to me and still figured in my last seminar:

(1) That book is part of an extended reflection on the historical threshold that separates Baroque and Rococo from the Enlightenment, an age of faith from an age of reason. But that threshold is also the threshold of our modern world. There is thus a sense in which this book is also a reflection on our spiritual culture, on both the legitimacy and the limits of that objectifying reason that presides over it. Kant, especially his *Critique of Judgment*, has remained important to me because he occupies that same threshold and offers us a key to understanding its significance. So does the Antinomy of Being.

(2) A reviewer called this book a preamble after the fact to my first book, *The Meaning of Modern Art*[36] of 1968, which was a greatly expanded version of just one brief chapter of my dissertation. In a sense he was right. That earlier book called for a step beyond modern art, and not just modern art, but beyond the nihilistic understanding of reality that, I claimed, much modern art presupposed, an understanding that renders nature mute, to be used and abused by human beings as they see fit. Since writing that book I have come to see more clearly what the step for which I called presupposes: an overcoming of what Nietzsche calls "the spirit of revenge," of that "ill will against time and its 'it was'"[37] that has supported metaphysics ever since Plato and at the same time prevents us from fully affirming all that binds us to time, prevents us from affirming ourselves as the mortals we are: finite and embodied. Much of my philosophical work has continued to circle around the possibility of such an overcoming, as it did already in my dissertation.

(3) Closely linked is the need to question that aesthetic approach to art and architecture, which, at least since Alexander Gottlieb Baumgarten's establish-

---

[35] Karsten Harries, *Die Bayerische Rokokokirche. Das Irrationale und das Sakrale* (Dorfen: Hawel Verlag, 2009).

[36] Karsten Harries, *The Meaning of Modern Art: A Philosophical Interpretation*, (Evanston: Northwestern University Press, 1968).

[37] Friedrich Nietzsche, *Thus Spoke Zarathustra*, *The Portable Nietzsche*, Walter Kaufmann (Trans.), (New York: Penguin Books, 1954), p. 252.

ment of aesthetics as a philosophical discipline in the orbit of Cartesian rationalism, has presided both over the production and the theory of art. That approach leads with some necessity to an understanding of works of architecture as decorated sheds, as functional buildings to which an aesthetic component has been added. And similarly it leads to an understanding of art as an aesthetic addendum to an often all too prosaic life. As its title suggests, in *The Ethical Function of Architecture*[38] I argued that whatever distinguishes architecture from mere building needs to be understood differently.

Wittgenstein claims that philosophical problems have the form, "I do not know my way about," a quote that recalls Aristotle who would have philosophy begin in wonder. Of course, not all problems having this form are therefore already philosophical. To lose one's way in a strange city is not sufficient to make one a philosopher. Nor is failure to understand a new piece of equipment. Say my computer misbehaves and I don't know what to do; I don't know my way about. But why does such loss of way not present us with a philosophical problem? I would suggest that it fails to do so because in such cases our disorientation is only superficial. Thus in the first case I might study a map; in the second I might ask an expert for help. The problem poses itself against a background of established and accepted ways of doing things to which we can turn to help us decide what is to be done. Genuinely philosophical problems, I would like to suggest, have no such background. They emerge wherever human beings have begun to question the place assigned them by nature, society, and history, and searching for firmer ground demand that this place be more securely established.

So understood, philosophy comes to an end, either when it despairs of responsibly addressing the questions that haunt it, or when it steps on what it takes to be firm ground and establishes what is now accepted as a secure foundation. When the latter happens philosophy gives birth to a science. There is thus a sense in which science and skepticism may be said to bound philosophy. Science today presents philosophy with a challenge resembling that which photography presented to representational painting.

But science itself is anything but unquestionable. There is a sense in which everyone of us, I suspect, stands in an ambiguous relationship to science and its offspring, technology. On one hand we have to affirm science. Given countless problems we face, it would be irresponsible not to do so. On the other hand science cannot know anything of persons as persons. Nor can it know anything of

---

[38] Harries, *The Ethical Function of Architecture* (Cambridge, MA: MIT Press, 1997).

values. To give an account of both the legitimacy and limits of scientific understanding, and that means also of technological thinking, seems to me one of the main tasks facing philosophy today. This book offers such an account.

Such an account must be guided by some understanding of where we should be going. In this broad sense all philosophy is at bottom "ethical reflection," reflection concerning the ethos, concerning the question: how should we take our place in this fragile world? This I take to be philosophy's fundamental question.

But is philosophy able to determine our proper place? Traditionally such determinations were given not by philosophers, but by prophets, poets, and statesmen. Plato's *Republic* gives expression to the claim that the philosopher should take over from the poet the task of establishing what our place should be. The ethical function that religion, art, and politics once had now comes to be claimed by reason.

Unfortunately reason has proved unequal to the assumed task. As Nietzsche saw, we live today in the ruins of the inherited value system. To support this claim I would have to show that, notwithstanding the efforts of philosophers from Plato to Kant and indeed right down to the present, reason alone has been unable to meet the challenges we face effectively. Let me give just one example: That we all need to make sure that those natural resources on which we depend for our survival will continue to be available, not just to us, but to future generations, has become almost a cliché. Given a still rising life expectancy, a still growing population, and demands for an ever higher standard of living, the conclusion seems inevitable: the road on which the world has been traveling has to lead to disaster, or rather disasters – not only to the expected disasters, such as mass starvation, wars for land, global warming, a deteriorating environment that will make clean water, air, and soil, not to speak of relatively unspoiled nature, increasingly scarce resources, but also to moral disaster. But if we all at bottom should know this, why do our responses remain so half-hearted? Needed is more than reason. The individual who says after me the deluge, who cares neither for his neighbor nor for coming generations, is not unreasonable. His is a different problem: he has a heart of stone. Needed is a change of heart. But how do we change hearts? Schiller's *Letters on the Aesthetic Education of Man* remains relevant: to change the way we relate to the environment we need more than just cold reason. We need to experience and cherish this earth as our home, the only home that we shall ever have.

In this sense I have called in my book *Infinity and Perspective,* as well as in quite a number of lectures and articles, for a post-Copernican geo-centrism.[39]

---

39 See Karsten Harries, "What Need is There for an Environmental Aesthetics," *The Nordic Jour-*

Full self-affirmation requires an affirmation of the never quite resolved tension between our need for freedom and our need for place, between dreams of journeying into the unknown and dreams of homecoming. In that tension the Antinomy of Being finds one expression. We are curious creatures, and curiosity calls us again and again away from home, beyond the places and the associated points of view and perspectives assigned to us by our situation. The loss of paradise will be repeated over and over by human curiosity. Relentlessly it bids us embark on ever new voyages of discovery, lets us repeat the Copernican revolution over and over again. To quote Nietzsche, "Since Copernicus, man seems to have got himself on an inclined plane – now he is slipping faster and faster away from the center into – what? into nothingness? into a *penetrating* sense of his own nothingness?"[40] As science has opened our life-world to the universe, this earth has become ever less homelike, more and more like a ship lost in an endless ocean, embarked on a journey with no discernible goal. But just as we have come to see the insignificance of human life here on earth, when measured by the space and time of the cosmos, we also have come to an increased awareness that for all practical purposes we are alone in the cosmos, that this earth is the only home we will ever have. That space exploration and the environmental movement should have developed in the very same years is no accident. There is a sense in which the exploration of space, including the vain search for extraterrestrial intelligence, have led to an ever clearer sense that we have no other home than this fragile, beautiful earth, which we should leave to those who come after us in a state that will allow them to flourish.[41] Despite our freedom, we remain earth-bound mortals. Our bodies and this earth to which we belong remain the ground of all meaning. In this sense we can speak of the need for a post-Copernican geo-centrism.

Despite the Copernican confidence that our reason and reality are commensurable, we have to accept their final incommensurability. The confidence that our human reason is in principle able to fathom reality, a confidence that finds expression in the principle of sufficient reason, which holds that every-

---

nal of Aesthetics, no. 40 – 41, 2010 – 2011, pp. 7– 22 and "Longing for Ithaca: On the Need for a Post-Copernican Geocentrism," *From the Things Themselves, Architecture and Phenomenology*, Jacquet and Vincent Giraud (Eds.), (Kyoto: Kyoto University Press. École francaise d'Extrême-Orient, 2012), pp. 495 – 522.

40 Friedrich Nietzsche, *On the Genealogy of Morals and Ecce Homo*, Walter Kaufmann and R. J. Hollingdale (Trans.), (New York: Vintage, 1989), p. 155.

41 Hans Blumenberg, *Die Genesis der kopernikanischen Welt* (Frankfurt am Main: Suhrkamp, 1975). Robert M. Wallace (Trans.), *The Genesis of the Copernican World* (Cambridge, MA: MIT Press, 1987). See also Karsten Harries, *Infinity and Perspective* (Cambridge, MA: MIT Press, 2001).

thing has a reason, suffers shipwreck, I want to insist, on the Antinomy of Being. That antinomy demands a distinction between two senses of Being. The first transcendental sense makes Being relative to our human being. The second transcendent sense grounds our being and thus also Being understood transcendentally. But any attempt to conceptually lay hold of that ground must fail. Here our thinking bumps against the limits of language and logic. And yet this ground is present to us whenever we experience the reality of the real, that something is, as opposed to what it is. To be open to the givenness of things, to the gift of their being, is to open a window in the house built for us by our reason, in which phenomena have to take their place if they are to be for us at all, a window in the world of phenomena to their transcendent ground. Every time we respond to a person as a person we open such a window. And the same can be said of our experience of a genuine work of art; or of the beauty of a daffodil. The Wittgenstein of the *Tractatus* might have said: a window to what is higher. This seminar, too, attempts to open such a window.

I The Antinomy of Being

1 The Antinomy of Being

As I pointed out in the Introduction, the title I have given this seminar is meant to invoke both Kant and Heidegger, especially the latter. Not that Heidegger used that expression, but he had to confront this antinomy in *Being and Time* (1927) in his attempt to think what he came to call the ontological difference, the difference between beings and their being – and his central concern was to remain until the very end of his life the question of Being. We are tempted to say: without Being beings would not be. Not that we ever encounter Being apart from our encounter with beings. Being is not some entity in the world that we might somehow discover. But in every encounter with some entity Being is co-present as the mode of its presencing, the way we encounter it, even if Being so understood remains almost always unthematized and not attended to. There is not just one such mode: the being of a tool is not that of a scientific object, the being of a person not that of a work of art. There are modes of Being. But without Being beings would not enter our consciousness, would not be. Being is constitutive of and in this sense transcends beings. So understood Being can be said to be transcendental.

As George Berkeley recognized, beings can present themselves only to a being that in some sense experiences or perceives them. *Esse est percipi*. Mind-independent things cannot be thought. Heidegger would not disagree. But while Berkeley could appeal to a divine knower who sustains all there is, Heidegger cannot think mind except as our human mind. Being, *Sein*, is thus made dependent on Dasein, i.e., on human being. Not that this commits Heidegger to solipsism: Dasein is not to be thought as an atomic subject, but as essentially a being-with-others. For Being, so understood, "to be" there must be human beings.

But this attempt to ground Being in the constitution of Dasein, of human being, has to call itself into question. In Heidegger's lecture course *The Basic Problems of Phenomenology* (1927), where Heidegger first uses the expression *ontologische Differenz*, "ontological difference" (GA24, 22), the difficulty shows itself in a paragraph in which he takes up the problem of truth in a way that remains close to the somewhat earlier parallel discussion in *Being and Time*. "The problem concentrates itself in the question: how does the existence of truth relate to Being and the way and manner in which Being is?" (GA 24, 318). Truth had long been related to mind. Think of Thomas Aquinas' famous definition: *veritas est adaequatio rei and intellectus*, "truth is the adequacy of the thing and the intellect."⁴² That makes truth essentially mind-dependent. Heidegger, who knew his scholastics very well, remains within the orbit of that definition. But the only intellect he recognizes is the human intellect. That is to say, for him there is no truth and that means for him also no Being, without Dasein (GA 24, 316).

But what about things? Is it not obvious that things such as dinosaurs existed long before there were human beings? And so Heidegger asks: "Is there Being only, when truth exists, i.e., when Dasein exists? Does whether there is Being or not depend on the existence of Dasein?" (GA 24, 317).

Heidegger's fundamental ontology would seem to demand that we answer this question affirmatively. But can this mean that there was no Being before human beings came into existence? His answer invites questioning: "The kind and manner, in which Being is and alone can be, prejudges nothing concerning whether and how beings can be as beings" (GA 24, 317). Earlier he had explained: "Before their discovery Newton's laws were neither true nor false. That cannot mean that the beings that are uncovered with the revealed laws before that were not so, as they showed themselves after their uncovering, and, as showing themselves thus, are. The discovering, i.e., the truth, reveals beings precisely as what they already were, without regard to their being discovered or not" (GA 24, 314). To be what it is, Heidegger rightly insists, nature does not need to disclose itself to human beings, i.e., does not need truth. But do we not want to say then that nature transcends Dasein and thus truth? And if we have to think nature in this way, do we not also have to think of Being as transcending the Dasein-dependent transcendental Being to which *Being and Time* sought to lead us?

The discussion of truth and Being in *The Basic Problems of Phenomenology*, and more especially the cited Newton passage, tracks and expands on the parallel discussion in paragraphs 43 and 44 of *Being and Time*. I shall consider it in more detail in Chapter Two. In *Being and Time* already Heidegger faced the need to take a step beyond an understanding of Being that makes it dependent on Dasein and thus beyond his own existential analysis. To be sure, no more than in the *Basic Problems* did Heidegger recognize at this point a deep challenge to his project:

> But the fact that Reality is ontologically grounded in the Being of Dasein does not signify that only when Dasein exists and as long as Dasein exists, can the Real be as that which in itself it is.

---

42 Thomas Aquinas, *Questiones disputatae de veritate*, qu. 1, art. 1. Here I would like to thank George Lindbeck, with whom I first studied *De Veritate*.

> Of course only as long as Dasein is (that is only as long as an understanding of Being is ontically possible [that is only as long as human beings are able to exist]), 'is there' Being. When Dasein does not exist, 'independence' 'is' not either, nor 'is' the 'in-itself.' In such a case this sort of thing can be neither understood nor not understood. In such a case even entities within-the world can neither be discovered nor lie hidden. In such a case it cannot be said that entities are, nor can it be said that they are not. But now, as long as there is an understanding of Being and therefore an understanding of presence-at-hand, it can indeed be said that in this case entities will still continue to be (GA2, 280–281; 212).

Like the Newton passage cited above, this would seem to force us to think "beings" as transcending "Being." But to think them in that way, must we not attribute to them some sort of transcendent Being? But such Being, Heidegger warns us, cannot be understood.

Heidegger, as I pointed out, had to confront the Antinomy of Being in *Being and Time* in his attempt to think the ontological difference. When we approach that difference from the perspective of the transcendental phenomenology Heidegger then embraced, we will want to say: Being is constitutive of and in this sense transcends beings. Beings can present themselves only to a being that is such as we are, a being that, embodied and dwelling in language, is open to a world in which beings have to take their place and present themselves if they are "to be" at all. And so Heidegger came to call language the house of Being. The way beings present themselves is always mediated by the body, by language, by history and founded in the being of Dasein as care.

In the "Letter on Humanism" (1947) Heidegger will repeat thus the sentence: "Only as long as Dasein is, is there [*gibt es*] Being" (GA9, 336). But Heidegger qualifies this when he speaks in par. 43 of *Being and Time* of the dependence of Being, but not of beings, of reality, but not of the real, on care, i.e., on the always understanding and caring being of human beings. In "The Letter on Humanism" this qualification becomes: "But the fact that the Da, the lighting as the truth of Being itself, comes to pass is the dispensation of Being itself..." (GA9, 336). There is therefore a sense in which beings and the real can be said to transcend that Being (*Sein*), which is said to be relative to Dasein. To be sure, these beings could not "be" in the first sense without human beings. Only human consciousness provides the open space, the clearing that allows things to be perceived, understood, and cared for. That space is a presupposition of the accessibility of things, of their Being. But this is not to say that we in any sense create these beings. They are given to us. Our experience of the reality of the real is thus an experience of beings as transcending Being so understood. This invites a distinction between two senses of Being, the first transcendental sense relative to Dasein and in this sense inescapably historical, the second transcendent sense, gesturing towards the ground or origin of Dasein's historical being and thus also of Being understood transcendentally. Transcendent Being dispenses "the Da, the lighting as the truth of Being" (GA9, 336; 216).

To distinguish Being, transcendentally understood, from this transcendent Being, Heidegger will at times, taking his cue from Hölderlin, write *Seyn* instead of *Sein* or cross *Sein* out. *Sein* and *Seyn* are the two sides of my antinomy. Being understood as the transcendent ground of experience (*Seyn*) transcends Being understood transcendentally (*Sein*). This demands that we think of Being (*Sein*) not just as dependent on Dasein, but as belonging to *Seyn*. The happening of truth thus comes to be understood by Heidegger as the presencing (*das Wesen*) of *Seyn*. The attempt to comprehend this happening, however, inevitably will become entangled in some version of the Antinomy of Being. This is suggested by Heidegger's explanation: "*Seyn* needs the human being for it to be (*wesen*), and the human being belongs to *Seyn*, so that he fulfill his ultimate vocation as *Da-sein*" (GA65, 251). For *Seyn* "to be," it must disclose itself as *Sein*.

Any attempt to conceptually lay hold of that originating ground threatens to transform it into a being, such as God or the thing in itself and must inevitably fail. Here our thinking bumps against the limits of language. Being refuses to be imprisoned in the house of language. And yet this elusive ground is somehow present to us, calls us, if in silence, opening a window to transcendence in our world, a world shaped for us by the progress of philosophy, i.e., of metaphysics. The evolution of Heidegger's thought following *Being and Time* thus supplements the silent call of conscience, which plays such a central part in that book, providing a key to Heidegger's understanding of authenticity, with the equally silent call of transcendent Being (gestured towards by his understanding of "earth"[43]), where there is now a suggestion that only as a response to the latter can there be authentic speech and authentic dwelling. To speak here of a *Kehre*, a U-turn, as Heidegger himself does for the first time in print in the "Letter on Humanism" (GA9, 328), is misleading, in that it suggests a reversal in his thinking. But, as Heidegger points out, "there has been no change of standpoint." The question of Being remains central. The so-called *Kehre* is thus better understood, as Heidegger himself here describes it, not as a philosophical advance, but as a more thoughtful attempt to attend to the matter to be thought (GA9, 343). What makes this step necessary is the antinomial essence of Being, which denies the thinker a foundation. The Antinomy of Being shows us why we cannot dispense

---

[43] See Karsten Harries, *Art Matters: A Critical Commentary on Heidegger's "The Origin of the Work of Art"* (New York: Springer, 2009), pp. 109–123.

with something like the Kantian understanding of the thing in itself as the ground of phenomena, even as the thing in itself eludes our understanding.

2 Word and Thing

Again and again Heidegger was to return to what I have called the Antinomy of Being. So in the essay *Das Wesen der Sprache* (1957), "The Esssence of Language."[44] Heidegger here comments on Stefan George's poem *Das Wort* (1919), "The Word".

> *Wunder von ferne oder traum*
> *Bracht ich an meines landes saum*
>
> *Und harrte bis die graue norn*
> *Den namen fand in ihrem born –*
>
> *Drauf konnt ichs greifen dicht und stark*
> *Nun blüht und glänzt es durch die mark ...*
>
> *Einst langt ich an nach guter fahrt*
> *Mit einem kleinod reich und zart*
>
> *Sie suchte lang und gab mir kund:*
> *›So schläft hier nichts auf tiefem grund‹*
>
> *Worauf es meiner hand entrann*
> *Und nie mein land den schatz gewann ...*
>
> *So lernt ich traurig den verzicht:*
> *Kein ding sei wo das wort gebricht.*

And here the English translation by Peter D. Hertz:

> Wonder or dream from distant land
> I carried to my country's strand
>
> And waited till the twilit norn
> Had found the name within her bourn –
>
> Then I could grasp it close and strong
> It blooms and shines now the front along ...
>
> Once I returned from happy sail,
> I had a prize so rich and frail,

---

44 Martin Heidegger, GA12, 145–204; 57–108.

> She sought for long and tidings told:
> "No like of this these depths enfold."
>
> And straight it vanished from my hand,
> The treasure never graced my land ...
>
> So I renounced and sadly see:
> Where word breaks off, no thing may be.

The last two lines suggest a transcendental interpretation of language: without language no thing can be. Only language gives things the space that allows them to be. Thinking of Wittgenstein's *Tractatus*,[45] we may want to substitute for language logical space: whatever can be has to find its place in logical space. Heidegger has a less reductive understanding of language. But the point is essentially the same:

> Only where the word for a thing has been found is the thing a thing. Only thus *is* it. Accordingly, we must stress as follows: no thing *is* where the word, i.e., the name is lacking. The word alone gives being to the thing. Yet how can a mere word accomplish this – to bring a thing into being? The true situation is obviously reverse. Take the sputnik. This thing, if such it is, is obviously independent of that name which we later tacked on to it. But perhaps matters are different with such things as rockets, atom bombs, reactors, and the like, different from what the poem names in the first stanza of the first triad (GA12, 154; 62).

What does Heidegger have in mind when he wonders whether there might not be a significant difference between the being of things such as "rockets, atom bombs, reactors, and the like" and the being of the "wonder or dream" of which the first triad of the poem speaks? The latter does seem in an obvious sense language-dependent. i.e., on the existence of human beings. But the stated reservation is difficult to dismiss. Consider the way Heidegger speaks in *Being and Time* of the independence of beings, but not of Being, from human Dasein, and that is to say also from language, which he thinks with an architectonic metaphor as the house of Being. In order to be for us things must find their place in the house of Being, i.e. in language. But countless things would seem to be, without being for us. Continuing with Heidegger's metaphor, we have to ask: but is Being really at home in this house?

It is not easy to simply answer that question with a firm "yes." Language is after all a product of human beings, and the arrival of human beings capable of speech is a rather late event in the history of the earth, let alone the cosmos.

---

[45] Ludwig Wittgenstein, *Tractatus Logico Philosphicus*, C. K. Ogden (Trans.), (London: Routledge and Kegan Paul, 1922).

Here Nietzsche's fable of the insignificance of human life seen from a cosmic perspective, which, following Kant and Schopenhauer, he places at the beginning of "On Truth and Lie in an Extramoral Sense":

> Once upon a time, in some out of the way corner of that universe which is dispersed into numberless twinkling solar systems, there was a star upon which clever beasts invented knowing. That was the most arrogant and mendacious minute of "world history," but nevertheless, it was only a minute. After nature had drawn a few breaths, the star cooled and congealed, and the clever beasts had to die. – One might invent such a fable, and yet still would not have adequately illustrated how miserable, how shadowy and transient, how aimless and arbitrary the human intellect looks within nature. There were eternities during which it did not exist. And when it is all over with the human intellect, nothing will have happened. For this intellect has no additional mission which would lead it beyond human life (TL 79).

Who could deny what Nietzsche here is saying about the insignificance of human life in the context of the cosmos?

But how are we to understand the being of this "universe which is dispersed into numberless twinkling solar systems?" Can it be understood without any relation to some sort of understanding? Berkeley's *esse est percipi* is not easily dismissed. We may be tempted to try to refute Berkeley as Samuel Johnson did, by kicking some stone: Are we not kicking something real, something that is? But this, too, is a perception, a *Wahrnehmung*, a taking for true. Philosophically speaking, we seem to be kicking into the void. And yet the realist's objection to the idealist will not be dismissed.

I already suggested that when Heidegger insists that there is no *Sein* without Dasein, no Being without human being, he does not seem so very distant from Berkeley's idealism. And thus we read in *Being and Time:*

> If what the term "idealism" says, amounts to the understanding that Being can never be explained by entities but is already that which is 'transcendental' for every entity, then idealism affords the only correct possibility for a philosophical problematic. If so Aristotle was no less an idealist than Kant (GA2, 275; SZ, 208).

But, as the appeal to Aristotle is meant to suggest, this is not to say that all that is depends on a human subject or consciousness. On this point Heidegger sides with realism. This ineliminable opposition of idealism and realism is an expression of what I have called the Antinomy of Being. It finds striking expression in Schopenhauer:

> For, "No object without a subject," is the principle that renders all materialism forever impossible. Suns and planets with no eye to see them and no understanding to know them

can of course be spoken of in words, but for the representation, these words are a *sideroxylon*, an iron wood. On the other hand, the law of causality, and the consideration and investigation of nature which follow on it, lead us necessarily to the certain presumption that each more highly organized state of matter succeeded in time a cruder state. Thus animals existed before men, fishes before land animals, plants before fishes, and the inorganic before that which is organic; consequently, the original mass had to go through a long series of changes before the first eye could be opened. And yet the existence of this whole world remains forever dependent on that first eye that opened, were it even that of an insect.[46]

Our experience of the reality, the thingliness of things, is an experience of something to which Being, understood idealistically, cannot do justice. It is an experience of what I call material transcendence. Such an experience resists being captured in concepts. We touch here the limits of our language, which are also the limits of our conceptual space.

Let me return to the last two lines of the poem by Stefan George:

So I renounced and sadly see:
Where word breaks off, no thing may be.

Just what is it that the poet has to renounce? A wordless understanding of the being of things? But why does he call this lesson sad? The poem speaks of a treasure that refuses to be grasped by the poet's hand.

Einst langt ich an nach guter fahrt
Mit einem kleinod reich und zart

Once I returned from happy sail,
I had a prize so rich and frail,

What is this *Kleinod*, this treasure, that will not be grasped or comprehended? Is it the true being of things, their being as things in themselves?

Heidegger could have cited the George poem already in *Being and Time*. Here already he understands *Rede*, speech, as one of the existentials, i.e., the fundamental structures constitutive of human Dasein. The word *Rede* Heidegger understands as a translation of the Greek *logos*. As the *zoon lógon échon*, the *animal rationale*, the animal endowed with reason, the human being is the being in which nature become conscious of itself, opens itself to itself. And so Heidegger calls the human being the clearing of Being, thinking of a forest clearing, using a metaphor that suggests an open space into which light falls, a metaphor that in-

---

[46] Arthur Schopenhauer, *Die Welt als Wille und Vorstellung*, 2 vols. (Wiesbaden: Brockhaus, 1965). E. F. J. Payne (Trans.), *The World as Will and Representation*, 2 vols. (New York: Dover, 1966), vol. 1, pp. 29–30.

vites us to think of the "distance" that separates the Cartesian subject and object; also of the Cartesian *lumen naturale,* the natural light. Does Descartes not also rely on metaphors, supported by the analogy of seeing and understanding that has supported philosophical thinking from the very beginning, even as his insistence that philosophical thinking be clear and distinct would rid language of its reliance on such metaphors? Resisting that demand Heidegger makes them conspicuous, lets us stumble over them, inviting us to question what philosophy all too often takes for granted.

In order to be for us things must find their place in that open space Heidegger calls the clearing of Being. But such placement presupposes something like coordinates that determine places. Wittgenstein speaks thus in his *Tractatus* of logical space, in which all possible things must find their place. The coordinates of this space are our concepts. In his dissertation and *Habilitationsschrift* Heidegger spoke a similar language. But just like Wittgenstein, Heidegger, too, had to recognize that, as Vico and Herder already knew, it is not an abstract logic, but our language that first opens up our world. And so he writes in *Being and Time:*

> The intelligibility of Being-in-the-world – an intelligibility which goes with a state-of-mind – *expresses itself [aussprechen] as discourse [Rede].* The totality-of-significations of intelligibility is put into words. To significations words accrue. But word-things do not get supplied with significations.
>
> The way in which discourse gets expressed [*hinausgesprochen*] is language [*Sprache*]. Language is a totality of words – a totality in which discourse has a 'worldly' Being of its own; and as an entity within the world, this totality thus becomes something which we may come across as ready-to-hand. Language can be broken up into word-things which are present-at-hand. Discourse is existentially language, because that entity whose disclosedness it articulates according to significations, has, as its kind of Being, Being-in-the-world – a Being which has been thrown and submitted to the 'world' (GA 2, 214; SZ, 161).

The difference between *aussprechen* and *hinausprechen* is lost in the translation, which uses "express" for both. But the latter suggest a speaking that sends the spoken, as an entity among entities, into the world: *Die Rede ist existenzial Sprache,* "Discourse is existentially language" – What would it mean to deny this? Heidegger's immediately following explanation seems convincing. If Dasein is essentially a being-in-the-world, also a being with others, *Rede* would seem to have to be equally essentially *Sprache.* The essence of language is then to be *Sprache. Rede* (*logos*) should then not be construed as a core or essence that could be reached by eliminating from *Sprache* all that is not essential, as Wittgenstein attempted to do in his *Tractatus.* Compare the claim "Discourse is existentially language" with the analogous claim: Dasein is existentially embodied.

But is Dasein adequately understood as being-in-the-world and as such essentially embodied? Can Heidegger's *Rede*, his translation of the Greek *logos*, really be said to be existentially *Sprache*? Are we human beings not able to raise ourselves above our embodied selves in a way that allows us to oppose an ideal language to whatever language we happen to speak, as the young Wittgenstein, Russell, and Frege attempted, a *Begriffsschrift*, i.e., a conceptual notation that would "break the domination of words over the human mind"[47]? Is this power of self-elevation not constitutive of human being?[48]

Consider these words by Meister Eckhart: "Yesterday as I sat yonder I said something that sounds incredible: 'Jerusalem is as near to my soul as this place is.' Indeed a point a thousand miles beyond Jerusalem is as near to my soul as my body is, and I am as sure of this as I am of being human, and it is easy to understand for learned priests."[49] To be sure of being human, Eckhart claims, is to know that something in us, Eckhart calls it our soul, is not bound by our body. Strange as the claim that Jerusalem is as close to me as my body may seem, what allows Eckhart to say this is nonetheless easy to understand. When I think of Jerusalem and Rome, is one city closer to my thinking self than the other? Closer in what sense? Is there not a sense in which all objects of thought are equally close to the thinker? Not only is Jerusalem as close to the thinker as her body is, but so is a place a thousand miles beyond, so indeed is every place. Following Plato, Augustine had thus insisted that the soul knows itself to be a thinking being and as such a spiritual substance to be essentially different from body and place. Descartes was to speak of a *res cogitans*. How could such a substance, grasped in its essence only in a movement of introversion, be said to be nearer one place than another? Meister Eckhart would seem to be quite in agreement with the philosophical tradition when he speaks of the soul as exempt from the limitations imposed on us by our embod-

---

[47] Gottlob Frege, *Begriffsschrift, eine der arithmetischen nachgebildete Formelsprache des reinen Denkens* (Halle: Louis Nebert, 1879), S. Bauer-Mengelberg (Trans.), *Concept Script, a formal language of pure thought modelled upon that of arithmetic*, in J. van Heijenoort (Ed.), *From Frege to Gödel: A Source Book in Mathematical Logic, 1879–1931* (Cambridge, MA: Harvard University Press, 1967), p. 7.

[48] See Theodor Litt, *Mensch und Welt. Grundlinien einer Philosophie des Geistes* (München: Federmann, 1948).

[49] *Meister Eckharts Predigten*, Josef Quint (Ed. and Trans.), 3 vols. (Stuttgart: Kohlhammer, 1936–1976), "Adolescens, tibi dico: surge!" 2:305. *Meister Eckhart* Raymond B. Blakney (Ed. and Trans.), (New York: Harper, 1957), p. 134. Translation changed.

ied existence: no matter how distant some place may be, the soul can leap to it and beyond. Had Plato not already attributed wings to thought?

To be sure, the embodied self will have difficulty identifying with Eckhart's soul, just as it has difficulty recognizing itself in the Cartesian *res cogitans.* As long as I understand myself concretely, as this individual, I understand myself as cast into the world, subject to place and time. Thus placed, I also know that my vision and understanding remain bound by perspective. Only to disembodied thought, only to a pure "I", would all things be equally close. I cannot recognize myself in that "I." Pure thought remains an elusive ideal. And so does a pure language that would break the domination of words. But even if we were to replace Heidegger's language with a *Begriffsschrift*, words with concepts, the dependence of the being of things on words or concepts would go unchallenged.

I conclude with the last line of the poem by Stefan George:

Where word breaks off, no thing may be.

Why does this sadden the poet? Presupposed is the dream of an access to things not mediated by any language. George's poem thus speaks to something like a dissatisfaction with, an ill will against language, this house of Being. To repeat the question: Is Being really at home in that house? Or is it perhaps a prison? The architectonic metaphor invites thought. It speaks to a certain reluctance to surrender all claim to that treasure, that *Kleinod,* of which the poem speaks.

II The Antinomy of Truth

1 The Ill Will Against Language

Already in Plato's dialogues we meet with the suspicion that our language not only uncovers, but covers up things, that words fail us when we attempt to do justice to the being of things. That such anxiety should find expression especially in poetic and philosophical texts from the first decades of the 20th century invites thought. In George and Hofmannsthal, in Wittgenstein and Heidegger, again and again we meet with a sense that our language has somehow let us lose touch with reality, meet with the desire to gain a more immediate access to things. In Hugo von Hofmannsthal's *Letter of Lord Chandos* (1902), a letter, supposed to have been sent in August 1603 by this fictional English Lord to Sir Francis Bacon, this anxiety is captured in extraordinarily convincing fashion.

The case of Hofmannsthal's Elizabethan Lord is simple: a figure of the Austrian poet, who, when still a teenager, had been celebrated as a master of the German language, only to be assailed by Nietzschean doubts concerning the power of language to reveal reality, the young Lord writes a letter to his well-intentioned older friend, the scientist and philosopher Sir Francis Bacon, in an attempt to explain to this founder of our then just emerging modern world his decision to abandon all literary activity. At issue is the rift that the young poet's merely aesthetic play with words had opened up between language and reality:

> My case in short is this: I have lost completely the ability to think or to speak of anything coherently.
>
> At first I grew by degrees incapable of discussing a loftier or more general subject in terms of which everyone, fluently and without hesitation, is wont to avail himself. I experienced an inexplicable distaste for so much as uttering the words spirit, soul, or body. I found it impossible to express an opinion on the affairs at Court, the events in Parliament, or whatever you wish. This was not motivated by any personal deference (for you know that my candor borders on impudence) but because the abstract terms of which the tongue must avail itself as a matter of course in order to voice a judgment – these terms crumbled in my mouth like moldy fungi.[50]

Like a corroding rust this inability to use words, because they have lost touch with what they supposedly are about, spreads to ordinary language, which the Lord experiences increasingly as indemonstrable, mendacious, hollow. At first

---

[50] Hugo von Hofmannsthal, "The Letter of Lord Chandos," *Selected Prose*, Mary Hottinger and Tania and James Stern (Trans.), (New York: Pantheon, 1952), 134–135.

this distrust is directed only towards certain lofty terms, which have all but lost touch with what they are supposed to say, words such as spirit, soul, body, hero, virtue, courage, words that too often used and worn out now idle.

But do not all our words necessarily cover up the unique particularity of things, their thingliness? Is our speaking not first of all and most of the time idle talk, as Heidegger understands it in *Being and Time?* We say what one says in a given situation without being much concerned with what makes that situation unique. Do not all our words lie, as the young Nietzsche argued in "On Truth and Lie in an Extra-Moral Sense"?[51] I shall have to return to that text.

Not so very different is how Hofmannsthal's Lord understands the insufficiency of language.

> My mind compelled me to view all things occurring in such conversations from an uncanny closeness. As once, through a magnifying glass, I had seen a piece of skin on my little finger look like a field full of holes and furrows, so I now perceived human beings and their actions. I no longer succeeded in comprehending them with the simplifying eye of habit. For me everything disintegrated into parts, those parts again into parts; no longer would anything let itself be encompassed in one idea. Single words floated round me; they congealed into eyes which stared back at me and into which I was forced to stare back – whirlpools which gave me vertigo and, reeling incessantly, led into the void.[52]

But the void left by this disintegration is not completely mute. As language gains an autonomy that threatens to render it meaningless by losing contact with reality, a minimal, but intense contact with beings is established. The tearing of language by silence grants epiphanies of presence.

> Since that time I have been leading an existence which I fear you can hardly imagine, so lacking in spirit and thought is its flow: an existence which, it is true, differs little from that of my neighbors, my relations, and most of the landowning nobility of this kingdom, and which is not utterly bereft of gay and stimulating moments. It is not easy for me to indicate wherein these good moments subsist; once again words desert me. For it is, indeed, something entirely unnamed, even barely nameable which, at such moments, reveals itself to me, filling like a vessel any casual object of my daily surroundings with an overflowing flood of higher life. I cannot expect you to understand me without examples, and I must

---

51 I prefer Walter Kaufmann's translation of the title to Daniel Breazeale's "On Truth and Lie in a Nonmoral Sense," although only Breazeale gives us a complete translation of Nietzsche's fragment, abbreviated as TL, in *Philosophy and Truth: Selections From Nietzsche's Notebooks of the Early 1970's* (Atlantic Highlands: Humanities Press, 1979).

See also *The Portable Nietzsche*, Walter Kaufmann (Ed. and Trans.), (New York: Penguin Books, 1954).

52 Hugo von Hofmannsthal, "The Letter of Lord Chandos," *Selected Prose*, Mary Hottinger and Tania and James Stern (Trans.), (New York: Pantheon, 1952).

plead your indulgence for their absurdity. A pitcher, a harrow abandoned in a field, a dog in the sun, a neglected cemetery, a cripple, a peasant's hut – all these can become the vessel of my revelation. Each of these objects and a thousand others similar, over which the eye usually glides with a natural indifference, can suddenly, at any moment (which I am utterly powerless to evoke), assume for me a character so exalted and moving that words seem too poor to describe it. Even the distinct image of an absent object, in fact, can acquire the mysterious function of being filled to the brim with this silent but suddenly rising flood of divine sensation. Recently, for instance, I had given the order for a copious supply of rat-poison to be scattered in the milk cellars of one of my dairy-farms. Towards evening I had gone off for a ride and, as you can imagine, thought no more about it. As I was trotting along over the freshly-ploughed land, nothing more alarming in sight than a scared covey of quail and, in the distance, the great sun sinking over the undulating fields, there suddenly loomed up before me the vision of that cellar, resounding with the death-struggle of a mob of rats. I felt everything within me: the cool, musty air of the cellar filled with the sweet and pungent reek of poison, and the yelling of the death cries breaking against the moldering walls; the vain convulsions of those convoluted bodies as they tear about in confusion and despair; their frenzied search for escape, and the grimace of icy rage when a couple collide with one another at a blocked-up crevice. But why seek again for words which I have foresworn! You remember, my friend, the wonderful description in Livy of the hours preceding the destruction of Alba Longa: when the crowds stray aimlessly through the streets which they are to see no more ... when they bid farewell to the stones beneath their feet. I assure you, my friend, I carried this vision within me, and the vision of burning Carthage, too; but there was more, something more divine, more bestial; and it was the Present, the fullest, most exalted Present. There was a mother, surrounded by her young in their agony of death; but her gaze was cast neither toward the dying nor upon the merciless walls of stone, but into the void, or through the void into Infinity, accompanying this gaze with a gnashing of teeth. – A slave struck with helpless terror standing near the petrifying Niobe must have experienced what I experienced when, within me, the soul of this animal bared its teeth to its monstrous fate.[53]

In the most insignificant things the Lord senses the infinite:

> Forgive this description, but do not think that it was pity I felt. For if you did, my example would have been poorly chosen. It was far more and far less than pity: an immense sympathy, a flowing over into these creatures, or a feeling that an aura of life and death, of dream and wakefulness, had flowed for a moment into them – but whence? For what had it to do with pity, or with any comprehensible concatenation of human thought when, on another evening, on finding beneath a nut-tree a half-filled pitcher which a gardener boy had left there, and the pitcher and the water in it, darkened by the shadow of the tree, and a beetle swimming on the surface from shore to shore, when this combination of trifles sent through me such a shudder at the presence of the Infinite, a shudder running from the roots of my hair to the marrow of my heels? What was it that made me want to break into words which, I know, were I to find them, would force to their knees those cherubim in whom I do not believe? What made me turn silently away from this place? Even

---

[53] Ibid., pp. 135–136.

now, after weeks, catching sight of that nut-tree, I pass it by with a shy sidelong glance, for I am loath to dispel the memory of the miracle hovering there round the trunk, loath to scare away the celestial shudders that still linger about the shrubbery in this neighborhood![54]

With "a shudder running from the roots of my hair to the marrow of my heels," the young Lord senses the infinite: "What was it that made me want to break into words which, I know, were I to find them, would force to their knees those cherubim in whom I do not believe?" And so they would! For the words for which the Lord is longing would know nothing of the rift separating reality and language. The words of that language would be nothing other than the things themselves. But this is to say: they would have to be the creative words of that God in whom neither the Lord, nor the young Hofmannsthal could believe. Nevertheless, the idea of this divine language functions here as a measure that renders our language infinitely inadequate and condemns him who refuses to sully the dream of that language to silence.

2 Truth and Thing in Itself

We know how much Hugo von Hofmannsthal owed Nietzsche.[55] Especially the Chandos Letter recalls Nietzsche's critique of language. "Do not all our words lie?" asks the young Nietzsche in his early never completed essay "On Truth and Lie in an Extra-Moral Sense." But what sense does this question make? Most of the time we seem to have little difficulty distinguishing telling the truth from lying. To lie is to make what the speaker knows to be an untrue statement. Lying is a contrast term: it presupposes an understanding of what it means to tell the truth. What then does Nietzsche mean by "truth" when he asks whether all our words lie?

"On Truth and Lie" gives us a clear answer.

> The various languages placed side by side show that with words it is never a question of truth, never a question of adequate expression; otherwise, there would not be so many languages. The "thing in itself" which is precisely what the pure truth, apart from any of its consequences, would be, is likewise something quite incomprehensible to the creator of language and something not in the least worth striving for. (TL 82)

---

54 Ibid., p. 137.
55 See László V. Szabó, "Zu Hugo von Hofmannsthals Nietzsche-Rezeption," *Jahrbuch der ungarischen Germanistik*, 2006, pp. 69–93.

II The Antinomy of Truth

The idea of the pure truth and the idea of the thing in itself are, according to the young Nietzsche, one and the same idea. It is this understanding of truth as a congruence of designations and things (TL 81) that allows him to claim that "to be truthful means using the customary metaphors – in moral terms: the obligation to lie according to a fixed convention, to lie, herd-like, in a style obligatory for all."[56]

But is this not reason to reject what Nietzsche here calls "the pure truth?" As Nietzsche well knows, the identification of the pure truth with the thing in itself is difficult to square with our ordinary understanding of truth. Why call the latter a lie? When on a rainy day I say "It is raining today," am I not telling the truth?

Consider that passage in the *Critique of Pure Reason* (A58/B83), where Kant calls the question, "What is truth?" "the old and famous question" with which one sought to get logicians into trouble, only to dismiss it, writing that "the nominal explanation of truth, that is to say, that it is the agreement of knowledge with its object, is here taken for granted and presupposed, "*wird hier geschenkt und vorausgesetzt.*" Presupposed is an understanding of truth as correspondence. And such an understanding of truth does indeed seem to agree with the way we ordinarily understand truth, without giving the matter much thought. To be sure, as Kant recognized, we use "truth" in different senses. Kant thus distinguished such "material (objective) truth" (A60/B85) from merely formal or logical truth, such as the truth of tautologies, and from the truth of aesthetic judgments, such as "this rose is beautiful," where our understanding agrees with how the object affects the subject. In this chapter we are concerned first of all with the meaning and value of what Kant calls material or objective truth, such as the truth of the judgment "Saturn has rings." In no way do we claim here an identity of the assertion and what it asserts. What we do claim is that the assertion states what to the best of our knowledge is the case.

Kant's understanding of material or objective truth recalls the way truth is defined in a text that has not lost its authority: Thomas Aquinas' *De Veritate*. Consider once more Aquinas' definition of truth as "the adequation of the thing and the understanding": *Veritas est adaequatio rei et intellectus.*[57] Quite in keeping with our everyday understanding, the definition claims that there can be no truth where there is no understanding. But can there be understanding without human beings? Does truth then depend on the existence of human beings? Aquinas, of course, would have rejected such a suggestion: the truth of our

---

[56] Friedrich Nietzsche "On Truth and Lies in an Extra-Moral Sense," *The Portable Nietzsche*, Walter Kaufmann (Trans.), (Hamondsworth: Penguin, 1976), p. 47.
[57] Thomas Aquinas, *Questiones disputatae de veritate*, qu. 1, art. 1. See Heidegger, *Einführung in die phänomenologische Forschung*, (WS 1923/24) GA17, 162–194.

judgments or propositions has its measure in the way things really are, in the truth of things, and that truth is understood by Aquinas as the adequacy of the thing to the divine intellect – recall the claim of Lord Chandos that were he to find the words adequate to the things that let him sense the presence of the infinite, they would force to their knees those cherubim in whom he does not believe.

Aquinas has a theocentric understanding of truth that gives human discourse its measure in God's creative word, in the divine logos. The thing as it is in truth is here understood as nothing other than the thing thought as *noumenon*, a term that relates it to a pure, disembodied intellect, the divine *nous*. In this sense Aquinas could claim: *Omne ens est verum.* "Every being is true." Nietzsche's identification of pure truth with the thing itself should thus not seem all that strange to us. And given such an understanding of "the pure truth," truth is indeed denied to us finite knowers, as the young Nietzsche proclaimed and as Kant, too, would have granted.

Thomas Aquinas' understanding of God left no room for thoughts of a cosmos from which understanding would be absent. His, as I said, was a theocentric understanding of truth, where we should note that the definition *veritas est adaequatio rei et intellectus,* "truth is the adequation of the thing and the understanding," invites two readings: *veritas est adaequatio intellectus ad rem,* "truth is the adequation of the understanding to the thing" and *veritas est adaequatio rei ad intellectum,* "truth is the adequation of the thing to the understanding." And is the second not presupposed by the first? Is there not a sense in which the truth of our assertions presupposes the truth of things or what we can call ontological truth? If we are to measure the truth of an assertion about something, must that thing not disclose itself to us as it really is, as it is in truth? But what does "truth" now mean? How are we to understand "the truth of things?" Could it mean the adequation of the thing to our finite, perspective-bound understanding? Would that not substitute appearances for the things themselves?

Theology once had a ready answer: every created thing necessarily corresponds to the idea preconceived in the mind of God and in this sense it cannot but be true. The truth of things, understood as *adaequatio rei (creandae) ad intellectum (divinum),* "the adequacy of the (to be created) thing to the (divine) intellect," secures truth understood as *adaequatio intellectus (humani) ad rem (creatam),* "the adequacy of the (human) intellect to the (created) thing."[58] Such talk

---

58 See Martin Heidegger, "Vom Wesen der Wahrheit," GA9, 178–182.

of the truth of things does accord with the way we sometimes use the words "truth" and "true"—e.g., when we call something we have drawn "a true circle" we declare it to be in accord with our preconceived idea of what a circle is. What we have put down on paper accords with an idea in our intellect. Here the truth of things is understood as *adaequatio rei ad intellectum (humanum)*, "the adequacy of the thing to the (human) intellect." Similarly we may call someone a true friend. He meets our expectations concerning friendship. But in neither case is there an identity. The material object transcends whatever of our ideas it may satisfy.

What right do we have to think that our human intellect can bridge the abyss that separates God's infinite creative knowledge from our finite understanding? Or, to rephrase the question for a godless age, what right do we have to think that we can bridge the abyss that separates things in themselves from what we can perceive and understand? The young Nietzsche insists that there can be no such bridge.

But does the idea of the thing in itself even make sense? Must what it attempts to capture not be thought with reference to a pure creative intellect? Kant thus tends to understand the thing in itself as the noumenon, i.e., in relation to nous, to a pure intellect. Thoughts of God inevitably suggest themselves. Not surprising therefore that in the *Antichrist* Nietzsche should write "God became the 'thing in itself'"[59] By then he had come to reject, together with the idea of God, the idea of the thing in itself as a *contradictio in adjecto*.[60] Heidegger could have agreed: To be for Heidegger, is to be related to a being that understands. The thought of the thing itself is incoherent.

3 The Truth of Phenomena

As pointed out, Kant, despite his willingness to take the traditional understanding of truth as correspondence for granted, would have agreed with the young Nietzsche to this extent: if we understand truth as the agreement of our judg-

---

For a somewhat fuller discussion see Karsten Harries, "The Antinomy of Being and the End of Philosophy," *Division III of Being and Time: Heidegger's Unanswered Question of Being*, Lee Braver (Ed.), (Cambridge, MA: MIT Press, 2015), pp. 133–148.

59 Friedrich Nietzsche, *Der Antichrist* 17, *Sämtliche Werke, Kritische Studienausgabe*, Giorgio Colli and Mazzino Montinari (Eds.), (Munich, Berlin, and New York: Deutscher Taschenbuch Verlag and de Gruyter, 1980), vol. 6, p. 184.

60 Friedrich Nietzsche, *Jenseits von Gut und Böse* I, 16, *Kritische Studienausgabe*, vol. 5, p. 29. See Mattia Riccardi, "Nietzsche's critique of Kant's thing in itself," *Nietzsche-Studien* 39, 2010, 3.

ments and things in themselves, understood as noumena, another term that gestures towards the truth of things, then the truth is not available to us finite knowers for Kant either. But Kant does not conclude that therefore we cannot justify the human pursuit of truth. He would not have called our everyday truths lies. We just need to recognize the relevant relativities. To be sure, our understanding cannot penetrate beyond phenomena; things as they are in themselves are beyond the reach of what we can know. But this does not mean that laying hold of the truth of phenomena does not provide us with a meaningful goal. The truth pursued by science is more than a subjective illusion.

Telling is this footnote in the "Transcendental Aesthetic" of the *Critique of Pure Reason*

> The predicates of appearance can be attributed to the object in itself [*dem Objekte selbst*], in relation to our sense, e.g., the red color or fragrance to the rose; but the illusion can never be attributed to the object as predicate, precisely because that would be to attribute to the object for itself [*für sich*] what pertains to it only in relation to the senses or in general to the subject, e.g., the two handles that were originally attributed to Saturn. What is not to be encountered in the object in itself [*an sich*] at all, but is always to be encountered in its relation to the subject and is inseparable from the representation of the object, is appearance, and thus the predicates of space and of time are rightly attributed to the objects of the senses as such [*als solchen*], and there is no illusion in this. On the contrary, if I attribute the redness to the rose *in itself*, the handles to Saturn or extension to all outer objects *in themselves*, without looking to a determinate relation of these objects to the subject and limiting my judgment to this, then illusion first arises (A 69/B70).

When we ascribe to the rose its red color or its fragrance we are conscious of the subjectivity our judgments, of the way what we experience depends on the make-up of our senses. Given this context, we can call such assertions true. But we are not describing here the object "as such." As the example of Saturn shows, we can gain an understanding of the object that is not so dependent on the senses and in this sense more objective: what is first described as an object with handles, is more adequately described as a sphere encircled by rings. The measure of such adequacy is provided by our idea of the object, not as it is perceived by some particular embodied subject located in space and time and limited by its point of view, but the object "as such." This is not to say that what Kant here calls the object "as such" is not still thought with reference to the subject, but it is now thought with reference, not to a particular embodied self, but with reference to what is always to be encountered in that object, i.e., with reference to the subject presupposed by all possible experience, the transcendental subject. The idea of what "is always to be encountered in an object's relation to the subject and is inseparable from the representation of the object," i.e., the formal idea of a material object, is sufficient to provide science with a regulative ideal that renders its pursuit of truth meaningful. "In all the tasks that may come before us in the field of experience, we treat those appearances as objects in themselves, without worrying ourselves about the primary ground of their possibility (as appearances)" (A393). That is sufficient to make sense of the Kantian understanding of truth as "the agreement of knowledge with its object." Object here refers to an appearance considered as the object as such. Key here is this by now familiar thought: to understand that what we experience first of all is only a subjective appearance, bound by a particular point of view and limited by a particular perspective, is to be already on the road towards a more adequate, more objective, and that means here first of all less perspective-bound and in this sense freer understanding.

Copernicus relied on this pattern of thought to make his readers more receptive to his break with Aristotle and Ptolemy, who remained too much in thrall to subjective appearance.

> And why are we not willing to acknowledge that the appearance of a daily revolution belongs to the heavens, its actuality to the earth? The relation is similar to that of which Virgil's Aeneas says: "We sail out of the harbor, and the countries and cities recede." For when a ship is sailing along quietly, everything which is outside of it will appear to those on board to have a motion corresponding to the motion of the ship, and the voyagers are of the erroneous opinion that they with all that they have with them are at rest. This can without doubt also apply to the motion of the earth, and it may appear as if the whole universe were revolving.[61]

Ornamenting his remark with a reference to the *Aeneid*, Copernicus uses the simile likening the earth to a ship, a simile found already in Cusanus' *De docta ignorantia*, to call the reader's attention to the relativity of apparent motion. As Plato had already taught, reflection on the nature of perspective teaches us that whatever presents itself to the eye, or more generally, to perception, is no more than subjective appearance. To get closer to "actuality" or objective reality we have to reflect on the way our point of view governs what appears to us. Objective reality cannot in principle be seen as it is. It is invisible and we can begin to understand it only in terms of our thoughtful reconstructions.

Copernicus' distinction between appearance and actuality is a presupposition of the emerging new science and of our modern understanding of reality. Implied is a diminution of the authority of the senses. Nietzsche had good reason to celebrate in *Beyond Good and Evil* Copernicus, together with the "Pole" Bosco-

---

[61] Nicolaus Copernicus, *De revolutionibus orbium coelestium* (Nürnberg: Johannes Petreius, 1543). Translated in *The Portable Renaissance Reader*, James Bruce Ross and Mary Martin McLaughlin (Eds.), (New York: Viking, 1953), p. 591.

vich (actually a Jesuit from Ragusa, now Dubrovnik) as the *grösste und siegreichste Gegner des Augenscheins*, "the greatest and most victorious opponents of visual appearance." Note the nature of this victory: *Augenschein* is devalued as mere *Augenschein* by being shown to be no more than perspectival appearance. The world revealed to us by the scientist is opposed to that comparatively superficial world given to the senses, especially to the eye. Nietzsche speaks of this victory over the senses as *der grösste Triumph über die Sinne, der bisher auf Erden errungen ist,* "The greatest triumph over the senses that has been won so far."[62] And if we understand with Kant the truth that matters to science as adequacy of our understanding to "the objects of the senses as such" that victory can be celebrated as a victory of the truth.

To be sure, what Kant here calls "the objects of the senses as such" are still appearances in space and time and constituted as such by the subject, leading necessarily to thoughts of what so appears, of the transcendental object, as a necessary condition of all experience. "The word 'appearance' must already indicate a relation to something the immediate representation of which is, to be sure, sensible, but which in itself, without this constitution of our sensibility (on which the form of our intuition is grounded), must be something, i.e., an object independent of sensibility" (A 252). As the word "transcendental" suggests, just as the transcendental subject should not be thought as a concrete subject located in time and space, so the transcendental object should not be thought as so located. It provides only the form of objectivity. "This transcendental object cannot even be separated from the sensible data, for then nothing would remain through which it would be thought" (A251). But although inseparable from our experience of appearances understood to be more than mere illusions, whose being is exhausted by their being for a subject, we cannot give any content to what transcends their phenomenal being. The transcendental object remains a mere X (A46, A109, B236/A191).

With his concept of the transcendental object Kant touches on what I have called the Antinomy of Being. On the one hand, many of Kant's remarks on the transcendental object invite an idealistic reading such as that offered by Fichte, a reading that would deny that Kant is thinking here of a transcendent ground of reality. Kant's transcendental object is indeed thought by him in essential relation to the transcendental subject as "only a pure concept of the understanding whose role is to govern the synthesis of any unified manifold ('ob-

---

[62] Friedrich Nietzsche, *Jenseits von Gut und Böse* I, 12, *Kritische Studienausgabe*, vol. 5, p. 26.

ject of experience')."⁶³ It therefore should not be identified with the noumenon or thing in itself.

But, on the other hand, such a reading has to contend with Kant's characterization of the transcendental object as the cause of appearance: "We may, however, entitle the purely intelligible cause of appearances in general the transcendental object, but merely in order to have something corresponding to sensibility as receptivity. To this transcendental object we can ascribe the whole extent of possible perceptions, and can say that it is given in itself prior to all experience" (A494/B522; cf. A288/B344). The transcendental object, so understood, announces itself in our sense of the givenness of the objects we experience. There is, to be sure the obvious objection to an understanding of the transcendental object as the cause of appearances, which invites a blurring of the distinction between transcendental object and thing in itself. Causality is a category. Categories can only be applied to appearances. That was the point of Friedrich Heinrich Jacobi's complaint that without the thing in itself he could not enter into Kant's critical philosophy, but with it he could not remain in it.⁶⁴ In what Kant has to say about the transcendental object we meet with an irresolvable tension between passages that support an idealistic reading and others that argue for a realistic interpretation. But the presence of that tension is not an argument against Kant who with the concept of the transcendental object struggles with what I have called the Antinomy of Being. The significance of this concept of the transcendental object = X, of a transcendent cause or ground of appearance, a ground that remains elusive, lies in the fact that it protects us from equating the objects that science seeks to understand with reality. In attempting to name that ground, we bump inevitably against the limits of language, as shown by Kant's metaphorical use of the word "cause" in the following passage. That it cannot be understood in terms of Kant's category of causality, which can be applied only to experience, is evident.

> The understanding accordingly bounds sensibility without thereby expanding its own field, and in warning sensibility not to presume to reach for things in themselves but solely for appearances it thinks of an object in itself, but only as a transcendental object, which is the cause of appearance (thus not itself appearance), and that cannot be thought of either as magnitude or as reality or as substance, etc. (since these concepts always require sensible forms in which they determine an object); it therefore remains completely unknown whether such an object is to be encountered within or without us, whether it would be canceled

---

63 See Lance Hickey, "Kant's concept of the transcendental object," *Manuscrito* 24, 1, 2001: pp. 103–139.
64 *Friedrich Heinrich Jacobi's Werke*, vol. 2 (Leipzig: Fleischer, 1815), "Beylage. Ueber den transcendentalen Idealismus," pp. 304–5.

out along with sensibility or whether it would remain even if we took sensibility away (A288/B344).

As will become clearer in the following chapters, we need such protection to preserve a meaningful life. Kant could not have claimed that their victory over deceptive appearance allowed Copernicus and Boscovich to grasp reality as it is in itself.

4 Truth as Disclosure

Nietzsche would have agreed. By the time he wrote *Beyond Good and Evil* he had come to dismiss the Kantian thing in itself as incoherent. Not that he could have presupposed and taken for granted Kant's understanding of material truth as the agreement of knowledge with its object. He might have asked: how is "object" to be understood here? He certainly would have rejected Kant's appeal to the transcendental object as the indispensable counterpart of the transcendental subject and a presupposition of our understanding of objective truth.

In his support we might cite Heidegger, who in *Being and Time* explicitly rejects the attempt to ground truth in some version of the transcendental subject, behind which he still senses the God whose death Nietzsche had proclaimed.[65] Absolute truth and the absolute subject are declared by Heidegger to be rests of Christian theology that philosophy ought to leave behind:

> The idea of a 'pure I' and of a 'consciousness in general' are so far from including the *a priori* character of actual subjectivity that the ontological characters of Dasein's facticity and its state of Being are either passed over or not seen at all....

> Both the contention that there are 'eternal truths' and the jumbling together of Dasein's phenomenally grounded 'ideality' with an idealized absolute subject, belong to those residues of Christian theology within philosophical problematics which have not as yet been radically extruded (GA2, 303–304; SZ, 229).

Heidegger would thus have us reject the appeal to a transcendental subject and the associated understanding of objective truth. But what account can we then give of progress, be it in science, in ethics, or in culture? This question was at

---

[65] For a thorough discussion of Heidegger on truth see Ernst Tugendhat, *Der Wahrheitsbegriff bei Husserl und Heidegger*, 2nd. ed. (Berlin: de Gruyter, 1970) and Daniel O. Dahlstrom, *Heidegger's Concept of Truth* (Cambridge: Cambridge University Press, 2001), which includes an unusually thoughtful critical discussion of Tugendhat's probing critique.

the heart of the objections Ernst Cassirer raised at his Davos disputation with Heidegger: "Is Heidegger willing to renounce all objectivity, this form of absoluteness, which Kant represented in the ethical realm, in the theoretical realm, and in the *Critique of Judgment*? Is he willing to retreat completely to the finite essence, or, if not, where for him is the breakthrough to this sphere?" (GA3, 278). The question bears repeating: Having rejected a Kantian account of phenomenal truth, what can Heidegger substitute for the truth of things, for Aquinas' *ens verum*? Or is the concept of "the truth of things" dispensable?

Without breaking with the scholastic understanding of truth as *adaequatio rei et intellectus*, Heidegger puts in the place of the infinite divine intellect the finite human knower, or Dasein, as the only intellect known to us. But what sense can we now give to the everyday understanding of truth as the agreement of knowledge with its object that Kant is willing to presuppose and take for granted?

Heidegger raises a number of questions about this traditional view. Knowledge is said to agree with its object: but how are we to think such agreement (GA 2, 285–286; SZ, 215–216) ? Does the often invoked metaphor of a picture help us? No doubt, just as sight has furnished our understanding of knowing with perhaps its leading metaphor so has truthful pictorial representation presided over our understanding of truth. Here two phenomena, the picture and the pictured, are said to agree in certain respects. Such an account, although often quite to the point—think of comparing a map to its corresponding satellite image—left Heidegger, as it left Frege,[66] dissatisfied.

---

66 In *"Der Gedanke,"* "The Thought," Frege begins his attack on the correspondence theory with the observation that when we call representations and thoughts all true, we throw together things that can and things that cannot be perceived. "This indicates that shifts of sense have taken place." The truth of pictures has furnished the model according to which truth in general is interpreted. This model suggests that truth must be sought "in an agreement (*Übereinstimmung*) of a picture with the pictured." *Übereinstimmung* suggests that the picture is completely adequate to the pictured. But this would eliminate the tension which must be preserved if pictures are to remain pictures. Agreement must be only in certain respects. To understand a picture, to grasp its sense, we have to know its form of representation. To learn whether a picture is true "We should have to investigate whether it would be true that—let us say a representation and something real agreed in a specified manner." We would have to discover whether it is true that picture and reality correspond. How is the second "true" to be understood? Again as correspondence? But does this not lead to an infinite regress? If in some cases truth can be understood as correspondence, e. g., the truth of pictures, this truth presupposes truth in a more fundamental sense. What is this more fundamental truth? Frege refuses to give us a definition. And must not every such attempt fail? "For in a definition one furnishes certain characteristics. And in the application to a special case what mattered would always be whether it were true that these characteristics applied. Thus we would move in a circle." See Gottlob Frege, "*Der Ge-*

To approach the meaning of truth Heidegger offers this example:

> Let us suppose that someone with his back turned to the wall makes the true assertion that "the picture on the wall is hanging askew." This assertion demonstrates itself when the man who makes it, turns around and perceives the picture hanging askew on the wall. What gets demonstrated in this demonstration? What is the meaning of "confirming" [*Bewährung*] such an assertion? Do we, let us say, ascertain some agreement between our 'knowledge' or 'what is known' and the Thing on the wall? Yes and no, depending upon whether our interpretation of the expression 'what is known' is phenomenally appropriate. If he who makes the assertion judges without perceiving the picture, but 'merely represents' it to himself, to what is he related? To 'representations' shall we say? Certainly not, if "representation" is here supposed to signify representing as a psychical process. Nor is he related to "representations" in the sense of what is thus "represented," if what we have in mind here is a 'picture' of that Real Thing which is on the wall. The asserting which 'merely represents' is related rather, in that sense which is most its own, to the Real picture on the wall. What one has in mind is the Real picture and nothing else. Any Interpretation in which something else is here slipped in as what one supposedly has in mind in an assertion that merely represents, belies the phenomenal facts of the case as to that about which the assertion gets made. Asserting is a way of Being towards the Thing itself that is (GA2, 288; SZ, 217–218).

To recognize this fit of the assertion and the real picture hanging on the wall is to be certain of its truth. We recognize the fit by perceiving the picture. The perception, we can say, fulfills the intention.

> The entity itself which one has in mind shows itself *just as* it is in itself, that is to say, it shows that it, in its selfsameness, is just as it gets pointed out in the assertion as being—Representations do not get compared, either among themselves or in relation to the Real Thing. What is to be demonstrated is not an agreement of knowing with its object, still less of the psychical with the physical; but neither is it an agreement between 'contents of consciousness' among themselves. What is to be demonstrated is solely the Being-uncovered [*Entdeckt-sein*] of the entity itself—that entity in the 'how' of its uncoveredness (GA2, 288–289; SZ, 218).

What gets demonstrated is the being-uncovering of the assertion, i.e., its truth. This, Heidegger suggests, gives us a first understanding of truth: it is a being uncovering:

> To say that an assertion "is true" signifies that it uncovers the entity as it is in itself. Such an assertion asserts, points out, 'lets' the entity 'be seen' (*apophansis*) in its uncoveredness. The *Being-true (truth)* of the assertion must be understood as *Being-uncovering*. Thus

---

danke," in *Logische Untersuchungen*, Günther Patzig (Ed. and Intro.), (Göttingen: Vandenhoeck und Rupprecht, 1966), p.4 and pp. 31–33.

truth has by no means the structure of an agreement between knowing and the object in the sense of a likening of the one entity (the subject) to another (the Object) (GA2, 289; SZ, 218–219).

There are of course questions and objections: how reliable are our perceptions? Are they not by their very nature partial? And do expectations and preconceptions not help to determine what we see? Thus we often "see" what we want to see or perhaps fear to see. How are we to distinguish such a perhaps hopeful or fearful seeing from a seeing that discloses the entity "as it really is?" Such questions suggest that certainty is rarely absolute. Often, it can be shaken by other evidence. This is recognized by Kant's definition of formal truth as the fit of knowledge with itself.[67] The necessity of such a fit may well lead us to question the reliability of perception. It invites a coherence theory of truth.

But bracketing such concerns for the time being, we can agree with Heidegger when he writes: "To say that an assertion 'is true' signifies that it uncovers the entity as it is in itself." But "the entity as it is in itself" invites questioning: How would Heidegger have us understand it? What access do we have to the entity "as it is in itself?" Did Nietzsche not have good reason to call such an access into question, to question indeed the meaning of the expression, the entity "as it is in itself?" Without an answer to these questions, the whole discussion leaves us swimming.

Matters are not helped much by Heidegger's suggestion that we understand truthful assertion as uncovering or disclosing (*Entdecken*) and truth as disclosure. "Disclosing" already suggest a successful exhibition of the thing as it is in itself. But this leads us back to the question: how are we to understand "the thing as it is in itself?" Often, however, Heidegger uses the term "discloses" in a broader sense that makes no reference to "the thing as it is in itself," for example: "To Dasein's state of Being, *disclosedness in general* essentially belongs" (GA2, 293; SZ, 221).

This is to say, we human beings are essentially open to the world in which we find ourselves and of which we are part. But such openness does not mean that things have disclosed themselves to us as the things they are. Often we are misled by the way things appear or are made to appear. Disguising and covering up are thus understood by Heidegger as modes of disclosing or uncovering. But is this not to grant that if we are to understand the essence of truth, we have to distinguish different modes of uncovering? Only some of these would seem to uncover what is as it is in itself. And this returns us once more to the question: how are we to understand "the thing as it is in itself?" Must we not

---

67 Immanuel Kant, *Logik*, A 72.

attend to the way it shows itself? Consider in this connection Johann Heinrich Lambert's understanding of phenomenology as "the theory of illusion (*Schein*) and its influence on the correctness and incorrectness of human knowledge."[68] Kant accepted that definition.

The presence of things is first of all presence "for me," dependent on the makeup of my body, its location, dependent especially on the eyes, dependent also on language, dependent also on various prejudices. Consider in this connection what Heidegger has to say about what he calls the essential fallenness of Dasein:

> Because Dasein is essentially falling, its state of Being is such that it is in 'untruth'. This term, like the expression 'falling', is here used ontologically. If we are to use it in an existential analysis, we must avoid giving it any ontically negative 'evaluation'. To be closed off and covered up belongs to Dasein's facticity. In its full existential-ontological meaning, the proposition that 'Dasein is in the truth' states equiprimordially that 'Dasein is in untruth'. But only in so far as Dasein has been disclosed has it also been closed off (GA2, 294; SZ, 222).

Heidegger's distinction between truth in its full existential-ontological meaning as disclosure and truth in its familiar everyday sense as correctness raises the question whether the former can be considered more than a perhaps necessary, but hardly sufficient condition of the latter. But if so, does the former deserve to be called "truth" at all?

Consider once more Heidegger's example of some painting that looks to me askew. Might I be mistaken? Implicit in my understanding of a perspective as a perspective is an awareness of the possibility of other perspectives, which may give me or someone else another and perhaps better access to what I see, the possibility of a more objective description. When I make the assertion, "the picture is hanging askew," I not only claim that it looks to me that way, but I claim it as a fact. How does this fact present itself? Do I see the fact that the picture is hanging askew? No! I see the picture. How then does this fact disclose itself? Often the evidence that fulfills the intention will demand more than a simple seeing, will demand a particular appropriation of what is seen. The appropriation presupposes something like an understanding of what I "see" as a fact that is there also for others to "see." Can this fact present itself to me? At this point the idea of presence begins to blur. Given an understanding of presence

---

[68] Johann Heinrich Lambert, *Neues Organon Oder Gedanken Über Die Erforschung Und Bezeichnung des Wahren Und Dessen Unterscheidung Vom Irrtum Und Schein* (Leipzig: Wendler, 1764), p. 218.

based on the paradigm of sight, is it not more plausible to say of facts that they are not present at all? That they are not so much "seen" as constituted or constructed from the available evidence? Inseparable from such constitution is a projection of what I see unto a background of other actual and possible ways in which what I now see could be seen or interpreted. Assertion of fact is in such cases not fulfilled just by what presents itself to my senses. It presupposes the power of transcending what appears towards the object that might possibly appear in ways that would lead me to revise my first impression. Consider once more Kant's formal understanding of truth as the fit of knowledge with itself.

Ernst Tugendhat has called our attention to Heidegger's problematic replacement in *Being and Time* of Husserl's claim that an assertion is true when it exhibits or discovers what is "as it is in itself" with the simple "an assertion is true when it discovers."[69] Truth in its most fundamental sense is understood by Heidegger as *aletheia*, disclosure that inseparably joins the discoverer and the discovered. So understood truth is constitutive of human existence (GA2, 291; SZ, 220).[70]

But how then is it possible to give disclosure a measure in the disclosed as it is in itself? Heidegger's conception of truth as disclosure blurs the distinction between semblance and truth, between truth and error. With his blurring Heidegger's understanding of truth as *aletheia* threatens to lose all connection with what we usually call "truth."

This is indeed suggested by Heidegger's claim that "the proposition that 'Dasein is in the truth' states equiprimordially that 'Dasein is in untruth'" (GA2, 294; SZ, 222). We should, however, not be too quick to draw such a conclusion from these two statements. The former asserts that Dasein is the place where disclosure happens, the clearing in which beings can alone present themselves; the latter asserts that that presentation is never unclouded by deceptive appearances; and more especially, it is ruled by ordinary language and its ways of seeing and understanding; there is no pure seeing, no pure thinking; understanding is "dominated by the way things are publicly interpreted." We might want to say that ordinary language is here recognized in its "quasi-transcendental"[71] signifi-

---

69 See Ernst Tugendhat's *Der Wahrheitsbegriff bei Husserl und Heidegger*, 2nd. ed. (Berlin: de Gruyter, 1970), and Daniel O. Dahlstrom, *Heidegger's Concept of Truth* (Cambridge: Cambridge University Press, 2001).
70 See Karsten Harries, "Truth and Freedom," *Edmund Husserl and the Phenomenological Tradition*, Robert Sokolowski (Ed.), (Washington: Catholic University Press, 1988), pp.131–155.
71 The expression *quasi-transzendental* offers a key to understanding Karl-Otto Apel's "transformation of philosophy," which is first of all a transformation of Kant's transcendental philosophy, although the place occupied by the transcendental unity of the apperception and by the catego-

cance, as constitutive of the way things disclose themselves to us first of all and most of the time. But no one, certainly not Heidegger, would claim that to understand as one understands is to understand what is so understood as it is in itself. Quite the opposite: ordinary language, Heidegger insists, tends to cover up what it lets us understand, even as we understand it in some fashion. First of all and most of the time our understanding is dominated by public ways of seeing and speaking and as such inauthentic. Consider once more Hofmannsthal's Lord Chandos.

Even this much too brief sketch suggests that Heidegger does not want to blur the distinction between truth and untruth. *Being and Time's* call to authenticity is at the same time a call to truth. Heidegger thus demands that Dasein "explicitly appropriate what has already been uncovered, defend it against semblance and disguise, and assure itself of its uncoveredness again and again" (GA2, 294; SZ, 222). We have to see and think for ourselves. But that presupposes that we really are ourselves. In *Being and Time* Heidegger thus attempts to give knowledge something like a foundation by making a particular mode of disclosure primary: To be in the truth is to be authentic. To be authentic, as Heidegger understands it, is to project oneself resolutely unto one's own death and thus to appropriate one's finitude, one's facticity, and historicity. Having thus gained possession of itself, authentic Dasein is in a position to see and think for itself.

As Heidegger points out, in *Being and Time* the anticipation of death and the sense of self that such anticipation yields play a part not unlike that given by Kant to the transcendental subject (GA2, 421–422; SZ, 318). But the self that is gained in the resolute anticipation of death is not constitutive of all possible experience, but a self that in every case is the individual's own, essentially bound into a specific situation. The same has to be said of authentic disclosure. Can such disclosure, as such, then still be said to be true? Is authentic Dasein not

---

ries has been assigned to other structures, which, however, are no longer quite transcendental in Kant's sense, but "quasi-transcendental," a term Jürgen Habermas, too, is fond of. Kant's transcendental subject has been historicized and brought down to earth. The "transcendental" has been incarnated. Phenomena that are part of the world and as such can be investigated by science are assigned a transcendental value, e. g., language or the body. They can be assigned such a value if they can be shown to be conditions of the possibility and validity of knowledge (I, p. 72). This opens up the possibility of a collaboration of transcendental philosophy with science, especially with such sciences as linguistics, sociology, and cognitive science. From the point of view of a purer transcendental philosophy, to be sure, such collaboration must appear to blur the profound difference that should separate what is purely transcendental from what is merely factual or ontic. But is such purity not incompatible with the situatedness of all our knowledge? See Karl-Otto Apel, *Transformation der Philosophie*, 2 vols. (Frankfurt: Suhrkamp Taschenbuch Verlag, 1976).

often mistaken? Karl-Otto Apel is right to insist, following Tugendhat, on the difference between disclosure, even authentic disclosure, and the truth of assertions.[72] To claim truth is not to be content with the evidence presented by subjective disclosure. Truth demands objectivity. When I assert something to be true I presuppose that the facts are there, not just for me, or for some particular group or culture, but for everyone to grasp. Anyone who seeks to know has to think himself capable of drawing a distinction between semblance and reality. Claims to truth presuppose an ability on the part of the concrete subject to transcend itself as it first of all finds itself, bound by all sorts of perspectives. The direction of such self-transcendence is indicated by Kant's transcendental subject. The thought of such a subject is part of the self's self-emancipation.[73] It would seem to be a presupposition of any adequate understanding of truth.

A defender of Heidegger might reply that far from neglecting this issue, *Being and Time* does give an account of the kind of objectivity that has here been demanded and of an understanding of truth as a correspondence between our thoughts or propositions and the objects themselves. Does Heidegger not point out that such an understanding of truth rests on a reduction of experience? To arrive at such an understanding Dasein must disengage itself from the world, as the usual readiness-to-hand of things is transformed into mere presence-at-hand. Dasein becomes a subject confronting a world that is now understood as the totality of objects or facts. Like pictures, propositions, too, come to be understood as such facts. Truth comes to be understood as correctness, as an ontic relation of correspondence between facts in the world.

Such an account, however, still cannot do justice the kind of objectivity demanded by an adequate understanding of truth, because it continues to think the object to which the true proposition has to correspond relative to a particular subject and to its point of view. Objectivity as it is demanded by the concept of truth must be thought as free from such relativity. It implies freedom from perspectival distortion. The being of objects as such is not being for a subject imprisoned in some particular here and now, but for an ideal subject that transcends the accident of location. Objectivity and truth presuppose that we human beings possess the power of self-transcendence in reflection. Our experience is indeed

---

[72] Karl-Otto Apel, "Sprache und Wahrheit in der gegenwärtigen Situation der Philosophie, Zur Semiotik von Ch. Morris," in *Transformation der Philosophie*, vol. I, pp. 138–166. See also Karsten Harries, "On the Power and Limit of Transcendental Reflection," *From Kant to Davidson. Philosophy and the Idea of the Transcendental*, Jeff Malpas (Ed.), (London and New York: Routledge, 2002), pp. 139–161.

[73] Cf. Karl-Otto Apel, *Transformation der Philosophie*, 2 vols. (Frankfurt: Suhrkamp Taschenbuch Verlag, 1976), vol. 2, p. 317.

bound to the body and to the accident of its location in space and time, and to that extent first of all and most of the time inescapably perspectival. But as soon as this becomes an object of reflection, the difference between appearance and reality has to open up. To think a particular perspective as a perspective is already to have transcended, at least in thought, its limitations.

Heidegger himself eventually came to recognize the inadequacy of his understanding of truth as *aletheia*[74] and came to offer this correction of what he had once maintained:

> The natural concept of truth does not mean unconcealment, not in the philosophy of the Greeks either. It is often and justifiably pointed out that the word *alēthes* is already used by Homer only in the *verba dicendi*, in statements, thus in the sense of correctness and reliability, not in the sense of unconcealment. But this reference means only that neither the poets nor everyday linguistic usage, nor even philosophy, see themselves confronted with the task of asking how truth, that is, the correctness of statements, is granted only in the element of the clearing of presence.
>
> In the scope of this question, we must acknowledge the fact that *aletheia*, unconcealment in the sense of the clearing of presence, was originally experienced only as *orthotes*, as the correctness of representations and statements. But then the assertion about the essential transformation of truth, that is, from unconcealment to correctness, is also untenable. Instead we must say: *aletheia*, as clearing of presence and presentation in thinking and saying, immediately comes under the perspective of *homoiosis* and *adaequatio*, that is, the perspective of adequation in the sense of the correspondence of representing with what is present.[75]

We can indeed not arrive at an adequate understanding of truth as correctness by some sort of transformation of truth as unconcealment. We need to appeal to the human power of self-transcendence.

The transcendental subject is thus not dismissed as easily as Heidegger suggested in *Being and Time*. As thinkers we are capable of a self-elevation[76] that leaves behind our time-and-space-bound situation, capable of arriving at the ideal of a "pure I" and of a "consciousness in general," that is to say, of arriving at the ideal of a "view from nowhere"[77] or of an "ideal observer." The transcen-

---

[74] In part in response to criticism offered by Ernst Tugendhat in *Der Wahrheitsbegriff bei Husserl und Heidegger* and by Paul Friedländer, "Aletheia" in *Plato: An Introduction* (vol. 1 [l.c.]. New York: Pantheon Books, 1958), pp. 221–229.
[75] Martin Heidegger, GA14, 87; "The End of Philosophy and the Task of Thinking" in D. F. Krell, (Ed.), *Basic Writings* (New York: Harper Collins, 1993), p. 447.
[76] See Theodor Litt, *Mensch und Welt. Grundlinien einer Philosophie des Geistes* (München: Federmann, 1948).
[77] See Thomas Nagel, *The View From Nowhere* (New York: Oxford University Press, 1986).

dental subject, so understood, has its counterpart in the idea of the transcendental object, the object as it is thought to exist "distinct from our knowledge" (A104).[78] With his idea of the transcendental object Kant posits an ideal that presides over the human quest for truth. This in no way calls into question that a knowledge of things in themselves is denied to us.

Heidegger to be sure would object. So let us consider once more his claim that the conception of the pure subject rests on a confusion of theology and philosophy. It is indeed hard to deny that there is a historical and systematic connection between the Christian idea of God and the transcendental or ideal subject, which comes to replace God as the foundation of all that can be. But while both imply a point of view beyond all definite perspectives, there is also a crucial difference: God provides not only the form but also the matter of what is. While the transcendental subject is radically opposed to material transcendence, formal and material transcendence are reconciled in God.[79]

Furthermore, to suggest a historical connection between God and the transcendental subject—a point we have to grant—is not to discredit the latter. Challenging Heidegger, I want to insist that the idea of such a subject has its foundation in the self-understanding of concretely existing human beings, who aware of themselves as occupying particular points of view with such awareness already transcend them. This movement of self-transcendence comes to rest only when we arrive at the thought of a "point of view" that transcends all perspectives. Our subjective awareness has its measure in the never completely realized ideal of a genuinely a-perspectival understanding.

---

[78] See Lance Hickey, "Kant's Concept of the Transcendental Object," *Manuscrito*, 2001. XXIV(1), pp. 103–139, April.

[79] I distinguish material from formal self-transcendence as follows: In the latter case what actually presents itself to my senses is transcended as the spirit elevates itself and considers, first, how what is experienced might present itself, given different points of view, then how it might present itself to an understanding no longer burdened by perspectival distortions at all, yielding the idea of a pure subject. I speak of formal transcendence to suggest that the idea of such a subject lacks content.

In the former case, what is transcended is precisely that linguistic or conceptual space in which things must find their place if they are to be understood and comprehended. "Material transcendence" points in the same direction as the Kantian "thing-in-itself," which is present to us only as appearance, more precisely in the experience of the givenness of appearance, in the experience of the thing as a gift. Inseparable from our experience of things is a sense of this gift, an awareness that our understanding is finite, and that means also that the reach of our words is limited. As Hofmannsthal's Lord Chandos recognized, everything real is infinitely complex and thus can never be fully translated into words.

To understand the subject as a subject that transcends all particular points of view is to presuppose that consciousness is tied to perspectives, but transcends these perspectives in the awareness that they are just perspectives. The transcendental subject has its foundation in the self-transcending subject. As this self-transcending subject, the human being is a bridge between the concrete and the ideal, between time and eternity. A transcendental argument inquiring into the possibility of transcendental arguments returns us thus to concrete and perspectival experience. To an ontology of objectivity, which corresponds to the pure transcendental subject, we must oppose something like Heidegger's fundamental ontology. Or perhaps, as Wittgenstein thought, traditional philosophy must be led back to its home in ordinary language. But such formulations are misleading in that they suggest that the perspectival is prior to the trans-perspectival without inquiring into the meaning of this priority. Perhaps the perspectival should be given temporal priority; but temporal priority is not transcendental priority. What we have to recognize is that the perspectival and the trans-perspectival cannot be divorced. If we recognize that man in his self-transcendence stands essentially in between the two, we have to admit that the supposedly fundamental ontology of *Being and Time*, like Wittgenstein's *Philosophical Investigations*, is also one-sided and no more fundamental than traditional transcendental philosophy. This suggests itself when Heidegger briefly considers the possibility that his fundamental ontology might be too tied to our modern western perspective to be of much help in the interpretation of more primitive cultures (GA2, 119; SZ, 82). To even entertain this possibility, we have to admit that in thought Heidegger's fundamental ontology can be transcended. Similarly, Wittgenstein invites us to imagine language-games very different from the ones we are as a matter of fact playing. Neither the existentials of fundamental ontology nor the grammar of our language furnish limits that we cannot transcend. Neither provides a foundation in the sense in which traditional transcendental philosophy thought it could furnish a foundation that could not, in turn, be transcended.

But can there be such a final foundation at all? It could be established only if it were possible to pass beyond concrete experience and to survey all possible experience. But how can we ever know whether the possibilities we can conceive are indeed all possibilities? What content can we give to "all possibilities?" What we can conceive depends on what and where we are, and this includes the language we speak. Perhaps others, better equipped and more imaginative than we happen to be, could do better. And even they could never claim to have an understanding of all possible experience or of all possible language. Transcendental arguments remain tied to possibilities that we can conceive and are willing to admit at a given time. Thus the transcendental philosopher remains tied to a given language and subject to the perspectives it imposes, even as he attempts to take a step beyond them. The absolute of which he dreams must elude him. The pursuit of objectivity cannot escape its ground in the concrete.

5 The Antinomy of Truth

I want to conclude this with a consideration of the much quoted answer Nietzsche gave in *"On Truth and Lie"* to the question: "What is truth?"—where truth no longer is understood as that pure truth he had earlier equated with the thing in itself, but as it is generally understood.

> What then is truth? A movable host of metaphors, metonymies, and anthropomorphisms: in short, a sum of human relations which have been poetically and rhetorically intensified, transferred, and embellished, and which, after long usage, seem to a people, to be fixed, canonical, and binding. Truths are illusions which we have forgotten are illusions; they are metaphors that have become worn out and have been drained of sensuous force, coins which have lost their embossing and are now considered as metal and no longer as coins (TL 84).

I want to focus especially on the very last part of the quote:

> *Metaphern die abgenutzt und sinnlich kraftlos geworden sind, Münzen die ihr Bild verloren haben und nun als Metall, nicht mehr als Münzen in Betracht kommen.*

Metaphors that have become *abgenutzt und sinnlich kraftlos* have, I take it, lost their metaphorical force. We no longer experience the collision of different images, indeed no image at all. What now counts is only their measurable weight. But such *Kraftlosigkeit des Sinnlichen* is one of the requirements of objective truth as Kant understands it and with him our science and our modern world. It is truth so understood that has called forth the ill will against the thought structures philosophy and science have raised. The discourse of science is necessarily *entfärbt*, drained of color, *kühler*, cooler, as Nietzsche writes (TL 84). This is required by the pursuit of truth that governs science. This is to say also that such discourse must seek to free itself from metaphor. The direction of this discourse towards non-metaphoricity has its foundation in the ideality of the objects of knowledge.

But the process should not be understood simply as an *Abnutzung*, a wearing out. *Sinnlich kraftlos,* "drained of sensuous force," has to be opposed to *geistig kraftvoll,* filled with spiritual force." Is it not the task of spirit to spiritualize and that is to humanize all that is sensible, as Hegel thought?

The second part of the statement is more confusing. What are we to understand by coins that have lost their image? Money subjects everything to a single measure and is such a subjection not a condition of all conceptualization? The economic metaphor is indeed suggestive, but just what does it suggest? What was it that one could exchange coins for when they still carried their image? Dream images?

The loss of the *Bild*, the image on the coin, agrees with what I have said about the whiteness of scientific discourse. But what are we to make here of *Metall?* Schopenhauer, to whom the young Nietzsche remains indebted, had pointed out that our concepts have generality, not because they have been abstracted from particulars, but because generality belongs to the concept as an abstract representation of reason. Using this account, the metal Nietzsche speaks of would seem to be that altogether heterogeneous material Schopenhauer mentions, the medium of generality. That does indeed remain empty without reference to the sensible and imaginable. As Kant had put it, "*Gedanken ohne Inhalt sind leer, Anschauungen ohne Begriffe sind blind,*" "Thoughts without content are empty, intuitions without concepts are blind" (A51/BN75). But this is to say that the truth sought by philosophy and science, by its essential generality, cannot do justice to the truth of things. To the Antinomy of Being corresponds an Antinomy of Truth. Just as we are forced to think Being in two senses, we are forced to think truth in two senses.

III The Architecture of Reason

1 Spider and Bee

What I have called the Antinomy of Being has found one expression in the ways philosophers have invoked architectural metaphors. There are those philosophers who have liked to speak of laying foundations, of raising conceptual edifices. Consider Descartes, who in his *Replies* to the *Objections* by Père Bourdin writes: "Throughout my writings I made it clear that my method imitates that of an architect."[80] The conceptual edifice he raised, which Descartes comes to liken to a chapel, is said to rest on firm foundations. Or consider Kant, who liked to speak of the architectonics of a philosophical system. But there are also philosophers who have used architectural metaphors to challenge system building philosophy. One of these was Nietzsche.

In this chapter, I want to return to Nietzsche's *On Truth and Lie*. In that brief, never completed text he uses a number of architectural metaphors such as *Turmbau*, the building of a tower (we are made to think of the Tower of Babel), *Zwingburg* (a stronghold that lords it over the surrounding community), *Kolumbarium* (a building meant to house ashes, life turned to dust), to call the system building of philosophy and science into question.

Especially suggestive is Nietzsche's comparison of human beings with bees:

> Just as the Romans and Etruscans cut up the heavens with rigid mathematical lines and confined a god within each of the spaces thereby delimited, as within a *templum*, so every people, has a mathematically divided conceptual heaven above themselves and henceforth thinks that truth demands that each conceptual god be sought only within his own sphere. Here one may certainly admire man as a mighty genius of construction, who succeeds in piling up an infinitely complicated dome of concepts upon an unstable foundation, and, as it were, on running water. Of course, in order to be supported by such a foundation his construction must be like one constructed of spider's webs; delicate enough to be carried along by the waves, strong enough not to be blown apart by every wind. As a genius of construction man raises himself far above the bee in the following way: whereas the bee builds with wax that he gathers from nature, man builds with the far more delicate conceptual material which he first has to manufacture from himself. In this he is greatly to be admired, but not on account of the drive for truth or for pure knowledge of things (TL 85).

---

[80] René Descartes, *The Philosophical Writings of Descartes*, 2 vols., John Cottingham, Robert Stoothoff, Dugald Murdoch (Trans.), (Cambridge: Cambridge University Press, 1985), vol. 2, p. 366.

That brings to mind the example of a piece of wax that Descartes had used in the *Second Meditation* to show that the essence of things can only be grasped by thought. At first it seems to Descartes, too, that the corporeal things we encounter are more clearly known to us than the self. We are outward-oriented. Consequently we are reluctant to make that inward turn that Descartes demands of us. To counter such reluctance, Descartes chooses an object that presents itself to all five senses. The wax is then heated. The same wax is said to remain nonetheless, although all the evidence with which my senses had supplied me now has changed. What then is this wax that remains the same in spite of the fact that everything I sense seems to be different? After we have abstracted from all that has changed and therefore cannot belong essentially to the wax, what remains? An extended thing that is flexible and movable.

> But what is meant here by 'flexible' and 'changeable'? Is it what I picture in my imagination: that this piece of wax is capable of changing from a round shape to a square shape, or from a square shape to a triangular shape? Not at all, for I can grasp (*comprehendo*) that the wax is capable of countless changes of this kind, and yet I am unable to run through this immeasurable number in my imagination, from which it follows that it is not the faculty of the imagination which gives me my grasp of the wax as flexible and changeable.[81]

Whatever can be sensed does not belong to this essence. And thus the clearly and distinctly grasped piece of wax loses what remained of the taste of honey, of the fragrance of the flowers, loses color and smell. What remains is a construction of thought, which, to be sure, remains dependent on experience, but must also leave it behind. And is this not also true of the world picture presented to us by our science?

Nietzsche does not think that such construction has its foundation in a concern for truth, but in the need to raise over the flowing water of the stream of experience a lasting architecture in which we can feel spiritually at home.

But how can Nietzsche say that such construction does not arise from "the drive for truth or for pure knowledge of things?" Is not precisely the drive for truth that would have us raise such an architecture?

2 A Social Contract Theory of Truth

We saw that the pure truth, as Nietzsche understands it, is denied to us human knowers. Given his understanding of pure truth, it is impossible to disagree. But

---

[81] Ibid., vol. 2, pp. 20–21.

how then are we to understand that there should be such a thing as a drive for truth? In answer Nietzsche comes up first with what we can call a social contract theory of truth. The drive for truth is said to have its foundation in the social being of man.

> Insofar as the individual wants to maintain himself against other individuals, he will under natural circumstances employ the intellect mainly for dissimulation. But at the same time, from boredom and necessity, man wishes to exist socially and with the herd; therefore he needs to make peace and strives accordingly to banish from his world at least the most flagrant *bellum omnium contra omnes*. This peace treaty brings in its wake something which appears to be the first step towards acquiring that puzzling truth drive: to wit, that which shall count as "truth" from now on is established. That is to say, a uniformly valid and binding designation is invented for things, and this legislation of language likewise established the first laws of truth (TL 81).

This allows us to make sense of lying:

> The liar is a person who uses the valid designations, the words, in order to make something which is unreal appear to be real. He says for example, "I am rich," when the proper designation for his condition would be "poor." He misuses fixed conventions by means of arbitrary substitutions or even reversals of names. If he does this in a selfish and moreover harmful manner, society will cease to trust him and will thereby exclude him (TL 81).

Sensible as it appears at first, the passage is yet difficult to make sense of. Consider the characterization of the liar as someone who makes arbitrary substitutions, who misuses fixed conventions. This presupposes that there is a proper use of these conventions. That proper use links things to valid and binding designations. But does this not presuppose that the things are in some sense already available to those who would enter into such a contract, that they have disclosed themselves? This does not mean those who enter the contract have to understand things as they are in themselves, but it does presuppose that they understand their appearances in the same way. The sameness of experience is a necessary condition of Nietzsche's social contract theory. But this is to say that something like Kant's understanding of perception as *Wahrnehmung*, as taking for true, is being presupposed. In what, if any sense, then did Nietzsche challenge Kant? As I pointed out, if we understand truth as a correspondence between our propositions and things in themselves, then there is no truth for Kant either.

And yet, as we saw, Nietzsche refuses to content himself with truth in the sense in which Kant claims truth for science. Nietzsche might have replied that it is not so much a matter of refusal as a necessity of thought that must appear once we raise Kant's Copernican reflection to a still higher level and reflect on the way our thinking remains tied to our language. Even if Kant insists that we shall never know things as they are in themselves, does he not still have too much faith in our ability to free ourselves from the prison of perspectives? Must further reflection not reveal that transcendental reflection can never secure the objectivity of scientific knowledge, because it can never extricate itself from its dependence on inevitably situated, ordinary language? As Karl-Otto Apel reminds us, Johann Georg Hamann already insisted that the *Critique of Pure Reason* should be preceded by a *Metakritik*, which would be a critique of language,[82] a demand repeated by Johann Gottfried Herder,[83] who protests against the elision of both, the concrete person and of language, in Kant's critical project. Challenging Kant, Herder insists that we think with words, not abstract concepts, and that we cannot think in any language other than our own. In the same vein Wilhelm von Humboldt argued that we cannot consider language the means to represent an already known truth; rather it is language that first discloses what would otherwise remain unknown, that provides the space in which alone anything can present itself.[84] An inevitably historical culture and language is the transcendental (or rather quasi-transcendental)[85] presupposition of thinking and experience. The incarnation of logos in everyday language here appears as a transcendental necessity.

But to insist that there are many languages that disclose the world in different ways is not to deny that such disclosure lays hold of reality in a way that allows for a distinction between deceptive and truthful talk, even if truth must be thought as relative to language. To be part of a community is to demand the proper use of language, recognizing that fiction, too, has its place.

> Thus, even at this stage, what they hate is basically not deception itself, but rather the unpleasant, hated consequences of certain kinds of deception. It is in a similarly restricted sense that man now wants nothing but truth: he desires the pleasant, life preserving consequences of truth. He is indifferent toward pure knowledge which has no consequences; towards those truths which are possibly harmful and destructive he is even hostilely inclined (TL 81).

---

82 Karl-Otto Apel, *Transformation der Philosophie*, 2 vols. (Frankfurt: Suhrkamp Taschenbuch Verlag, 1976), vol. I, pp. 138–139. Cf. Johann Georg Hamann, *Metakritik über den Purismus der reinen Vernunft* (1785), *Hamanns Schriften*, Friedrich Roth (Ed.), vol.7, (Berlin: Riemer, 1825).
83 See Johann Gottfried Herder, "Eine Metakritik zur Kritik der reinen Vernunft," aus "Verstand und Erfahrung," *Sprachphilosophische Schriften*, Erich Heintel (Ed.), (Hamburg: Meiner, 1960), pp. 183–186.
84 Wilhelm von Humboldt, *On Language, On the Diversity of Human Language Construction and its Influence on the Mental Development of the Human Species*, Michael Losonsky (Ed.), Peter Heath (Trans.), (Cambridge: Cambridge University Press, 1999).
85 See footnote 71 above.

The truth that is demanded here is relative to the language- and interest-bound appearance of things. If truth demands the congruence of our designations with things as they are in themselves there is no truth.

> It is only by means for forgetfulness that man can ever reach the point of fancying himself to possess a "truth" of the grade just indicated. If he will not be satisfied with truth in the form of tautology, that is to say, if he will not be content with empty husks, then he will always exchange truths for illusions (TL 81).

Nietzsche here admits truth in the form of tautology. But why does he devalue the everyday truths that matter to us as "illusions?" Does Nietzsche have a right to this label? Or does he, perhaps under the spell of Schopenhauer's rhetoric, move too easily from the Kantian *Erscheinung* to *Schein*, i.e., from appearance to illusion?

Does the following reflection give him this right?

> What is a word? It is the copy in sound of a nerve stimulus. But the further inference from the nerve stimulus to a cause outside us is already the result of a false and unjustifiable application of the principle of sufficient reason (TL 81).

How convincing are these reflections? The word is said to be a copy (*Abbildung*) of a nerve stimulus (*Nervenreiz*) in sound (*Lauten*). What sense can we give here to the idea of a copy? Copy would seem to presuppose a certain structural similarity. How are we to understand this similarity in this particular case? And Nietzsche's claim that this nerve stimulus does not permit the inference to a cause without us also invites question. As a physical event, must it not have a cause of some sort?

The second part of Nietzsche's remark suggests a critique of Schopenhauer's causal theory of perception. According to Schopenhauer, when I see the sun, the understanding passes immediately from what Nietzsche calls a nerve stimulus to the object that causes that stimulus: I see the sun. Schopenhauer is aware that there is no necessity here: my seeing can be mistaken. But these are exceptions. There is a sense in which the seen sun is both cause and effect. We are tossed back and forth between two ways of looking at the matter: cause and effect reverse themselves. This reversal is inseparable from perception as Schopenhauer understands it. Nietzsche would seem to disagree.

But Nietzsche is concerned here not so much with the nature of perception as with the nature of language:

> If truth alone had been the deciding factor in the genesis of language, and if the standpoint of certainty had been decisive for designations, then how could we still dare to say "the

stone is hard," as if "hard" were something otherwise familiar to us and not merely a purely subjective stimulation. We separate things according to gender, designating the tree as masculine [*der Baum*] and the plant as feminine [*die Pflanze*]. What arbitrary assignments! How far this oversteps the canons of certainty! We speak of a "snake": this designation touches only on its ability to twist itself and could therefore also fit a worm. What arbitrary differentiations! What one-sided preferences, first for this, then for that property of a thing!" (TL 81–82).

Nietzsche is here arguing against those who think that words somehow express the essence of the thing. To return to a passage we considered in the preceding chapter:

The various languages placed side by side show that with words it is never a question of truth, never a question of adequate expression; otherwise, there would not be so many languages. The "thing in itself" which is precisely what the pure truth, apart from any of its consequences, would be) is likewise something quite incomprehensible to the creator of language and something not in the least worth striving for (TL 82).

As noted before, it is Nietzsche's understanding of truth as, not just a correspondence, but a congruence of designations and things (TL 81) that allows him to say that pure truth would be the thing in itself. What we can grant him is that the thing in itself remains quite incomprehensible. What we are dealing with are always only appearances.

It is this way with all of us concerning language: we believe that we know something about the things themselves when we speak of trees, colors, snow, and flowers, and yet we possess nothing but metaphors for things—metaphors which correspond in no way to the original entities. In the same way that the sound appears as a sand figure, so the mysterious X of the thing in itself first appears as a nerve stimulus, then as an image, and finally as a sound. Thus the genesis of language does not proceed logically in any case, and all the material within and with which the man of truth, the scientist, and the philosopher later work and build, if not derived from never-never land, is at least not derived from the essence of things (TL 82–83).

The question remains: what are we to make of the idea of this mysterious thing in itself? Where does it come from? Why is it needed? Nietzsche here would seem to blur the all-important distinction between the thing-in-itself and objective appearance, i.e., the object science seeks to know.

In the next paragraph Nietzsche addresses the problem of concepts and their generality:

In particular, let us further consider the formation of concepts. Every word instantly becomes a concept precisely insofar it is not supposed to serve as a reminder of the unique and entirely individual original experience to which it owes its origin: but rather, a word becomes a concept insofar as it simultaneously has to fit countless more or less similar cases – which means purely and simply, cases which are never equal and thus altogether unequal. Every concept arises from the equation of unequal things. Just as it is certain that one leaf is never totally the same as another, so it is certain that the concept "leaf" is formed by arbitrarily discarding these individual differences and by forgetting the individual aspects. This awakens the idea that, in addition to the leaves, there exists in nature the "leaf": the original model according to which all the leaves were perhaps woven, sketched, measured, colored, curled, and painted—but by incompetent hands, so that no specimen turned out to be a correct, trustworthy, and faithful likeness of the original model (TL 83).

Common to empiricists and rationalists had been the belief that concepts and percepts could be placed in a continuum. For the former concepts are washed out, if you want white percepts; for the latter percepts are confused concepts. Kant breaks this continuum. In the realm of aesthetics this has its counterpart in Lessing's rejection of the *ut pictura poesis* thesis. Like Schopenhauer, I find it impossible not to go along with Kant on this matter. The young Nietzsche's position is not altogether clear, as shown by his tendency to approach the problem of truth in terms of the picture theory. But is understanding like picturing? Lessing's rejection of the *ut pictura poesis* thesis invites a reconsideration of the picture theory of truth.

Nietzsche is of course right when he argues in the following lines that we should not reify and attribute causal efficacy to these concepts. And yet his reference to Schopenhauer's *qualitas occulta* invites questioning:

We call a person "honest," and then we ask "why has he behaved so honestly today?" Our usual answer is: "on account of his honesty." Honesty! This in turn means that the leaf is the cause of the leaves. We know nothing whatever about an essential quality called "honesty"; but we do know of countless individualized and consequently unequal actions which we equate by omitting the aspects in which they are unequal and which we now designate as "honest" actions. Finally we formulate from them a *qualitas occulta* which has the name "honesty." We obtain the concept, as we do the form, by overlooking what is individual and actual; whereas nature is acquainted with no forms and no concepts, and likewise with no species, but only with an X which remains inaccessible and undefinable for us. For even our contrast between individual and species is something anthropomorphic and does not originate in the essence of things (TL 83).

In this connection we may want to consider Plato's *Cratylus:* does the way we group objects have no foundation in these objects? Is there nothing like an *eidos* in *physis?* In that case, whether or not we group elephants and giraffes in different species would have to be considered completely arbitrary. Not that such groupings are necessary. No doubt we could group things differently, depending on different interests and experiences. But something like Schopenhauer's argument for a *qualitas occulta* has to be right. Indeed Nietzsche's own account presupposes it. Otherwise leaves would not have been grouped together. There has to be something like a similarity perceived in phenomena if concept formation is to make any sense. Furthermore, this similarity has to be experienced similarly by different human beings, otherwise Nietzsche's social contract theory of language makes no sense. But that theory does not account for the human unwillingness to settle for a knowledge of appearances.

3 Mother and Father of Our Concepts

> We still do not yet know where the drive for truth comes from. For so far we have heard only of the duty which society imposes in order to exist: to be truthful means to employ the usual metaphors. Thus, to express it morally, this is the duty to lie according to a fixed convention, to lie with the herd and in a manner binding upon everyone (TL 84).

Given the preceding, the claim is easily understood. "Lie" here operates against the background of the strong understanding of truth discussed earlier. It should be clear also that within the realm of the lie, so understood, we must distinguish between lying and truth-telling:

> As a *"rational"* being, he now places his behavior under the control of abstractions. He will no longer tolerate being carried away by sudden impressions, by intuitions. First he universalizes all these impressions into less colorful cooler concepts so that he can entrust the guidance of his life and conduct to them. Everything which distinguishes man from the animals depends upon this ability to volatilize perceptual metaphors in a schema, and thus to dissolve an image into a concept. For something is possible in the realm of these schemata which could never be achieved with the vivid first impressions: the construction of a pyramidal order according to castes and degrees, the creation of a new world of laws, privileges, subordinations, and clearly marked boundaries – a new world, one which now confronts that other vivid world of first impressions as more solid, more universal, better known, and more human than the immediately perceived world, and thus as the regulative and imperative world (TL 84).

The main thought should be familiar by now. Note, however, the tone of the key words: *verallgemeinern,* "universalize," *die anschaulichen Metaphern zu einem Schema verflüchtigen, also ein Bild in einen Begriff auflösen,* "to volatilize perceptual metaphors in a schema, and thus to dissolve an image into a concept."

> Whereas each perceptual metaphor is individual and without equals and is therefore able to elude all classification, the great edifice of concepts displays the rigid regularity of a Roman columbarium and exhales in logic that strength and coolness which is characteristic of mathematics. Anyone who has felt this cool breath [of logic] will hardly believe that even the concept—which is as bony, foursquare, and transposable as a die—is nevertheless

merely the residue of a metaphor, and that the illusion which is involved in the artistic transference of a nerve stimulus into images is, if not the mother, then the grandmother of every single concept (TL 84).

But remembering the earlier discussion (TL 82), if the grandmother of every concept is the transference of a nerve stimulus into an image (perceptual metaphor), and their mother the transference of images into words (original poetry), that transference also invites us to inquire into the father and perhaps the grandfather. The father would refer to what lets human beings universalize impressions, to that which, according to Nietzsche, lets every word immediately become a concept, i.e., to what Schopenhauer calls reason, while the grandfather would refer perhaps to what Schopenhauer calls the principle of sufficient reason.

Given the fact that *On Truth and Lie* first became available to most English speakers in Walter Kaufmann's greatly abridged edition, it is perhaps not surprising that the paternity of the concept should have been suppressed and at any rate gone pretty much unrecognized. Its significance becomes more apparent in the part of the essay not included in Kaufmann's selection. Let me return once more to the passage that I quoted in the very beginning of this chapter:

> As a genius of construction man raises himself far above the bee in the following way: whereas the bee builds with wax that he gathers from nature, man builds with the far more delicate conceptual material which he first has to manufacture from himself. In this he is greatly to be admired, but not on account of the drive for truth or for pure knowledge of things (TL 85).

The material of which this conceptual edifice is constructed is not the same as the ground that precariously supports it. While the former is manufactured by the subject, the latter may be thought of as the Heraclitean river, considered as a stream of perceptions.

For the Kant of the *Critique of Pure Reason* the understanding was the source of the laws of nature and of our concepts. Source should here be understood in terms of the paternity of our concepts. Nietzsche understands this paternity as anthropomorphism.

> That is to say, it is a thoroughly anthropomorphic truth which contains not a single point which would be "true in itself" or really and universally valid apart from man. At bottom, what the investigation of such truths is seeking is only the metamorphosis of the world into man (TL 85–86).

But how is *anthropos* (*der Mensch*) to be understood here?

> Similar to the way in which astrologers considered the stars to be in man's service and connected with his happiness and sorrow, such an investigator considers the entire universe as the infinitely fractured echo of one original sound—man; the entire universe as the infinitely multiplied copy of one original picture—man. His method is to treat man as the measure of all things... (TL 86).

Kant might have insisted that "man" be thought here in terms that would include any understanding, i.e., as the transcendental subject. Would Nietzsche have disagreed? If not, his use of the copy metaphor is quite misleading: "*als das verfielfältigte Abbild des einen Urbildes, des Menschen,*" "as the infinitely multiplied copy of the one original picture—man." We have an uncertainty here similar to the one I noted before with respect to the word. At issue is what we can call a third Copernican revolution, which inquires into the possibility of Kant's Copernican revolution and recognizes with Herder and Humboldt its dependence on ordinary language. At stake is the legitimacy of substituting for Kant's transcendental structures a natural language. Does it rest on a confusion of what Kant had been careful to separate: on a failure to give full weight to the heterogeneity of percept and concept, a heterogeneity to which the picture theory cannot do justice?

The last statement of this paragraph demands our special attention:

> ... but in doing so he again proceeds from the error of believing that he has these things [which he intends to measure] immediately before him as mere objects. He forgets that the original perceptual metaphors are metaphors and takes them to be the things themselves (TL 86).

There are two problems here that should not be blurred:
(1) The problem of the metamorphosis of things into perceptions. This metamorphosis is meant by the original perceptual metaphors that cut us off from the truth.
(2) Then there is the metamorphosis of these metaphors into words and concepts. This involves the human knower in a very different way. Schopenhauer would have said it involves reason.

The heterogeneity of these two "metaphors" must be acknowledged. Nietzsche tends to lump them together, inviting confusion.

When Nietzsche speaks of the forgetting of this primitive world of metaphor, we may want to add that this forgetting takes two quite different forms: we forget this world, i.e., we cover up what we perceive with our words and concepts, and we forget that this world is itself a world of metaphors.

Nietzsche is of course right: there can be no such thing as a correct perception. What would it mean?

> ... but in any case it seems to me that "the correct perception" – which would mean "the adequate expression of the object in the subject" is a contradictory impossibility, for between two absolutely different spheres as between subject and object, there is no causality, no correctness, and no expression; there is at most an *aesthetic* relation. I mean a suggestive transference, a stammering translation into a completely foreign tongue—for which there is required in any case, a freely inventive intermediate sphere and mediating force. "Appearance" is a word that contains many temptations, which is why I avoid it as much as possible (TL 86).

This recalls Kant's discussion of the schematism, where he insists that there must be something that mediates between the categories of the understanding and sense impressions. The schema is understood by Kant as a third thing, as a product of the imagination, which is understood as a representation of a "*Verfahren der Einbildungskraft einem Begriff sein Bild zu verschaffen* (B 179)," "of a procedure of the imagination to furnish a concept with its picture." The schema thus bridges the gap that has opened up between concept and percept, where Kant subordinates the work of the imagination to the transcendental unity of the apperception, subjects it to the logos.

But if there is a need to furnish a concept with its picture, there is also a need to furnish a percept with its concept. This is the problem of the genesis of empirical concepts such as "elephant" or "rose." Required here is what Kant called a reflective judgment. Here the imagination must first recognize in particulars a kind of family resemblance. Such recognition is at work in the creation of any concept. Metaphor formation is a similar process, but here the family resemblance would seem to be between concepts rather than particulars.

I do think that the imagination needs to be given an even more important role than Kant here gives it. But to a Kantian Nietzsche appears confused in his own metaphorical use of metaphor. And this confusion, it would seem, is not forced on us by the matter to be thought. It depends on what seems almost a deliberate blindness. At any rate, we can distinguish between:

(a) what Nietzsche calls perceptual "metaphors," the transference of a nerve stimulus into an image;
(b) the metaphor of the word, the transference of images into words, and
(c) metaphor in the usual sense, which presupposes a proper, i.e., generally accepted discourse.

4 Nietzsche and Kant

Did Nietzsche himself think that he had seriously challenged Kant? His rejection of the Kantian *Erscheinung* and its replacement with *Schein* may suggest this. And yet with his view of science he would seem to grant Kant most of what matters. To be sure, at first there would seem to be an obvious difference.

> But when the same image has been generated millions of times and has been handed down for many generations and finally appears on the same occasion for all mankind then it acquires at last the same meaning for men it would have if it were the sole necessary image and if the relationship of the original nerve stimulus to the generated image were a strictly causal one. In the same manner an eternally repeated dream would certainly be felt and judged to be reality. But the hardening and congealing of a metaphor guarantees absolutely nothing concerning its necessity and exclusive justification (TL 87).

Nietzsche is very much aware that such reflections are difficult to reconcile with our faith in science, faith that we daily affirm in our everyday behavior.

> Every person who is familiar with such considerations has no doubt felt a deep mistrust of all idealism of this sort just as often as he has quite clearly convinced himself of the eternal consistency, omnipresence, and infallibility of the laws of nature. He has concluded that so far as we can penetrate here—from the telescopic heights to the microscopic depths—everything is secure, complete, infinite, regular, and without any gaps. Science will be able to dig successfully in this shaft forever, and all the things that are discovered will harmonize with and not contradict each other. How little does this resemble a product of the imagination, for if it were such, there should be some place where the illusion and unreality can be divined (TL 87).

What would Kant have thought of the following observation, which would call what here is asserted into question?

> Against this, the following must be said: if each of us had a different kind of sense perception—if we could only perceive things now as a bird, now as a worm, now as a plant, or if one of us saw a stimulus as red, another as blue, while a third even heard the same stimulus as a sound—then no one would speak of such a regularity of nature, rather nature would be grasped only as a creation which is subjective in the highest degree (TL 87).

A Whorfian kind of reflection is raised to the physiological level, which presupposes, however, some understanding of an objective nature. So it is not surprising that Nietzsche should return to a position that would seem very much in keeping with what Kant has to say:

> But everything marvelous about the laws of nature, everything that quite astonishes us therein and seems to demand our explanation, everything that might lead us to distrust idealism: all this is completely and solely contained within the mathematical strictness and inviolability of our representations of time and space. But we produce these representations in and from ourselves with the same necessity with which the spider spins. If we are forced to comprehend all things only under these forms, then it ceases to be amazing that in all things we comprehend nothing but these forms. For they must all bear within themselves the laws of number, and it is precisely number which is most astonishing in things (TL 87).

Does this not grant the Kantian all that he might demand? Nietzsche here grants that our representations of space and time are necessary conditions of experience.

> All that conformity to law, which impresses us so much in the movement of the stars and in chemical processes, coincides at bottom with those properties which we bring to things. Thus it is we who impress ourselves in this way. In conjunction with this it of course follows that the artistic process of metaphor formation with which every sensation begins in us already presupposes these forms and thus occurs within them. The only way in which the possibility of subsequently constructing a new conceptual edifice from metaphors themselves can be explained is by the firm persistence of these original forms. That is to say, this conceptual edifice is an imitation of temporal, spatial, and numerical relationships in the domain of metaphor (TL 88).

This passage makes clear that in this essay Nietzsche understands the problem of metaphor formation against the background of what looks very much like the Kantian *a priori*, which remains the *a priori* of metaphor formation. This is to say, metaphor formation presupposes a world of objects in Kant's sense.

5 The Tower of Babel

The second part of Nietzsche's essay changes the tenor of the discussion.

> We have seen how it is originally language which works on the construction of concepts, a labor taken over in later ages by science. Just as the bee simultaneously constructs cells and fills them with honey, so science works unceasingly on this great columbarium of concepts, the graveyard of perceptions (TL 88).

Science seeks to complete the work of language. Language : science = life : death. This burial work would seem to begin as soon as there is speech. Interesting is the analogy with the bee. But science replaces honey with ashes.

Nietzsche next shifts to an image of science as a Tower of Babel:

> It is always building new, higher stories shoring up, cleaning and renovating the old cells; above all, it takes pains to fill up this monstrously towering framework and to arrange therein the entire empirical world, which is to say, the anthropomorphic world. Whereas the man of action binds his life to reason and its concepts so that he will not be swept away and lost, the scientific investigator builds his hut right next to the tower of science so that he will be able to work on it and find shelter for himself beneath these bulwarks which presently exist. And he requires shelter, for there are frightful powers which continuously break in upon him, powers which oppose scientific "truth" with completely different kind of "truths" which bear on their shields the most varied sorts of emblems (TL 88).

What then is the difference between the discourse of science and everyday language? Schopenhauer had suggested that science is distinguished from ordinary language by its systematic form of description. Nietzsche here follows Schopenhauer. Science subordinates particular truths under ever more general principles, insists on closure and completeness.

The ground of everyday language and its truths, on the other hand, is metaphor formation.

> The drive toward the formation of metaphors is the fundamental human drive, which one cannot for a single instant dispense with in thought, for one would thereby dispense with man himself. This drive is not truly vanquished and scarcely subdued by the fact that a regular and rigid new world is constructed as its prison from its own ephemeral products, the concepts (TL 88–89).

There is thus tension in human beings between the demands of reason and the imagination. "Prison" does not seem to me a quite adequate translation of *Zwingburg*, which refers to a tyrant's strong castle. The metaphoric drive, the imagination, appears as an anarchic element, which challenges what science would have us accept as reality by opposing to it the realms of myth and art. Metaphor now comes to mean more what we usually mean by that term. By contrast, proper discourse is discourse whose propriety is tied to obedience to the rule of that tyrant living in the strong castle. Metaphor keeps us open to the infinite life and richness of the life of perception. In that sense metaphor opposes to what is accepted as waking reality a reality that is quite different, closer to that of the dream.

> In fact, because of the way that myth takes for granted that miracles are always happening, the waking life of a mythically inspired people—the ancient Greeks for instance—more closely resembles a dream than it does the waking world of a scientifically disenchanted thinker (TL 89).

Myth is tied to an enchantment that, Nietzsche would seem to claim, true humanity requires. *The Birth of Tragedy* had developed this point. There is in us an innate tendency to allow ourselves to be enchanted:

> But man has an invincible inclination to allow himself to be deceived and is, as it were, enchanted with happiness when the rhapsodist tells him epic fables as if they were true, or when the actor in the theater acts more royally than any real king. So long as it is able to deceive without *injuring*, the master of deception, the intellect, is free; it is released from its former slavery and celebrates its Saturnalia (TL 89).

Nietzsche here pleads for a liberation of the imagination:

> In comparison with its previous conduct, everything that it now does bears the mark of dissimulation [*Verstellung*], just as the previous conduct did of distortion [*Verzerrung*]. The free intellect copies human life. But it considers this life something good and seems to be quite satisfied with it. That immense framework and planking of concepts to which the needy man clings his whole life in order to preserve himself is nothing but a scaffolding and toy for the most audacious feats of the liberated intellect. And when it smashes this framework to pieces, throws it into confusion, and puts it back together in an ironic fashion, pairing the most alien things and separating the closest, it is demonstrating that it has no need of these makeshifts of indigence and that it will now be guided by intuitions rather than concepts. There is no regular path which leads from these intuitions into the land of ghostly schemata, the land of abstractions. There exists no word for these intuitions; when man sees them he grows dumb, or else he speaks only in forbidden metaphors and in unheard-of combinations of concepts. He does this so that by shattering and mocking the old conceptual barriers he may at least correspond creatively to the impression of the powerful present intuition (TL 90).

There is something volcanic about this imagination. It refuses to bind itself to the regulative ideal of truth as a correspondence of our discourse to the things. And yet the imagination, too, knows something like correspondence, an analogue to truth: Nietzsche speaks of a *schöpferische Entsprechung* to a *gegenwärtige Intuition*, "a creative correspondence to the present intuition." The imagination appears here free from the rule of reason. This is to say also that truth as ordinarily understood no longer functions as a regulative ideal. What has been substituted for it is what one might call truth of an altogether different sort.

Nietzsche goes on to juxtapose the intuitive and the rational man, one scornful of abstraction and the architecture of reason, the other fearful of anarchic intuition and the deconstructive impulse:

> The latter is just as irrational as the former is inartistic. They both desire to rule over life: the former, by knowing how to meet his principal needs by foresight, prudence, and regularity; the latter by disregarding these needs and, as an "overjoyed hero," counting as real only that life which has been disguised as illusion and beauty. Whenever, as was perhaps

the case in ancient Greece, the intuitive man handles his weapons more authoritatively and victoriously than his opponent, then, under favorable circumstances, a culture can take shape and art's mastery over life can be established (TL 90).

The fragment "*On Truth and Lie*" ends on the same note as the closely related essay *On the Pathos of Truth*. As he did there, Nietzsche reminds the reader of the Stoic sage as Schopenhauer described him: the man of reason. That Schopenhauer here sides with the artist is evident, and siding with the artist, he also sides, at least as Nietzsche reads him, with the formation of culture. The opposition of reason and culture had been a central theme in *The Birth of Tragedy*.

Nietzsche suggests a deep connection between rationality as it manifests itself in science and death. Remember the image of a *Kolumbarium der Begriffe*, a columbarium of concepts," a *Begräbnisstätte der Anschauungen*, "a graveyard of intuitions." Concepts, this suggests, are the ashes of lived intuition. The pursuit of truth, the attempt to understand things as they really are, unclouded by all too human interests and perspectival distortions, threatens to lead us out of life. The pathos of truth may want to translate life out of time, may want a semblance of eternal life, and yet the idea of such a translation is for Nietzsche the most seductive deception. The pursuit of truth so understood is really the pursuit of nothing, a nothing whose seductive promise we bear within ourselves. The attempt to defeat the essential insecurity of human existence by turning to reason threatens to transform human life, even before death, into a living death, where Nietzsche is no doubt also thinking of the Christian understanding of an afterlife. A civilization that has subjected itself to the tyrant in his castle lives death.

This forces us to take seriously Geoffrey Hartmann's claim that "Everything that blows the cover of reified or superobjective thinking is important."[86] But we should note that Nietzsche's essay gives us no hope that the *Zwingburg* that science has built will collapse when we realize that all concepts originate with the imagination, that the mother of all concepts is the poetic imagination. We have to keep in mind also the father, i.e., reason. The essay thus suggests that what endows the father and his castle with their suffocating authority is our overly great preoccupation with our indigence, is our own attempt to secure our existence. It is we who allow this patriarch to rule our lives and that rule, Nietzsche would seem to suggest, will be broken, not by reasoning more carefully, but by a different pathos, a pathos that counteracts the pathos of truth. The problem we face is not so much one of epistemology as one of ethics.

---

[86] Geoffrey Hartmann, "Literary Criticism and its Discontents," *Critical Inquiry*, vol. 3, no, 2, p. 216.

IV The Devil as Philosopher

1 Knowing Knowledge

The title I have given this chapter demands some explanation: We do not tend to think of the devil as a philosopher. Is the devil not the father of lies (*John* 8:44)? And is the philosopher not supposed to be the lover of wisdom and as such opposed to whatever the devil stands for? The devil as seducer, as liar – these are familiar characterizations. But should we think of the devil as a philosopher, as a lover of truth?

And yet, that there is a connection is hinted at by the Biblical understanding of the devil as Lucifer, the light bringer, the morning star, who wanted to ascend to the heavens and raise his throne above the stars of God, only to be brought down to the realm of the dead (*Isaiah* 14:12–14)? Does the philosopher's love of truth, the "pathos of truth," to cite the title of one of Nietzsche's essays, not answer to the snake's promise: "*Eritis sicut Deus, scientes bonum et malum*," "you will be like God, knowing good and evil" (*Genesis* 3:5)? Goethe has Mephistopheles, disguised as Faust, write these words into the family album of the student who has come to the university eager to understand all that is on earth and in heaven.[87] And are we human beings, especially the philosophers among us, not haunted by the snake's promise? Think of Spinoza, Fichte, or Hegel. And even the atheist Sartre, who declared the idea of God to be a contradiction, nevertheless insisted that the fundamental project of us human beings is what he knew to be the vain project to become God.[88] The philosopher, possessed by the pathos of truth, does indeed look a lot like Goethe's Mephistopheles.

But what made me first think of the devil as a philosopher was not Goethe's Mephistopheles, but the way the devil is portrayed as a "sort of scholar and philosopher" in a story written in 1813 by the romantic poet Adelbert von Chamisso: "*Peter Schlemihls wundersame Geschichte*" or "Peter Schlemihl's Remarkable Story."[89] This, too, like Goethe's *Faust*, is the story of a pact with the devil. In 1804 the young Chamisso had indeed published a one-act tragedy, which he

---

[87] Johann Wolfgang von Goethe, *Faust*, Erster Teil, 2048.
[88] Jean-Paul Sartre, *Being and Nothingness*, Hazel E. Barnes (Trans. and Intro.), (New York: Philosophical Library, 1956), p. 615.
[89] Adelbert von Chamisso, *Peter Schlemihl*, John Bowring (Trans.). Project Gutenberg EBook , transcribed from the 1889 Cassell & Company edition by David Price, p. 25.

later was to call it a *"fast knabenhaften metaphysisch-poetischen Versuch"*[90] an "almost boyish poetic-metaphysical experiment," dealing with the Faust theme.[91] But that experiment was thoughtful enough to draw the attention of the philosopher Johann Gottlieb Fichte, who was to become a fatherly friend.[92]

A good and an evil spirit fight here for the soul of Faust. The good spirit admonishes Faust not to listen to the snake's promise and to believe. But Faust wants to know. And at the price of his soul the evil spirit promises him truth and knowledge. Faust accepts the bargain and the evil spirit fulfills that promise in a fashion; but the knowledge that he ends up providing is the knowledge that the pursuit of truth ends in the recognition that all our access to reality is mediated, mediated by our language, our reason, our senses.

> The flower of faith bloomed to the child.
> Demanding truth, you proudly stepped on it.
> Well! I shout at you the terrible truth:
> From the contradictions of your wise men
> It glares at you, as you suspected:
> Doubt is the limit of what man can know.
> Shrouded in dust, he can know nothing.
> No light can shine for him born blind.
>
> Just as language, the sound of words,
> Mediates and is sign for you of thought;
> So what the sense perceives, the thought itself
> Are only words to you, an empty vacuous sign
> Of a reality forever hidden.
> You can think only with the mediator language
> See nature only with your senses,
> Think it only with the laws of the understanding.
> And even were you to possess a hundred senses and a thousand,
> You poorly endowed human, and if more freely
> Your thought lifted itself unto the universe,
> Perceived in many other ways; still you would always see,

---

90 Adelbert von Chamisso, *Reise um die Welt mit der Romanzoffischen Entdeckungs-Expedition in den Jahren 1815–1818 auf der Brigg Rurik, Kapitain Otto von Kotzebue* (Leipzig: Reclam, 1836), Einleitung.

91 Adelbert von Chamisso, "Faust. Eine Tragödie in einem Akt. Ein Versuch" (1803), *Musenalmanach auf das Jahr 1804*, L. A. v. Chamisso and E. A. Varnhagen (Eds.).(Leipzig: Carl Gottlob Schmidt), 1804, Sämtliche Werke, vol. 1 (München: Winkler, 1975), pp. 500–509.

92 Adelbert von Chamisso, *Reise um die Welt, Einleitung.*

Separated, united with it by the body's bonds,
Only your own shadows and know nothing.[93]

The truth is denied to us—that is the evil spirit's wisdom, anticipating Nietzsche and Hofmannsthal. If Heidegger called language the house of Being, Chamisso's Faust comes to experience that house as a prison and his desire to seize the truth only strengthens its walls.

Chamisso's youthful attempt presupposes an acquaintance with transcendental idealism. That Fichte should have taken an interest in the young poet is thus not surprising. Chamisso's evil spirit does indeed recall the spirit that convinces the "I" of the Second Book of Fichte's *The Vocation of Man*, [94] *Wissen* (Knowledge), of the truth of transcendental idealism. So let us turn to that Second Book.

2 Idealism and Nihilism

In the First Book of *The Vocation of Man* Fichte had developed the threat the scientific worldview poses to the dignity of man by making human beings but part of the mechanism of nature. That seems to leave no room for freedom and thus for a robust understanding of what makes a person a person. In the Second Book Fichte turns to the philosophy of Kant to blunt that threat. It is almost as if the Spirit that speaks here to Fichte's "I" were the spirit of the *Critique of Pure Reason*, although we should also keep in mind the resemblance to Descartes' evil genius.

The argument that Spirit advances is in substantial agreement with that advanced by Kant, as appropriated by Fichte in his *Wissenschaftslehre*. It holds that the world that the sciences seek to describe is a world of appearances only, not of things in themselves. But this means that the being of this world is essentially a being for the subject, which is therefore not part of that world. The subject stands before the world, understood as the totality of phenomena, somewhat as an observer stands before a picture.[95] That subject is thus not to be understood as just another part of nature, subject to its laws. To be sure, as an embodied self the

---

[93] Adalbert von Chamisso, "Faust. Eine Tragödie in einem Akt. Ein Versuch," *Sämtliche Werke*. vol. 1, p. 506. My translation.
[94] Johann Gottlieb Fichte, *Die Bestimmmung des Menschen* (1800). References in the text are to *The Vocation of Man*, Roderick M., Chisholm (Ed. and Intro), (New York, Liberal Arts Press, 1956)
[95] GA5, 75–115. "The Age of the World Picture," William Lovitt (Trans.), *The Question Concerning Technology and other Essays* (New York: Harper Torchbooks, 1977), pp. 115–154.

subject, too, experiences itself as part of nature. But as knowing subject the human being transcends nature. This gives you the outline of the argument.

But let us move a bit more slowly. The first thing that cannot be doubted is that objects are present to me (VM 35). How do I know about these objects? I sense them (VM 36). Things are given to me in sensation. Sensation is a particular determination of myself (VM 37). I do not have direct access to things; all I have access to are my own sensations.

This point has of course been challenged. In his "The Refutation of Idealism," for example, G. E. Moore sought to refute the thesis that *esse est percipi*, a thesis said by him to be presupposed by every idealism, arguing that when, e.g., I see a blue flower, I do have a direct perception of the blue of the flower as something that is there regardless of whether I perceive it or not.

> I am as directly aware of the existence of material things in space as of my own sensations; and what I am aware of with regard to each is exactly the same—namely that in one case the material thing, and in the other case my sensation does really exist. The question requiring to be asked about material things is thus not: What reason have we for supposing that anything exists corresponding to our sensations? but: What reason have we for supposing that material things do not exist, since their existence has precisely the same evidence as that of our sensations?[96]

The perceived, Moore argues, is independent of the act of perception. And that is indeed what I would be inclined to say. What supports this is the realist side of what I have called the Antinomy of Being. But the question returns: what meaning can we give here to "existence?" Can I really say of the blue of the flower that it exists without any perceiving subject? Moore would have us answer in the affirmative. But are secondary qualities such as blue, things in themselves? And what about the flower? Must its being, too, not be thought relative to some perceiving or understanding subject. Does the idea of a thing in itself even make sense?

Fichte, at any rate, would have us disagree with Moore: I can only think of the tree as an object of some sort of perception. According to Fichte we are directly aware only of our sensation, not of the objects before us. "In all perception you perceive only your own condition" (VM 38).

But how then do we come to interpret our sensations in such a way as to fashion out of them a world of objects out there in space that we take to be

---

[96] G. E. Moore, "The Refutation of Idealism," Originally published in *Mind*, 12 (1903), pp. 433–53. Reprinted in *Selected Writings*, Thomas Baldwin (Ed.), (London: Routledge, 2013), p. 44.

real? Fichte's Spirit leads his "I" to recognize that our experience of things presupposes what Kant called a pure intuition of space:

> *Spirit.* Thus there is nothing remaining of the object but *what is perceptible*, what is a property or attribute. This perceptibility you extend through a continuous space which is divisible to infinity; and the true bearer of the attributes of things which you have sought, is, therefore only the space which is thus filled? (VM 46).

The objects I experience present themselves to me. But, Fichte's "I" objects, must there then not be something, some thing in itself that does the presenting?

> *I.* I find a thing determined this way or that. I cannot rest satisfied with knowing that it *is* in this state. I assume that it has *become so*, and that not through itself, but by means of a foreign power. This foreign power, which made the thing what it is, *contains the cause*; and the manifestation of that power, which did actually make it so, *is the cause* of this particular determination of the thing. My sensation must have a cause: this means that it is produced within me by a foreign power (VM 53).

The Spirit counters:

> But how then do you know, and how do you propose to prove, *that* sensation must have a cause? (VM 54).

Can it be an immediate perception? Fichte answers, "No!" Perception establishes only that something is, not how it has become so, still less that it has become so by a power lying beyond perception. To generalize from an observation of external things would be to beg the issue (VM 54). All that remains is to say that within himself the human being has the power to break out of himself. We posit the things as other, they are not other in themselves.

> *Spirit.* You perceive then that all knowledge is merely a knowledge of yourself; that your consciousness never goes beyond yourself; and that what you assume to be a consciousness of the object is nothing but a consciousness of the fact that you have *posited* an object—posited it necessarily, in accordance with an inward law of your thought, at the same time as the sensation (VM 57).

Presupposed by consciousness is a polarity. In the *cogito* both subject and object are present. Our being is that polarity and we have to guard against thinking of the self first of all as an isolated subject that needs to establish relationships with an external world. The human being is not a thing, but a relation. The object is nothing apart from the subject nor is the subject apart from the object.

> You yourself art the thing; you yourself, by virtue of your finitude—the innermost law of your being—are thus presented before yourself, and projected out of yourself; and all that you perceive beyond yourself is still yourself alone. This consciousness has been well named "intuition." In all consciousness I am intuitively aware of myself; for I am myself: for the subjective, conscious being, consciousness is intuitive self-contemplation (VM 64).

We are always caught within the net of our own consciousness. The world we encounter is the product of our own mind. When we die we might as well be nothing.

"But is this not patently absurd?" the realist will object. Is it not obvious that the world existed before I was conscious of it and will exist when I will be dead? If Fichte is right, it must be impossible for a human being to really think of his own death. Of course, as a finite embodied being that is part of the world, I know that I will die. Other people die and I am like them. But when I say this, what I speak about is not myself as consciousness, but myself as object in the world. We should note: the human being here appears twice, once as an object in the world and once as consciousness. When we think about our own death we may imagine ourselves as objects dying or dead, but here our consciousness transcends that death. Thus we might imagine ourselves looking at our own funeral. As long as we understand reality as the world of objects we encounter and interpret ourselves as parts of that world, speaking of ourselves as positing that world makes no sense.

But for objects to be given at all must consciousness not be presupposed? Objects can be given only in consciousness. The opposite cannot even be thought. For to think of objects as not thought, Fichte's Spirit insists, is a contradiction. The world of objects must vanish with my death. Death negates the very condition of consciousness and can therefore be thought only as a limit.

Has the Spirit successfully banished the fear that we might be no more than insignificant parts of the world machine? This is what he claims to have shown:

> *Spirit.* From you, then, I need fear no objection to the principle now established: that *our consciousness of external things is absolutely nothing more than the product of our own presentative faculty*, and that, with respect to such things, we know only what is produced through our consciousness itself, through a determinate consciousness subject to definite laws (VM 74).

The Spirit's use of "our" and "we" invites question. How are we to understand this plural? Does idealism here not issue in a transcendental solipsism, as Moore insisted it had to?[97]

The Spirit claims to have shown the "I's" fear of science to have been groundless.

> *Spirit.* And with this insight, mortal, be free, and forever released from the fear which has degraded and tormented you! You will no longer tremble at a necessity which exists only in your own thought; no longer fear to be crushed by things which are the product of your own mind; no longer place yourself, the thinking being, in the same class with the thoughts which proceed from you (VM 75).

But, as we are not surprised to learn, Fichte's "I" is anything but grateful:

> *I.* Stay, deceitful Spirit! Is this all the wisdom towards which you have directed my hopes, and do you boast that you have set me free? You have set me free, it is true; you have absolved me from all dependence, for you have transformed me, and everything around me on which I could possibly be dependent, into nothing. You have abolished necessity by annihilating all existence (VM 76).

Fichte's Spirit would seem to be a nihilist. *Nihil*, nothing, will have the last word. In the end everything will vanish into nothing. Like Descartes' evil genius, Fichte's Spirit threatens to transform life into an empty dream. And even the dreamer dreaming that dream in the end dissolves into nothing. Given the Spirit's wisdom, it seems that in the end nothing matters, that my life is of no account. The good and the evil life are equally swallowed by nothing. The "I" finds itself utterly alone, surrounded by a nothingness that will devour all.

The mood in which this nothingness presents itself is dread, as Kierkegaard and Heidegger were to analyze it. What we dread is the nothing that will finally overtake us. That distinguishes it from fear, which has a definite object. Most of the time, to be sure, we are not in dread. The world keeps us too occupied. But there may be moments when an individual may ask herself: what is the point of it all? Take someone whose world has been shattered by war or some natural disaster. The world no longer seems to offer anything to hold on to. It has become mute.

We should keep in mind that 1800 was a time when the old religious, social, and political order seemed to be collapsing. "Nihilism," used already by Frie-

---

[97] G. E. Moore, "The Refutation of Idealism," Originally published in *Mind*, 12 (1903), pp. 433–53. Reprinted in *Selected Writings*, Thomas Baldwin (Ed.), (London: Routledge, 2013). Moore, "Refutation of Idealism," p. 43.

drich Heinrich Jacobi—I shall return to him a bit later—to describe the kind of Kantian idealism defended by Fichte's Spirit, was soon to describe a widely experienced state of mind. It was picked up by literary critics. In parapraph 2 of his *Vorschule der Ästhetik* the poet Jean Paul Richter speaks thus of "poetic nihilists." The passage is worth quoting:

> It follows from the lawless willfulness of the current spirit of the age—which in its intoxication with the self would rather destroy the world and the cosmos, in order to empty for itself an empty playing field in the nothing... that it has to speak in condescending terms of the imitation and study of nature. For as gradually the history of the age comes to resemble an historian and is without religion and fatherland, so self-centered willfulness finally has to bump against the hard and sharp decrees of reality and for that reason would rather fly into the desert of fantastic invention, where there are no laws to be followed except those that are its own, more confining, smaller, those of building with rhyme and assonance.[98]

As art emancipates itself from the task of representation, an empty formalism becomes ever more important. It would be interesting to look at the evolution of modern art from this perspective. Such art has its philosophical analogue.

It did not take nihilism long to make its appearance in literature. Ivan Turgenev's novel *Fathers and Sons* deserves special mention here. His Basarov became the paradigmatic nihilist. The pseudonymous author of volume one of Kierkegaard's *Either/Or*, the aesthete A, is another unusually articulate nihilist. But the most influential philosopher of nihilism is Nietzsche, whose proclamation of the death of God implies also the devaluation of all of what were once our highest values. And nihilism is a presupposition of the thought of existentialists such as Sartre and Camus. But the phenomenon is of course not confined to our modern age. We meet with it already in the *Gilgamesh Epic* and in the Bible's *Ecclesiastes* where the preacher proclaims that all is vanity.

But to return to Fichte: is this then what reason leads us to, to the recognition that all talk of God or absolute values or of a vocation of man is in the end but an escape from the truth? In the Third Book of *The Vocation of Man* Fichte attempts to answer such questions by showing that even though theoretical reason can know nothing of God, talk of a vocation of man is anything but idle. Faith comes to the rescue.

---

[98] Jean Paul Richter, *Vorschule der Ästhetik, Jean Paul's sämmtliche Werke* (Berlin: G. Reimer, 1827), vol. 41, par. 2, p. 32.

3 The Man Without a Shadow

Before I turn to Book Three of *The Vocation of Man* let me return to the story of Peter Schlemihl. As this story begins we are in the age of Enlightenment, that is to say the age of reason, which is also the age of emerging capitalism, just outside the northern gate of some seaport, with a garden party at the newly built country villa of the nouveau-riche Thomas John, who has made money the measure of value, asserting that people who do not possess at least a million are scum, a remark that meets with the young Peter Schlemihl's thoughtless agreement. Does not everything have a price? Was it such thoughtlessness that let our hero be approached at that party by a thin grey man who wants to buy his shadow in exchange for a never empty wallet? What good, after all, is one's shadow, compared to all that money can buy? The reader is invited to reflect on the relationship between the homogenizing power of money, which would subject everything to the same measure, and the loss of the shadow, which suggests a disturbed relationship to the body. The grey man's promise, at any rate, persuades our thoughtless Schlemihl to strike the bargain.

Having lost his shadow, he has to recognize almost immediately that this loss has made normal relationships with other human beings quite impossible. The bargain he has struck has made him an introverted, thoroughly displaced person. No surprise that he loses the woman he loves.

It does not take Peter long to regret his bargain. But when the devil offers to return him his shadow, but now at the price of his soul, Schlemihl turns down this offer and, disgusted with himself, throws away the ever full wallet that has brought him such unhappiness. Not that he regains his shadow, but, as if to compensate him for the loss of his shadow, Peter Schlemihl gains a new mobility, coming into possession of a pair of seven league boots that renders distance of little significance and that he puts to good use as a scientist.

What is the relationship between our hero's loss of his shadow and the mobility he is granted by the fortuitous acquisition of a pair of seven league boots? How is the devil related to the pursuit of science?

To give a first answer to the first question: the commitment to objectivity that is a presupposition of scientific inquiry presupposes a self-elevation that means also a self-displacement. There is a sense in which to a scholar studying, say, Israel, Jerusalem is as close as whatever place he happens to find himself in—we are speaking of spiritual, not physical proximity.[99] That is to say also, as a scientist such a scholar casts no shadow. So understood the loss of the shadow, that is

---

[99] See Karsten Harries, *Infinity and Perspective* (Cambridge, MA: MIT Press, 2001), pp. 160–161.

to say, the transformation of the embodied self into a disembodied thinker, into a Cartesian *res cogitans*, lies at the very origin of philosophy and of science. The scientist wants to understand what he observes as it really is, not as it appears, given a particular point of view. This desire to know is said to have already caused Thales to tumble into his well. Such absent-mindedness and the loss of the shadow belong together. They belong with that disinterested objectivity that is demanded of all who lay claim to the pursuit of truth. A Cartesian *res cogitans* does not cast a shadow. And human beings who understand themselves first of all as such free, thinking subjects, who just happen to find themselves in some particular body, in a particular place and time, will not allow such particularities to determine who they are, but will consider all they observe material to be fashioned into a successful life.

But how does such a free spirit measure success? Where do we find the proper measure? Does our reason hold the key? That was the snake's promise. By relieving us of our shadows, the devil would free us from whatever external reality would bind us, be it the body, be it society, be it God. But if such liberation lets us look more objectively at our world, does it also bring us a knowledge of good and evil, as the snake promised? Are we possessed of a practical reason that tells us with as much certainty what we ought to do as theoretical reason tells us what is the case? Is a self-centered egoist, who says "after me the deluge," unreasonable?

4 The Devil as Philosopher

With this question in mind, let me turn to Chamisso's decription of the devil as a philosopher. Our hero, having resisted the devil's offer to return him his shadow at the price of his soul, having learned that the loss of his shadow condemns him to be "a restless and solitary wanderer on the face of the earth,"[100] is joined by a traveler who, having first extolled the pleasure and power money brings, falls into a philosophical monologue:

> He unfolded his views of human life and of the world, and, touching on metaphysics, demanded an answer from that cloudy science to the question of questions—the answer that should solve all mysteries. He deduced one problem from another in a very lucid manner, and then proceeded to their solution.[101]

---

100 Adelbert von Chamisso, *Peter Schlemihl,* John Bowring (Trans.), Project Gutenberg EBook, transcribed from the 1889 Cassell & Company edition by David Price, p. 34.
101 Ibid., p. 34.

Although declaring himself unfit for metaphysical speculations, Peter is nevertheless impressed, if not edified, by the airy architecture raised by this philosopher's words.

> Now this skillful rhetorician seemed to me to expend great skill in rearing a firmly-constructed edifice, towering aloft on its own self-supported basis, but resting on, and upheld by, some internal principle of necessity. I regretted in it the total absence of what I desired to find; and thus it seemed a mere work of art, serving only by its elegance and exquisite finish to captivate the eye. Nevertheless, I listened with pleasure to this eloquently gifted man, who diverted my attention from my own sorrows to the speaker; and he would have secured my entire acquiescence if he had appealed to my heart as well as to my judgment.[102]

Chamisso's devil presents itself to our hero as a philosopher whose conceptual architecture, held together by an inner necessity, appears to support itself. This architecture is the work of a thinking that would subject everything to the principle of sufficient reason, an architecture that seems to rest on a foundation that supports itself. Such a foundation is provided by God thought as *causa sui*, and Spinoza's philosophy is perhaps the most rigorous working out of the philosophy represented by Chamisso's devil.

The reference to Spinoza is not out of place here. In 1813 the pantheism controversy into which Kant too was drawn and which put Spinoza at the very center of philosophical discussion had not yet been forgotten. That controversy had its origin in the publication of Friedrich Heinrich Jacobi's *Über die Lehre des Spinoza in Briefen an den Herrn Moses Mendelssohn* (1785).[103] In the beginning of these letters Jacobi tells of the first time he visited Lessing in Wolfenbüttel. He reports Lessing to have said: "There is no other philosophy than the philosophy of Spinoza."[104] That had to upset the Lessing admirer Mendelssohn, since Spinoza's system was generally thought to be atheistic. If that was not to be extended to all of philosophy, one had to reject or modify Lessing's assertion. But Jacobi agrees with Lessing. He, too, thinks that at bottom there is no other philosophy than that of Spinoza. For the God-believing Jacobi the only conclusion to be drawn was: what philosophy calls truth does not do justice to truth.

> The whole matter consists in this: assuming fatalism I immediately draw the conclusion against fatalism and everything that is connected with it.—If there are only efficient and

---

102 Ibid., p. 34.
103 Friedrich Heinrich Jacobi, *Über die Lehre des Spinoza in Briefen an den Herrn Moses Mendelssohn* (Breslau: Löwe, 1785).
104 Friedrich Heinrich Jacobi, *Jacobis Spinoza Büchlein nebst Replik und Duplik* (München: G. Müller, 1912), p. 67.

no final causes, the thinking faculty is in the whole of nature only an observer. Its only business is to accompany the mechanism of the effective forces.... We only believe that we act from anger, love, generosity, or for a good reason. All illusion! In all these cases what moves us is at bottom something that does not know anything of all that and that accordingly is completely without sentiment and thought... I do not know how to refute someone able to accept this. But someone unwilling to accept this has to become the antipode of Spinoza.[105]

Jacobi is willing to admit: A rigorous rationalism leads to Spinoza. But we cannot live with such a rationalism. It is existentially unbearable.

And this is how Peter Schlemihl reacts to the words of the devil. The only adequate response is to follow Jacobi and to turn away from every attempt to subject reality in its entirety to our reason and the principle of sufficient reason. But of this Jacobi's enlightened contemporaries did not want to hear. So they ridiculed him as an enemy of reason and a disguised Jesuit.

5 Science and Faith

Given the historical context, it is not surprising that the pantheism controversy should have been given a transcendental turn by the charge of atheism raised against Johann Gottlieb Fichte fifteen years later. Fichte himself recognized the affinity between his thought and that of Spinoza. Both are said by him to be the result of "the necessary striving to establish the highest unity in human knowledge." Had Kant not called reason by its very nature architectonic? Reason seeks to assign all knowledge a place in a systematic whole.[106] To pursue the truth is to be in search of such a whole. What Spinoza failed to see, according to Fichte, is that this unity could not be established by theoretical reason as an existing reality, but only provided practical reason with an ideal that we human actors ought to, but will never succeed in realizing.[107] In a way that recalls Descartes, Fichte attempts to ground his philosophical edifice in the I, which in reflection transcends itself and gives itself a measure in the idea of the infinite or absolute I, which would include all of reality, which is a presupposition of the pursuit of truth and more importantly of our sense of duty, where

---

105 Ibid., pp. 69–70.
106 With his antinomies, to be sure, Kant showed that this interest can never be satisfied. *Kritik der reinen Vernunft*, A 474/B 502. See Paula Manchester, "Kant's Conception of Architectonic in its Philosophical Context," *Kant Studien*, Volume 99, Issue 2, June, 2008, pp. 133–151.
107 Johann Gottlieb Fichte, *Grundlage der gesamten Wissenschaftslehre* (1794), (Hamburg: Meiner, 1956), pp. 18–21.

Fichte follows Kant in insisting on the priority of practical reason. This double pursuit is taken to be constitutive of the life of reason. It is taken to justify our confidence in a natural and a moral world order that should not be placed in some transcendent realm, but that it is our vocation to establish. This order does not depend on a personal God, but finds its sufficient reason in the subject certain of its vocation, for what we ought to do must also be something we can do. Certain of our vocation, we are also certain that our actions are not in vain. Such certainty, according to Fichte, is a presupposition of science; it is also a presupposition of the moral life.[108]

But is such confidence that our efforts are not futile justified? The question is more easily answered in the affirmative in the case of scientific inquiry than in the case of moral action. Can theoretical and practical reason really be bound together as Fichte attempted to do? Is Fichte's system more than another philosophical construct that reason itself calls into question as lacking a foundation? Is a selfish egoist, such as Kierkegaard's aesthete, unreasonable? Jacobi had already described such an egoist in his epistolary novel *Allwill* (1792)[109] and it is not surprising that Jacobi should have become a prominent critic of Fichte's enterprise. By then Fichte had replaced Spinoza in Jacobi's mind as *the* philosopher, the Messiah of Reason, as he called him.[110] But "Messiah of Reason" turns out to be one of the devil's masks.

Fichte, to be sure, rejected the charge of atheism, which his essay "On the Ground of Our Belief in a Divine World Government" had invited. But the atheism controversy ended up costing him his professorship in Jena. In 1800 he left Jena for Berlin, where, as I mentioned, he was to meet Chamisso, who speaks of him as a "fatherly friend" and got Fichte to contribute to the *Musenalmanach*, a literary journal Chamisso had helped found and finance. Schlemihl's response to the devil's elegant thought architecture may well represent Chamisso's own response to the kind of philosophy that provoked the atheism controversy.

---

108 Cf. Heinrich Rickert, *Fichtes Atheismusstreit und die Kantische Philosophie. Eine Säkularbetrachtung*, Sonderdruck aus den "Kantstudien." (Berlin: Reuther and Reichard, 1899).
109 Friedrich Heinrich Jacobi, *Allwill*, J. U. Terpstra (Ed. and Intro.), (Groningen: J.B. Wolters, 1957).
110 *Jacobi an Fichte*. (Hamburg: Perthes, 1799), Supplement II was republished in *Werke II*, 1815 (Jacobi, 1812–1825) under the title of *Über die Unzertrennlichkeit der Freiheit und Vorsehung von dem Begriffe der Vernunft*.

6 Fichte's Faith

Fichte admits that there is no argument that will force the nihilist to abandon his position. Fichte's faith is essentially what Kant calls practical reason and discusses in his *Critique of Practical Reason*.

> Now that I know this, I possess the touchstone of all truth and of all conviction. Conscience alone is the root of all truth. Whatever is opposed to conscience or stands in the way of the fulfillment of her behests is assuredly false; I could never become convinced, even if I should be unable to discover the fallacies by which it is produced (VM 90).

What is called conscience here is also the call of reality, which is submerged whenever the world is seen as the desiccated object of a detached, theoretical understanding. Our knowledge is interested. Bracket that interest and you lose reality.

> What is it which holds us within the power of this first natural belief? Not inferences of reason, for there are none such; it is our *interest* in a reality which we desire to produce: in the good, absolutely for its own sake, and the common and sensuous, for the sake of the enjoyment they afford. No one who lives can divest himself of this interest, and just as little can he cast off the faith which this interest brings with it. We are all born in faith; he who is blind, follows blindly the secret and irresistible impulse; he who sees, follows by sight, and believes because he resolves to believe (VM 90–91).

What separates the interested behavior of the child from the interested behavior of the philosopher is the intervening suspicion of nihilism. "With freedom and consciousness I have returned to the point at which Nature had left me. I accept that which she announces; but I do not accept it because I must; I believe it because I will" (VM 92). It follows that the good and the true are ultimately one. Nihilism is a matter of the will. It is a sin and sin is the forgetting of the true vocation of man. Man is someone called. This calling confronts him with what he ought to do. Conscience calls us in the categorical imperative to treat whatever rational beings we encounter as ends in themselves:

> Whatever these beings may be in and for themselves, you shall act towards them as self-existent, free, substantive beings, wholly independent of yourself. Assume it as already known, that they can give a purpose to their own being wholly by themselves, and quite independently of you; never interrupt the accomplishment of this purpose, but rather further it to the utmost of thy power (VM 95).

Kant had said that we should treat all persons as ends in themselves. This would seem to presuppose my ability to recognize them as indeed persons. But a purely theoretical knowledge cannot supply such an understanding. For it I have to turn somewhere else. For Fichte the reality of the other person is given with the moral imperative. I do not confront the other person first and then conclude that I ought to treat her or him as ends in themselves. Rather other human beings present themselves to me as beings to be respected in their being. Morality offers the key to the reality of the world:

> My world is the object and sphere of my duties, and absolutely nothing more; there is no other world for me, and no other qualities of my world; my whole united capacity, all finite capacity, is insufficient to comprehend any other. Whatever possesses an existence for me, can bring its existence and reality into contact with me only through this relation, and only through this relation do I comprehend it: for any other existence than this I have no organ whatever (VM 96–97).

For Fichte there are two coordinate ways of knowing: speculation and moral activity. Of these the latter is the more immediate. It is disrupted by reflection. Further reflection cannot lead us back to reality. The answer is not to be found in speculation but in the affirmation of our moral vocation.

7 The Loss of the Shadow

In conclusion let me return once more to our story. Who is this Peter Schlemihl? We are given a pointer by what may be Chamisso's most famous poem, *Das Schlosss Boncourt*," in which the poet recalls the ancestral castle of his family, destroyed by the French revolution. He first published that poem in the appendix to the 2nd edition of *Peter Schlemihl wundersame Geschichte*. As a child, the poet, born as Louis Charles Adélaide de Chamissot de Boncourt, had to leave with his family, first their castle in the Champagne, then their homeland, France. Thus uprooted he never was able to feel really at home in Prussia, in which his family had found refuge and which he served for a time as an officer. He still remained an outsider. Like his hero, the poet, too, is someone without a real home. What had been home to the child the French Revolution had destroyed.[111]

But this destruction was also an expression of a more encompassing destruction that accompanied the age of reason as an evil spirit. The loss of the shadow can also be understood as the result of an uprooting that is but the other side of

---

[111] Adelbert von Chamisso, *Reise um die Welt mit der Romanzoffischen Entdeckungs-Expedition in den Jahren 1815–1818 auf der Brigg Rurik, Kapitain Otto von Kotzebue*, (Leipzig: Reclam, 1836), Einleitung.

the liberation from religious and social bonds. To possess a shadow means to be able to call this earth home. The loss of home had however also a good side: it made Chamisso more mobile, gave him a new freedom. And science demands a freer, more objective way of relating to the earth. His loss of a shadow thus let the fictive Peter Schlemihl become a scientist. And his loss of home did something similar for Chamisso, as the many plants, animals, and landscapes that bear his name still witness. As a participant in a Russian research expedition he spent the years 1815 to 1819 circumnavigating the earth.

But what interests me here is not the biography, but the metaphor of the shadow. How are we to understand the offer of the devil to return Peter his shadow, but at the price of his soul? A presupposition of this offer is the loss of the shadow, i.e., that self-elevation of the human being that transforms him or her into an abstract subject. Such a subject has left the always space- and time-bound human being beneath itself. And does the search for the truth not demand such a self-elevation? With this the body becomes less important.

Shadows have long been understood as signs of a full embodied existence. Ghosts are said to cast no shadows. Thus in Richard Strauss's and Hugo von Hofmannsthal's opera *Die Frau ohne Schatten*, the beautiful daughter of the spirit king Keikobad not only is unable to bear children, but her barren beauty threatens to turn the emperor who loves her into stone. Only our shadows let us belong to the earth.

The devil would take our shadow, would liberate us from what binds us to the earth. He promises a freer existence. To cast a shadow a person must stand in the light, which in our story, too, as so often, stands also for a divine light. The offer of the devil promises thus an existence that is in no need of light other than that provided by our ego.

But the question remains: how are we to understand the devil's offer to return Peter his shadow, but at the price of his soul? The devil can make that offer because that self-elevation that robs the self of its shadow also denies the body, which does cast a shadow, anything like soul. Think of Descartes who opposes a shadow-less *res cogitans* to a soul-less *res extensa*. So understood nature has no room for anything like soul. To understand oneself as just such a *res extensa* is to lose sight of what makes human beings human.

Having rejected the devil's offer to return him his shadow, Peter has to make his peace with his now shadow-less existence. He has to accept that he will always remain an outsider. But as a compensation for what he has lost he discovers a pair of seven league boots. The loss of the shadow leads to a changed understanding of space: distance loses its former significance. We should think here of the way science and technology have transformed our sense of distance. Automobile, airplane, telephone, computer have brought things closer than ever before. But such proximity is shadowed by a distance that forbids real intimacy. Think of the internet: shadow-less spirits here meet shadow-less spirits.

Unlike the poet, Peter Schlemihl missed his chance to create a home for himself with the woman he loves. And thus he spends the rest of his life, like the hermits of long ago, in an Egyptian cave, but as a true modern, not lost in religious meditations, but making good use of his seven league boots, as a researcher, eager to observe and explore the earth.

V The Shipwreck of Metaphysics

1 Introduction

In the first chapter I mentioned Kant's antinomies and I referred to Heidegger's thinking of Being, which, I suggested, leads us into a related antinomy. I called it the Antinomy of Being. Today I would like to return to that antinomy and consider it in greater depth. What is at issue is the reach of our reason. Can we dismiss Nietzsche's suspicion that the thought structures raised by our reason leave us with constructions resembling a Roman columbarium, turning the honey of life into ashes? Chamisso develops a related thought when he presents his devil as a philosophical architect. The loss of the shadow is the other side of a self-elevation of the spirit that finds its philosophical expression in the seemingly self-supporting thought architectures raised by a Spinoza or a Fichte. But every attempt to force reality into such a framework does violence to reality. Scientists, to be sure, are well aware of the impossibility of constructing reality *a priori*, aware of the need for careful observation; but their attempts to comprehend nature nevertheless presuppose some metaphysics of nature that leaves the life-world behind. Thus Peter Schlemihl, even after he has sent the devil back to hell, having thus saved his soul, nevertheless remains tied to the devil by the shadow-less life of a scientist that he now embraces.

2 Time as the Ground of Being

Let me return to what I called the Antinomy of Being and that is to say also to Heidegger's *Being and Time*. That the book we have is only a fragment of the work Heidegger envisioned at the time is made clear in paragraph 8, which presents us with a sketch of the "Design of the Treatise" (GA2, 53–53; SZ, 39–40)— with its rushed publication Heidegger responded to pressure by the dean of the philosophical faculty at Marburg, which had chosen him to succeed Nicolai Hartmann, but was informed by the ministry in Berlin that a major publication was needed (GA14, 99). That "Design" not only tells us that the book we now have contains only the first two sections of Part One, that is to say roughly one third of the envisioned two-part work, but also gives us an idea of what the envisioned third section of Part One was supposed to accomplish. As Heidegger explains the overall design of the envisioned work:

> If we are to arrive at the basic concept of 'Being' and to outline the ontological conceptions which it requires and the variations which it necessarily undergoes, we need a clue which is concrete. We shall proceed towards the concept of Being by way of an Interpretation of a certain special entity, Dasein, in which we shall arrive at the horizon for the understanding of Being and for the possibility of interpreting it; the universality of the concept of Being is not belied by the relatively 'special' characteristic of our investigation. But this very entity, Dasein, is in itself 'historical,' so its ownmost ontological elucidation necessarily becomes an 'historiological' ('*historischen*') Interpretation (GA2, 52–53; SZ, 39).

This tells us that the projected third section of Part One would have returned to the task of determining the concept of Being, after an analysis of the temporality of Dasein had provided the necessary horizon.[112] Heidegger's "design" also suggests that such a determination could still only have been provisional in that an adequate determination of the concept of Being is said to call for the three step destruction of the history of philosophy that Part Two of *Being and Time* was supposed to accomplish, a destruction that would have led the reader back to the origin of Greek ontology and thus to the limit of philosophy as we know it and with it to a more original understanding of time and Being than allowed for by the phenomenological-transcendental approach adopted in *Being and Time*. Such a "destruction" has to call into question the phenomenological method for which Heidegger thanks his mentor Edmund Husserl in a footnote (GA2, 52; SZ, 38), a method that remains rooted in the tradition to be "destroyed." Already here we get a premonition of the collision between the claim of phenomenology to lay firm foundations and an ever growing awareness of the historical embeddedness of thought, a collision that dooms any attempt to arrive at a definitive determination of the concept of Being. That impossibility becomes explicit in subsequent works: there is indeed tension already in the very expression "concept of Being" in that Being resists being assigned its place in logical or linguistic space.

Much of the destruction of the history of philosophy promised for the projected Part Two is now available in one form or another, both in Heidegger's lectures and in his published essays. But what about the Third Section of Part One of *Being and Time*? Paragraph 8 gives only its title, "Time and Being." What strikes the reader immediately is the reversal that has taken place: instead of journeying from Being to time we now are to return from time to Being, raising the question of whether the much discussed *Kehre* or reversal in Heidegger's

---

[112] For a somewhat fuller discussion see Karsten Harries, "The Antinomy of Being and the End of Philosophy," *Division III of Being and Time: Heidegger's Unanswered Question of Being*, Lee Braver (Ed.), (Cambridge, MA: MIT).

path of thinking, supposed to have taken place several years after the publication of *Being and Time,* had not in fact already been anticipated in the original projection of the work.

Too much here remains unsaid to give us more than hints of how Heidegger came to think of the issue of "Time and Being," where the much later lecture of that title and the seminar that followed, in which he reconsiders what *Being and Time* had left unsaid, demand special attention. This much, however, is clear: Heidegger soon came to recognize the insufficiency of what he had envisioned when beginning work on *Being and Time,* an insufficiency that, having completed his analytic of Dasein, forced him to abandon the project. This, however, leaves the question, how might Section Three of Part One of *Being and Time* have looked as Heidegger initially envisioned it?

Heidegger himself answered this question. He had indeed worked out in great detail much of what was to be covered in this section. In a later marginal note to the second part of the title of Part One, "The Explication of Time as the Transcendental Horizon for the Question of Being," he thus refers us to *The Basic Problems of Phenomenology* (GA 2, 55).

In the beginning of that lecture course (1927) we find a note, calling it a working out of the third section of Part One of *Being and Time* (GA 24,1) and much later in that course he reaffirms that interpretation (GA24, 460–461). So the question, what would the third section of the first part of *Being and Time* have said, would seem to receive here its answer: It would have included much of the material now found in *The Basic Problems of Phenomenology,* especially in its second part. As Friedrich-Wilhelm von Herrmann suggested in his postscript: "For the thematic of 'Time and Being' the first chapter of Part Two is decisive. The text published here allows, even given its incompleteness, an understanding of the systematic design (*Grundriss*) of the question of Being, as it presented itself to Heidegger, given the point that he had reached at the time on his path of thinking" (GA24, 473). Heidegger here sums up the result of the existential analytic presented in *Being and Time:*

> The constitution of the Being of Dasein is founded in temporality (*Zeitlichkeit*)... As such, temporality (*Zeitlichkeit*) also *makes possible the thematic interpretation of Being and its articulation and many modes,* i.e. makes possible ontology. Out of this grows a distinct problematic, related to *Zeitlichkeit.* We call it *Temporalität.* The term '*Temporalität*' is not synonymous with *Zeitlichkeit,* although it is only its translation. It means temporality, in as much as it has been thematized as the condition of the understanding of Being and of ontology as such (GA24, 323–324).

The thematization developed in this chapter remains thus very much within the orbit of the still fundamentally transcendental approach of *Being and Time.* The essential temporality of Dasein is analyzed and said to make possible any understanding of Being (GA24, 429). And so Heidegger can claim that "all ontological propositions are, because assertions about Being, in light of time rightly understood, *a priori* propositions." (GA24, 461). *A priori*, he explains, refers to what is prior. Given our ordinary, i.e., as Heidegger puts it, vulgar concept of time, such a claim makes little sense: first of all and most of the time we encounter beings, not their Being. That is said to have misled philosophers again and again. "Because one fails to recognize the extent to which the interpretation of Being necessarily takes place in the horizon of time, one has to attempt to explain away the temporal determination of the *a priori*. One goes so far as to claim that the *a priori*, the essences, that is the determination of beings in their Being, was the extra-temporal, what is beyond time, the timeless" (GA24, 462). But such an understanding of the *a priori* is said to be misled by the vulgar understanding of time. To gain a more adequate understanding of the *a priori* we have to recognize that the vulgar understanding of time descends from and presupposes "original time (*ursprüngliche Zeit*) in which the constitution of the Being of Dasein has its ground. Only the temporality of the understanding of Being allows one to clarify why the ontological determinations of Being have the character of a priority" (GA24, 462). Key here is the concept of possibility. Referring to Kant, Heidegger states: "*A priori* means what makes beings as beings in *how* and *what* they are possible" (GA24, 461), i.e., *a priori* means their Being. But the very origin of possibility, Heidegger insists, is original time.

But in what sense can original time account for things being *what* they are? To be sure, first of all and most of the time we are preoccupied with things, without paying heed to the fact that Being has always already been understood in some way. "This, what is prior, factically existing Dasein has forgotten. If, then the Being, which as 'prior' has always already been understood even though forgotten, is to become the object, the objectification of this prior, of this forgetting, must have the character of a coming back to what was already and in advance understood" (GA24, 463). What Heidegger says here, summing up the preceding discussion, invites being read as a possible abstract for the missing third section of *Being and Time*, Part One, as originally envisioned: "A twofold possibility of the objectification of the pre-given lies essentially in the essence of Dasein. Factically the possibility of two basic kinds of science is given with the existence of Dasein: the objectification of beings as positive science, and the objectification of science as temporal, i.e., transcendental science, ontology, philosophy" (GA24, 466). What Heidegger here calls phenomenology is the effort to gain step by step "access to Being as such and to work out its structures" (GA24, 466). The key to phenomenology so understood is said to be the step back to original time. But Heidegger also warns us not to expect results that would allow us to say that we had finally arrived at our goal: "The only thing that is truly new in science and in philosophy is genuine questioning and the battle with things that serves them" (GA24, 467).

Far from having led Heidegger to some sort of foundation, the question of Being was rendered more questionable by his attempt to ground it in the constitution of Dasein and that in turn in original time. In the first chapter I already discussed the way this difficulty shows itself in *The Basic Problems of Phenomenology* and the parallel discussion in *Being and Time*.[113] There is no truth, Heidegger had claimed, without Dasein (GA 24, 316). But can this mean, I asked, that there was no Being before human beings came into existence? To be what it is, Heidegger rightly insists, nature does not need to disclose itself to human beings, i.e., does not need truth so understood. But do we not want to say then that nature transcends Dasein and thus truth and that primordial time, which Heidegger's fundamental ontology ties inseparably to Dasein? And if we have to think nature in this way, do we not also need to think of Being as transcending the Dasein-dependent Being to which *Being and Time* sought to lead us? This, as I pointed out, invites a distinction between two senses of Being, the first transcendental sense relative to Dasein and in this sense inescapably historical, the second transcendent sense, gesturing towards the ground or origin of Dasein's historical being and thus also of Being understood transcendentally? But that ground must remain elusive.

3 Sackgassen and Holzwege

Did the so-called *Kehre*, the turn from an understanding of Being as the transcendental-phenomenological presupposition of beings to an understanding of Being as the transcendent ground of beings, allow Heidegger to advance beyond the position at which he had arrived in *Being and Time*? Or does the question of Being as developed in *Being and Time* present itself as a limit where philosophy reaches some sort of end? In the *Letter on Humanism* Heidegger suggests just this: "It is everywhere supposed that the attempt in *Being and Time* ended in a blind alley (*Sackgasse*)" (G9, 343/222). Heidegger leaves that supposition standing, hinting that not only his philosophy, but perhaps all philosophy understood as metaphysics had reached here something like a dead end. "The thinking that hazards a few steps in *Being and Time* has even today not advanced beyond that

---

[113] See Chapter I, 1 above.

publication. But perhaps in the meantime it has in one respect penetrated further into its own matter" (GA9, 343/222).

This further movement led Heidegger to re-describe the path of his thinking, not as a *Sackgasse*, but as a *Holzweg* (GA13, 91). And so he gave the most important collection of essays he published the title *Holzwege* (GA5). But what is the difference? Do not *Sackgasse* and *Holzweg* both suggest a path that lets us miss the intended goal? The transcendental path Heidegger followed in *Being and Time* did indeed not lead him to the intended goal. But if *Sackgasse* lets us think of some urban cul-de-sac that invites us to retrace our steps, *Holzweg* has a very different connotation. As Heidegger explains in the very beginning of *Holzwege*:

> *Holz lautet ein alter Name für Wald. Im Holz sind Wege, die meist verwachsen jäh im Unbegangenen aufhören.*
> *Sie heißen Holzwege.*
> *Jeder verläuft gesondert, aber im selben Wald. Oft scheint es, als gleiche einer dem anderen. Doch es scheint nur so.*
> *Holzmacher und Waldhüter kennen die Wege. Sie wissen, was es heißt, auf einem Holzweg zu sein* (GA5, iii).
>
> *Holz* is an old name for a wood. In such a wood are paths that suddenly stop in the untrodden.
> They are called *Holzwege* (woodpaths).
> Everyone takes its separate course, but in the same wood. Often it seems as if one were the same as another. But it only seems that way.
> Wood cutters and foresters know these paths. They know what it means to be on a *Holzweg*.

Holzweg names a path that is cut into the forest to enable loggers to bring out the trees they have cut. This meaning should be kept in mind. A *Holzweg* is thus a path that does not lead where those who wanted to get somewhere were expecting to go. Such a path leads nowhere and suddenly stops. Because *Holzwege* are not commonly used, they tend to be overgrown and difficult to walk. Often such a *Holzweg* will lead to an open place in the forest where some trees have been cut down, i. e., into a clearing. But clearing, *Lichtung*, is, as I pointed out, a key metaphor Heidegger uses to describe the being of Dasein, where this choice of metaphor, which joins light and an open place, provides a good example of the point of Heidegger's metaphorical speaking. (In this connection consider Descartes' understanding of the open space or distance that separates subject and object and of the need for a *lumen naturale!*)

The expression, *auf einem Holzweg sein*, is used in German to suggest that we have lost our way, precisely the condition that Wittgenstein took to describe the form of a genuinely philosophical problem. Greek philosophy spoke of *apo-*

ria. To be on a *Holzweg* usually means that you have taken a wrong turn. And travelling with Heidegger you may well find yourself disappointed. Significant questions go unanswered. In an important sense Heidegger's path leads nowhere. And yet leading nowhere it leads us back to ourselves.

One last thing: a *Holzweg* begins in a familiar landscape, as Heidegger's path of thinking begins in the to many philosophers still familiar landscapes of Neo-Kantianism and transcendental phenomenology, only to end in the bewildering and unfamiliar.

Heidegger's late essay "*Zeit und Sein*" ("Time and Being") (1962), presents itself to us as another such *Holzweg*. The title may suggest that after thirty-five years, Heidegger had decided to complete in the only way he then still thought possible what he had left unfinished for so long, thus giving this belated version the title of the Third Section of the First Part of *Being and Time*. Instead, the essay casts further light on why that third part had to remain unwritten and the project of *Being and Time* unfinished. Especially illuminating with respect to the relationship of the essay to the unwritten Third Part of *Being and Time* is Alfredo Guzzoni's "Protokoll zu einem Seminar über den Vortrag 'Zeit und Sein,'" "Summary of a Seminar on the Lecture 'Time and Being'" that Heidegger chose to include in the original edition of *Zur Sache des Denkens* (1969). The very project of a fundamental ontology, i.e., the entire project of *Being and Time* is here called into question: As Heidegger described that project: "The decisive matter that here must be considered is the relationship of fundamental ontology to the one question in search of the meaning of Being for which *Being and Time* is the preparation. According to *Being and Time* fundamental ontology is the ontological analytic of Dasein. "Hence *fundamental ontology*, from which alone all others can arise, must be sought in the *existential analytic of Dasein*" (GA2, 18; SZ, 13). Accordingly, it appears as if fundamental ontology were the foundation for the still missing ontology itself, which is to be raised on this foundation" (GA14, 39). But this is a misleading impression. This supposedly fundamental ontology is unable to provide us with a *fundamentum inconcussum* on which we might then raise our philosophical edifice; rather it provides us with a *fundamentum concussum* (GA14, 40). What shakes this supposed foundation is what I called the Antinomy of Being. That antinomy is inseparable from the temporality of Dasein.

In *Being and Time*, as I suggested, this antinomy announces itself in the questions raised by Heidegger's claim that, while Being cannot be without Dasein, that cannot be said of beings. And of course, there were countless things before there were human beings. But how is this "were" to be understood? And what about the locution "Being cannot be without Dasein?" Is that to be understood as a tautology? In Heidegger's transcendental sense these beings that were before human beings had indeed no Being. But Heidegger does not deny that they were.

Thinking here bumps against the limits of language.

4 Theories of Double Truth

Let me shift gears to suggest in a much more concrete way why what I have called the Antinomy of Being matters. On May 13, 2009 I had a conversation over lunch with a colleague, Professor Drew McDermott of Yale's computer science department. What we then talked about has continued to occupy me. Professor McDermott told of how he had recently returned to the thought of Martin Heidegger, which he had encountered in college quite some time ago, but to which for many years had given little thought. But now he had come to see that what Heidegger had to say did do justice to our first person awareness of being in the world. In that sense much of what he had to say could be called true. From the third person perspective of the scientist, however, it had to be judged false. Two incompatible conceptions of Being collide here.

McDermott's comment made me think of Kierkegaard's distinction between subjective and objective truth.[114] Kierkegaard knew of course very well that first of all "the question about truth is asked objectively, truth is reflected upon objectively as an object to which the knower relates himself." Why then should we oppose to it a subjective truth and how are we to understand such a truth? Kierkegaard defines it as "An objective uncertainty, held fast through appropriation with the most passionate inwardness" – Kierkegaard was thinking of love and faith. This subjective truth he calls "the highest truth there is for an *existing* person." In such attainment the individual is said to perfect him- or herself. We may well wonder whether we should speak in such cases of knowledge at all. But what is at issue is clear enough: the value of objective truth:

> The way of objective reflection makes the subject accidental, and thereby transforms existence into something indifferent, something vanishing. Away from the subject the objective way of reflection leads to the objective truth, and while the subject and his subjectivity become indifferent, the truth also becomes indifferent, and this indifference is precisely its objective validity; for all interest, like all decisiveness, is rooted in subjectivity.[115]

---

[114] Søren Kierkegaard, *Concluding Unscientific Postscript*, David F. Swenson and Walter Lowrie (Trans.), (Princeton: Princeton University Press, 1974), pp. 182, 178.
[115] Ibid., p. 173.

Kierkegaard speaks of an objective uncertainty, not of an objective falsehood. That avoids the paradoxical claim advanced by McDermott that what we are convinced is absolutely true, e.g., for him the claim that there are absolute values, must yet be judged, without overturning such conviction, objectively false.

McDermott followed this conversation up by sending me the draft of a paper on which he was still working with the thought-provoking title: "How Moral Absolutism Can Be True and False at the Same Time; Or: Non-Phenomenological Existentialism." Here the paper's abstract:

> We examine ethics from the point of view of cognitive science. Science commits one to a view in which ethics is just an arbitrary aspect of culture, and the study of cultures is value-free, so that relativism seems axiomatically true. But intelligent agents cannot take the view of pure science, because certain built-in beliefs contradict it. These inescapable framework illusions (IFI's) include a belief in free will, the persistence of the self through time, and, among humans, the universalizability of moral statements.[116]

McDermott takes us moderns to be confronted with something rather like a Kantian antinomy: as intelligent agents we are compelled to believe certain things, most importantly that our will is free, that we are selves that persist through time, that there are moral truths that can be universalized, beliefs which as individuals committed to science we yet know to be false. A somewhat weaker version of this claim, closer to what Kierkegaard was going to maintain, is, as we have seen, familiar from the work of philosophers such as Kant and Fichte, who insist that as free, responsible actors we have to take as true what theoretical reason is unable to establish, indeed cannot even make sense of. But they would have refused to assert that what practical reason forces us to accept as true is from an objective, third person point of view false. Thus they would not have wanted to say that "moral absolutism can be true and false at the same time."

The title of McDermott's paper brought to mind that theory of double truth condemned by the theologians at the university of Paris in 1277.[117] Should I understand McDermott in the image of Siger of Brabant, the Aristotelian philosopher of nature, who was perhaps the leading target of that condemnation? Like our science, Aristotelian science also left no room for certain key beliefs and especially for the kind of freedom demanded by Christianity. Given Aristo-

---

[116] Drew McDermott, "How Moral Absolutism Can Be True and False at the Same Time; Or: Non-Phenomenological Existentialism," unpublished draft.
[117] See Karsten Harries, "The Theory of Double Truth Revisited," *Politics of Practical Reasoning. Integrating Action, Discourse, and Argument*, Ricca Edmondson and Karlheinz Hülser (Eds.), (Plymouth: Lexington Books, 2012), pp. 205–225.

tle's understanding of nature, such claims had to be judged false. How then could a good Christian be a follower of Aristotle? Could Aristotelian science and Christian theology, while they contradicted each other, both lay claim to truth? Must such a theory of double truth not be rejected by every right thinking person?—and there is indeed reason to wonder whether Siger ever really endorsed it. Similarly, we must ask today, how can we claim moral absolutism to be true and false at the same time, except by relativizing the truth in question? Does the very essence of truth not rule out the theory of double truth?—But what is truth? That question brought to my mind the young Nietzsche, who, as we saw, wrestled with it in "On Truth and Lie in an Extra-Moral Sense," which we considered in some detail in preceding chapters. Here I want to content myself with this suggestion: despite all that distinguishes the medieval Aristotelian philosopher of nature, the cognitive scientist very much of today, and the 19th century critic of objectifying reason and its truth, all three wrestle with what has remained fundamentally the same problem: rigorous reflection on the essence of truth leads us into an antinomy to which the title of McDermott's paper gives expression. Reason, however, refuses to accept such an antinomy; it is forced to go beyond it. But reason has nowhere to go. Thus, I will argue, as Kant did, that our reason is forced to recognize its own limits. As Nicolaus Cusanus might have put it, the antinomy of truth lets us becomes learned about our ignorance.

5 Neurath's Principle

Let me return to McDermott's draft. Is it really possible for us to hold something, take Moral Absolutism, to be true and false, as he insists we must do? As I pointed out, in the 13th century there were indeed philosophers who, in public at least, came close to defending some such view: then it was Aristotle's newly imported philosophy of nature, which clashed with Christian common sense, watched over by the theologians. McDermott is free of such theological commitments. He speaks instead of certain "built-in" "inescapable framework illusions," where the very words "built in" and "framework illusions" suggest that in the end he, too, may not hold a robust theory of double truth, but ends up making science the privileged custodian of truth.

There is much I agree with in his paper. First of all, I agree with the claim that science as we know it is ideally value free. McDermott invokes what, referring to *An Enquiry Concerning the Principles of Morals,* he terms Hume's principle: "No statement about the way things ought to be can be derived from any set of statements about the way things are."¹¹⁸ I would not want to endorse this principle without asking: how should we understand: "the way things are?" Does science hold the key?

Regardless of whether this question must be answered in the affirmative, we can conclude with McDermott: "Because science is entirely about the way things are, nothing in science bears on whether one moral system is superior to another, or whether there is some supersystem that encompasses all the little ones... Science is crushingly indifferent to our affairs... From the purely scientific point of view, the self doesn't exist at all; all that is observable are agents that *believe* they are selves."¹¹⁹

I agree with McDermott that science knows nothing of values, persons, or freedom, although I hesitate to conclude from this that for science relativism seems axiomatically true: If science knows nothing of values it cannot say with confidence that they are either time-bound or timeless, either relative or absolute. What it can say is that, as a matter of fact, there has been a great deal of disagreement about what human beings have taken to matter most profoundly or to value. In that sense value judgments have been relative. But that does not show that values are in fact relative. The fact that there has been disagreement about the possibility of squaring the circle does not mean that there is not a truth of the matter. Questions of truth and validity, it would seem, cannot be settled by appeals to what people happen to think. McDermott would seem to overplay his hand when he writes, "relativism is not just true, it is almost axiomatically true, given my premises."¹²⁰ He seems to me more nearly correct when he writes, "IFIs are illusions in the sense that they are false or meaningless."¹²¹ I think "meaningless" here is the better term: Given the scientific understanding of truth, McDermott's IFIs are meaningless.

But what is the scientific understanding of truth? I shall have to return to that question. If I pretty much agree with McDermott about what he calls Hume's Principle, at least if restricted to the scientific understanding of nature, I have questions about his second fundamental principle, McDermott calls it Neurath's Principle – the reference is to Otto Neurath's *Foundations of the Unity of Science: Toward an International Encyclopedia of Unified Science* (1971): "The world discovered (and yet to be discovered) by science *is* the world;"—Science here means fundamentally physics—"But it's the only world

---

[118] Drew McDermott, "How Moral Absolutism Can Be True and False at the Same Time; Or: Non-Phenomenological Existentialism," draft, p. 2
[119] Ibid., pp. 3 and 10.
[120] Ibid., p. 5.
[121] Ibid., p. 8.

there is. All the other sciences are reducible to it, in what is by now a well-known sense. Nothing happens in chemistry that can't be explained in terms of physics; nothing happens in biology that can't be explained in terms of physics and chemistry; and so forth."[122] This would mean that we really need only one concept of nature and that physics provides the key to that concept.

I find this principle questionable. I, too, want to say that "The world discovered (and yet to be discovered) by science is the world." But with Heidegger I would want to raise the question of the Being of the world thus discovered. Heidegger's question of Being is the question of our mode of access to beings. What justifies the equation of the world or of nature with the world or nature discovered or to be discovered by science? What about the way an artist discovers the world; or a religious person? Are they obviously in error?

What can be said in support of the equation of the world with "The world discovered (and yet to be discovered) by science?" I already suggested a first answer: it would seem to be entailed by our familiar everyday understanding of truth as the correspondence of our thoughts or propositions with the things – but with the things as they really are, not as they appear to be to an observer limited by his or her subjective perspective. This entails a privileging of the a-perspectival and objective.[123] Isn't such objectivity a presupposition of really understanding what is?

But what does it mean to "*really* understand" something? What conception of reality here being presupposed? Is our human reason able to fathom reality? Kant presents us with considerations that render the commensurability of human reason and reality, a presupposition of Neurath's principle, not just questionable, but untenable. What renders it untenable is what I have called, with reference to Kant's antinomies, the Antinomy of Being. But more on that later. Here I only want to state where I disagree with McDermott.

And yet, there is a great deal we agree on. I agree that we find it impossible to let go of what McDermott calls "inescapable framework illusions" and I, too, would include among these the belief in free will and the belief that we are selves that exist until we die. McDermott's "inescapable framework illusions" look a great deal like what Kant would have called ideas of reason. But although not supported by science, are such ideas therefore false?

---

[122] Ibid., pp. 2–3.
[123] Cf. Karsten Harries, *Infinity and Perspective* (Cambridge, MA: MIT Press, 2001), pp. 309–317; Karsten Harries, *Art Matters: A Critical Commentary on Heidegger's "The Origin of the Work of Art"* (New York: Springer, 2009), pp. 125–138.

According to McDermott "we are compelled to live by key foundational beliefs that are false."[124] The belief in the freedom of the will is said to be one such error:

> The odd thing about the free-will error is that it is impossible for us to correct it, at least when it comes to contemplating our own decisions. That's because our brains are "wired" in such a way as to treat a decision in the process of being made as exempt from causal laws. As explained in (McDermott 2001), it would be completely pointless for a brain to use causal reasoning, i.e., simulation or some other modeling technique, to predict what it was going to do, because what it is going to do depends on the computation it is in the middle of ... Evolution has made sure that any such attempt is blocked by the hard-wired belief that the decision currently under review is exempt from causal modeling. It is this hard-wired belief that we introspectively perceive as freedom.[125]

McDermott includes in these IFIs the belief in an absolute ethical truth. And so he concludes the paper with a plea for religious tolerance. He even takes it to be an absolute ethical principle:

> This principle was mostly unnecessary until the debut of multiple evangelizing monotheisms on the world stage, and it took a few centuries for Europeans to realize that without it too many people would perish in this life without really settling the question of who would control the next one. European culture then spread throughout most of the world, but there are still places where the idea of tolerance hasn't yet gotten through. I fervently hope that we can get it through without too many people getting killed in the process. Because, if you ask me, the principle of tolerance is an absolute ethical truth.[126]

But that absolute truth, he also insists, while he cannot renounce it, is really a falsehood. He explicitly agrees with J. L. Mackie[127], "that moral thinking is inevitably permeated by fundamental errors."[128] The beliefs in freedom, in a stable self, in absolute values, are said to be such errors.

McDermott is a materialist, and he holds that science holds the key to all that can reasonably be said to be. He is well aware of the unbelievability of such a materialism. Our first person experience of the world argues against it. But from the point of view of the scientist's sober third-person awareness such

---

[124] Drew McDermott, "How Moral Absolutism Can Be True and False at the Same Time; Or: Non-Phenomenological Existentialism," draft, p. 30.
[125] Ibid., pp. 6–7.
[126] Ibid., p. 32.
[127] J. L. Mackie, *Ethics, Inventing Right and Wrong* (New York City, Viking, 1977).
[128] Drew McDermott, "How Moral Absolutism Can Be True and False at the Same Time; Or: Non-Phenomenological Existentialism," draft, p. 5.

first person awareness supports us with a web of lies. For science to develop as it did, reason had to free itself from the grip of these lies. McDermott could have agreed with Nietzsche, when the latter calls Copernicus and Boscovich "the greatest and most victorious opponents of what appears to the eye." As I pointed out, this victory relies on a pattern I have called Copernican reflection: "Appearance to the eye" (*Augenschein*) is devalued by being shown to be no more than perspectival appearance. The world opened up by the scientist is opposed to the comparatively superficial world that continues to be our life-world. But as Nietzsche knew, this victory brings with it "the self-diminution of man, his will to self-diminution," which since Copernicus is said to be "in an unstoppable progress." "Since Copernicus, man seems to have got himself on an inclined plane – now he is slipping faster and faster away from the center into—what? into nothingness? into a *penetrating* sense of his own nothingness?" [129] Modern science is inescapably shadowed by nihilism. As we can read in Wittgenstein's *Tractatus*:

> 6.4 "All propositions are of equal value."
>
> 6.41 The sense of the world must lie outside the world. In the world everything is at it is and happens as it does happen. In it there is no value—and if there were, it would be of no value."[130]

McDermott could not have disagreed. But his theory of double truth suggests that the specter of nihilism is in fact banished, as soon as a first person point of view is adopted. I wonder. Can I really say: I know x is false, but I nevertheless believe x, indeed believe it to be an absolute truth?" I am unable to do so. I consider this the expression of a true antinomy, and, as Kant suggests, the solution of such antinomies lies in recognizing that the reason that lets us call McDermott's IFI's false does not circumscribe reality. That is to say, what McDermott calls Neurath's principle must be rejected.

McDermott suggests another way out: "But if materialism provides an explanation of its own unbelievability, an explanation I have sketched above, then this inferential step loses whatever plausibility it might have had."[131] In *Being*

---

129 Friedrich Nietzsche, *Zur Genealogie der Moral*, III, 25, *Kritische Studienausgabe*, vol. 5, p. 404. Walter Kaufmann and R. J. Hollingdale (Trans.), *On the Genealogy of Morals and Ecce Homo* (New York: Vintage, 1989), p. 155.
130 Ludwig Wittgenstein, *Tractatus Logico Philosphicus*, C. K. Ogden (Trans.), (London: Routledge and Kegan Paul, 1922).
131 Drew McDermott, "How Moral Absolutism Can Be True and False at the Same Time; Or: Non-Phenomenological Existentialism," draft, p. 13.

and Time Heidegger, according to McDermott, offers us a convincing account of our inescapable framework intuitions and in this sense can claim them to be true, but true only relative to our first-person awareness. McDermott thus claims "that first-person awareness is a belief system that brains inhabit, a web of IFIs that ensure it can never accept the whole truth as revealed by science."[132] I agree that science has to look at consciousness in some such way.

According to McDermott the progress of science has compressed the sphere of IFI's, but he insists that it won't be able to eliminate it altogether, even though as a scientist he is forced to admit that these IFI's are false. But this recognition that the progress of science "has compressed the sphere of IFI's" presupposes that the boundary that separates first and third person awareness is a shifting boundary, tending towards the progressive elimination of IFI's, although McDermott insists that this elimination never will be total. But such talk of a shift invites another look at the boundary supposed to separate subjective from objective truth and thus another look at the "theory of double truth."

---

132 Ibid., p. 9.

VI Limits and Legitimacy of Science

1 The Meaninglessness of the World

McDermott, as we saw, recognizes that the scientific world picture is difficult to reconcile with our common sense, without, however, challenging its truth. He recognizes that this world picture has no room for freedom, values, or God. So understood, the scientific world picture is essentially nihilistic. This, to be sure, does not seem to perturb McDermott. Subjectively he claims to be convinced that there are absolute ethical truths, even though as a scientist he knows that they are false. As I pointed out, I have difficulty with his way of separating subjective and objective truth.

With his separation of an objective, scientific understanding of reality from a subjective, personally engaged understanding McDermott is hardly alone, but has the support of a long tradition that includes Jacobi, Kant, Fichte, Schopenhauer, Nietzsche, and Wittgenstein. To quote once more Wittgenstein's *Tractatus*:

> 6.41 The sense of the world must lie outside the world. In the world everything is as it is and happens as it does happen. In it there is no value—and if there were, it would be of no value.
>
> If there is a value which is of value, it must lie outside all happening and being-so. For all happening and being-so is accidental.
>
> What makes it non-accidental cannot lie in the world, for otherwise this would again be accidental.
>
> It must lie outside the world.

The first proposition of the *Tractatus* defines the world as "everything that is the case." Compare with this 1.13: "The facts in logical space are the world." There is some tension between the two propositions. Only the second asserts the subordination of the world to logical space. But noting the tension buried in these two expressions, which we can understand as an intimation of the Antinomy of Being, clear is Wittgenstein's insistence that we cannot finally explain why the facts are just as they are. The world could be very different or not be at all. That the world is the way it is, is for us an accident. As such it lacks meaning.

What does Wittgenstein mean by meaning (*Sinn*)? We experience something as meaningful, he suggests, when we experience it as not accidental, i.e., as having to be just as it is. A successful work of art comes to mind. The world would be experienced by us as meaningful if we could experience it as being somehow like a successful work of art, i.e., as not accidental, say, as having its sufficient reason in God. This is how religion, and this is how Leibniz und Spinoza understand the world. But the presupposed idea of God is itself groundless. So understood, the world remains an aesthetic construction that leaps over reality.

Wittgenstein understands thoughts as logical pictures of facts.

> 3.1 In the proposition the thought is expressed perceptibly through the senses.
>
> Whether a meaningful proposition is true or false is decided by the facts. But the propositions of ethics cannot appeal to certain facts. They are therefore meaningless.
>
> 6.42 Therefore there cannot be any ethical propositions. Propositions cannot express anything higher.

But what does Wittgenstein mean here by "higher?" Higher would be what lets us experience the world as not accidental. In love or religion or art we experience what is higher. But this, according to the young Wittgenstein, cannot be comprehended or put into words. Recall Hofmannsthal's *Chandos Letter*, close to the spirit of the *Tractatus*.

> 6.421 It is clear that ethics cannot be put into words.
>
> Ethics is transcendental.
>
> (Ethics and aesthetics are one.)

There is an obvious objection to what Wittgenstein here assumes: can "putting into words" be reduced to a matter of stating meaningful propositions, as Wittgenstein understands them in the *Tractatus?* That this is misguided Wittgenstein soon was to recognize. In the *Philosophical Investigations* he thus was to place our everyday speaking between the logically correct and for that reason in principle translatable language that provides natural science with a regulative ideal and the language of poetry, which resists translation. Successful poetry may succeed in saying what is higher, but without claiming truth, as science has to demand it.

2 "Only Lawful Connections are Thinkable"

What is Wittgenstein's understanding of science in the *Tractatus*? A picture serves him as an explanation:

> 6.341 Newtonian mechanics, for example, brings the description of the universe to a unified form. Let us imagine a white surface with irregular black spots. We now say: Whatever kind of picture these make I can always get as near as I like to its description, if I cover the sur-

face with a sufficiently fine square network and now say of every square that it is white or black. In this way I shall have brought the description of the surface to a unified form. This form is arbitrary, because I could have applied with equal success a net with a triangular or hexagonal mesh. It can happen that the description would have been simpler with the aid of a triangular mesh; that is to say, we might have described the surface more accurately with a triangular, and coarser, than with the finer square mesh, or vice versa, and so on. To the different networks correspond different systems of describing the world. Mechanics determine a form of description by saying: All propositions in the description of the world must be obtained in a given way from a number of given propositions—the mechanical axioms. It thus provides the bricks for the building of the edifice of science, and says: Whatever building thou wouldst erect, thou shalt construct it in some manner with these bricks and these alone.

The empty page stands here for the space of all that is possible; the spots for what is real. They could of course be different; there are infinitely many possible worlds.

Natural science aims to represent reality in its totality by means of suitable forms of description. Decisive is the claim to provide a picture of the whole of reality, as is the claim to systematicity. The form of description on which mechanics relies is thus based on a small number of axioms. To fulfill their function, these axioms have to answer to the essence of nature in some way. They have their ground in some determination of the essence of nature. Every science thus presupposes something like a metaphysics of nature, even if it may want to reject the word and claim to have nothing to do with metaphysical speculation. A good example of such an axiom is the axiom proposed in Plato's *Timaeus* that the motion of the heavenly bodies is circular and uniform or composed of such motions. Only Kepler demonstrated the falsehood of the Platonic axiom. That necessitated a new foundation for natural science, work that occupied thinkers from Kepler to Newton.

Wittgenstein knows that such axioms, even if always responding to a supposed insight into the essence of nature, are only human constructions that cannot claim finality. For such axioms there can be no *a priori* foundation. What in science is *a priori* is, according to Wittgenstein, only what is constitutive of all possible forms of description: its logical, mathematical form.

> 6.342 And now we can see the relative position of logic and mechanics. (The net might also consist of more than one kind of mesh: e.g. we could use both triangles and hexagons.) The possibility of describing a picture like the one mentioned above with a net of a given form tells us nothing about the picture. (For that is true of all such pictures.) But what does characterize the picture is that it can be described completely by a particular net with a particular size of mesh. Similarly the possibility of describing the world by means of Newtonian mechanics tells us nothing about the world: but what does tell us something about it is the

precise way in which it is possible to describe it by these means. We are also told something about the world by the fact that it can be described more simply with one system of mechanics than with another.

Especially the proposition "But what does characterize the picture is that it can be described completely by a particular net with a particular size of mesh" invites questions: Can the spots in the picture ever be adequately described with the help of, say, a quadratic net? The spots would then have to have themselves a quadratic form. But suppose the spot to be described is a circle? A fully adequate description would mean the squaring of the circle. The impossibility of that attempt has been proven: π is an irrational number, notwithstanding the fact that the relation of the diameter to the circumference is readily seen. That shows that there is a sense in which our sight transcends our reason or *ratio*, which would have us express the relation we see as the relation of two natural numbers. It was only in 1768 that Johann Heinrich Lambert was able to prove the irrationality of π. But the relation can also not be expressed with the help of such algebraic operations as addition, squaring and drawing the square root; π also cannot be constructed geometrically. We thus call π not only, like the square root of 2, an irrational, but a transcendental number.

The irrationality of the world already upset the Greeks. The Pythagoreans are thus said to have been deeply disturbed by the discovery of the irrationality of the square root of 2. There is the story that at first one wanted to keep this discovery a secret and the unfortunate individual who is said to have divulged it is said to have drowned in the ocean.

But let us return to Wittgenstein:

> 6.343 Mechanics is an attempt to construct according to a single plan all the propositions that we need for the description of the world.
>
> 6.3431 The laws of physics, with all their logical apparatus, still speak, however indirectly, about the objects of the world.
>
> 6.35 Although the spots in our picture are geometrical figures, nevertheless geometry can obviously say nothing at all about their actual form and position. The network, however, is purely geometrical; all its properties can be given a priori. Laws like the principle of sufficient reason, etc. are about the net and not about what the net describes.

Wittgenstein takes the principle of sufficient reason to be given and determined *a priori*, something that reason in its attempt to understand nature always already brings with it.

The question remains: how are we to understand the ontological significance of this principle? Does it belong to the essence of Being?

> 6.36 If there were a law of causality, it might be put in the following way: There are laws of nature. But of course that cannot be said: it makes itself manifest.

It shows itself in the way science does its work. But that nature shows us this is more than a lucky accident; it is the necessary presupposition of our ability to think and explore nature.

> 6.361 One might say, using Hertz's terminology, that only connections that are subject to law are thinkable.

The young Wittgenstein thus understands the principle of sufficient reason as a presupposition of all connections that are thinkable.

But what allows us to claim that such thinking is fully adequate to nature in its entirety? Does the picture that Wittgenstein gives us not call such confidence into question? What in the pictured spots corresponds to the angles of the triangles, squares, and hexagons that form his nets? How do Wittgenstein's propositions relate to the pictured facts? In the *Tractatus* we meet with a certain lack of clarity which mirrors what I call the Antinomy of Being. The picture he offers us in 6.341 invites us to think the pictured reality as transcending any picture that science can give us. To generalize: reality transcends the reach of logic and in the *Tractatus* that means also of language. Reality transcends the reach of the *ratio*. Reality is transcendent.

But this conflicts with the understanding of the world as falling into logical space. To repeat it once more: everything that is capable of meaning anything to us, must be capable of being said. And is this not also true of reality? "*Kein Ding sei wo das Wort gebricht.*" The *ratio* builds being the house. So understood logic and language transcend reality. "Logic is transcendental." (6.13)

The Antinomy of Being has its foundation in the essence of Being. It was this that so disturbed the Pythagoreans.

3 Pictures and Models

Wittgenstein barely names those in the *Tractatus* to whom he owes a debt. In the Preface we read that it was of no concern to him whether something similar had been thought before him. Frege and Russell are mentioned – otherwise hardly anyone. That makes the cited reference to Heinrich Hertz all the more remarkable. Wittgenstein owes Hertz more than just a picture of his mechanics. Hertz offered the young Wittgenstein a model of how science should do its work and he extended it to all responsible thinking.

Hertz thought that to establish his *Principles of Mechanics* he needed only three basic concepts, space, time, and mass and just one basic law. Here some sentences from the very beginning of the Introduction to his *Principles of Mechanics*:

> The most direct, and in a sense the most important, problem which our conscious knowledge of nature should enable us to solve is the anticipation of future events, so that we may arrange our present affairs in accordance with such anticipation. As a basis for the solution of this problem we always make use of our knowledge of events which have already occurred, obtained by chance observation or by prearranged experiment. In endeavoring thus to draw inferences as to the future from the past, we always adopt the following process. We form for ourselves images or symbols of external objects; and the form which we give them is such that the necessary consequents of the images in thought are always the images of the necessary consequents in nature of the things pictured. In order that this requirement may be satisfied, there must be a certain conformity between nature and our thought. Experience teaches us that the requirement can be satisfied, and hence that such a conformity does in fact exist. When from our accumulated previous experience we have once succeeded in deducing images of the desired nature, we can then in a short time develop by means of them, as by means of models, the consequences which in the external world only arise in a comparatively long time, or as the result of our own interposition. We are thus enabled to be in advance of the facts, and to decide as to present affairs in accordance with the insight so obtained. The images which we here speak of are our conceptions of things. With the things themselves they are in conformity in one important respect, namely, in satisfying the above-mentioned requirement. For our purpose it is not necessary that they should be in conformity with the things in any other respect whatever. As a matter of fact, we do not know, nor have we any means of knowing, whether our conceptions of things are in conformity with them in any other than this one fundamental respect.[133]

The conformity of nature and our thoughts is confirmed by our experience; not by particular experiences, but by the essence of experience. Without such conformity there would be no experience. This conformity is thus given *a priori*.

When we decide to make ourselves pictures of nature, the question arises: which form should our pictures take? Here Hertz makes three demands:

> The images which we may form of things are not determined without ambiguity by the requirement that the consequents of the images must be the images of the consequents. Various images of the same objects are possible, and these images may differ in various respects. We should at once denote as inadmissible all images which implicitly contradict the laws of our thought. Hence we postulate in the first place that all our images shall

---

133 Heinrich Hertz, *Die Prinzipien der Mechanik in neuem Zusammenhange dargestellt. Unveränderter fotomechanischer Nachdruck der Ausgabe,* Leipzig 1894 (= *Gesammelte Werke*, Band III) (Darmstadt: Wissenschaftliche Buchgesellschaft, 1963). *Principles of Mechanics*, D. E. Jones and J. T. Walley (Trans.), (London: Macmillan, 1899), pp. 1–2.

be logically permissible or, briefly, that they shall be permissible. We shall denote as incorrect any permissible images, if their essential relations contradict the relations of external things, i.e., if they do not satisfy our first fundamental requirement. Hence we postulate in the second place that our images shall be correct. But two permissible and correct images of the same external objects may yet differ in respect of appropriateness. Of two images of the same object that is the more appropriate which pictures more of the essential relations of the object, the one which we may call the more distinct. Of two images of equal distinctness the more appropriate is the one which contains, in addition to the essential characteristics, the smaller number of superfluous or empty relations, the simpler of the two. Empty relations cannot be altogether avoided: they enter into the images because they are simply images, images produced by our mind and necessarily affected by the characteristics of its mode of portrayal.[134]

To sum up Hertz's three postulates:
(1) Images may not be incompatible with the laws governing our thinking. Logic must allow them. They must be permissible.
(2) They must be correct, i.e., agree with our experience of reality.
(3) They have to be appropriate: One picture is more appropriate than another when it gives us a more complete picture of the essential relations, i.e., when it is more distinct. And given two equally distinct images, that one is more appropriate which needs less, includes less that is superfluous, is simpler.

Hertz understands mechanics as an appropriate representation of nature, and his representation of mechanics as more appropriate because simpler, requiring only three principles and a single axiom.

Hertz's attempt to get by with three fundamental concepts, space, time, and mass recalls Schopenhauer. The young Wittgenstein, too, owes Schopenhauer a great deal. Schopenhauer, however, questioned the possibility of forming all propositions that we need for a full description of the world according to a single plan (6. 343). Were this possible, there would be at bottom only one science, only one mode of explanation. For McDermott, and of course not only for him, that would be physics.

Again and again we meet with the hope to reduce all descriptions of the world to mechanics, or even better, as already the Pythagoreans had hoped, to mathematics. But that last hope can be refuted with an *a priori* argument: to reduce all science to mathematics would be to lose sight of reality. We would then be unable to distinguish our picture of reality from reality. With this our picture would lose its character as a picture. But the reduction of all science to physics

---

[134] Heinrich Hertz, *Principles of Mechanics*, D. E. Jones and J. T. Walley (Trans.), (London: Macmillan, 1899), p. 2.

cannot similarly be rejected. Quite the opposite: does the logical essence of language, as, e.g., Wittgenstein understands it in the *Tractatus*, not demand some such reduction?

4 Kant's Metaphysical Foundations of Natural Science

Not only the young Wittgenstein was of this opinion. Kant already held what is essentially the same position. His understanding of what constitutes science in its proper sense is instructive:

> That only can be called science (*Wissenschaft*) proper whose certainty is apodictic: cognition that can merely contain empirical certainty is only improperly called science. A whole of cognition which is systematic is for this reason called science, and, when the connection of cognition in this system is a system of causes and effects, rational science. But when the grounds or principles it contains are in the last resort merely empirical, as, for instance, in chemistry, and the laws from which the reason explains the given facts are merely empirical laws, they then carry no consciousness of their necessity with them (they are not apodictically certain), and thus the whole does not in strictness deserve the name of science; chemistry indeed should be rather termed systematic art than science.[135]

How are we to understand the first proposition? Would this not mean that only mathematics can claim to be a science in the proper sense, since in all the other sciences experience makes a decisive contribution? Can or should the concept of science be narrowed in that way? Is not the systematic representation of nature, supported by careful observation, as so brilliantly executed in Kant's day by the botanist Carolus Linnaeus, greatly admired by both Rousseau and Goethe, science? Kant admits this. But he demands more of a "rational science": it has to provide us with a system of causes and effects, i.e., it has to posit causal laws. So understood the science of an Aristotle can be called a rational science, since it posits causal laws. And yet it leaves something decisive missing. To give just one example: by basing his table of the four elements on the properties hot and cold, dry and wet, thus presupposing the organization of our human senses, his physics cannot meet the demand for objectivity, which science in what Kant calls its proper sense must make. Only a discipline whose laws are not just based on experience can be called an "*eigentliche Wissenschaft*," science in the proper sense. This does not mean that such a science must not draw its content from

---

[135] Immanuel Kant, *Metaphysische Anfangsgründe der Naturwissenschaft*, (Riga: Hartknoch, 1786), Ernest Belfort Bax (Trans.), *The Metaphysical Foundations of Natural Science*, CreateSpace Independent Publishing Platform (June 12, 2015).

experience, but the form of these laws must be capable of *a priori* justification. This is to say, for Kant, it has to have its foundation in a metaphysics of nature that has an *a priori* foundation.

> A rational doctrine of nature deserves the name of natural science only when the natural laws at its foundation are cognized *a priori*, and are not mere laws of experience. A natural cognition of the first kind is called pure, that of the second applied, rational cognition. As the word nature itself carries with it the conception of law, and this again the conception of the necessity of all the determinations of a thing appertaining to its existence, it is easily seen why natural science must deduce the legitimacy of its designation only from a pure part of it, [a part] namely, which contains the principles *a priori* of all remaining natural explanations, and why only by virtue of this portion it is properly science, in such wise, that, according to the demands of the reason, all natural knowledge must at last turn on natural science and there find its conclusion. This is because the above necessity of law inseparably attaches to the conception of nature, and hence must be thoroughly comprehended. For this reason the most complete explanation of particular phenomena upon chemical principles, invariably leaves an unsatisfactoriness behind it, because from these accidental laws, learnt by mere experience, no grounds *a priori* can be adduced.[136]

If we follow Kant, in order to really deserve the title of a science, a discipline has to be supported by principles that are given it *a priori*. Logic, as Wittgenstein understands it, fails to meet what Kant demands, for it recognizes no causal laws. Presupposed by every science is indeed, as already stated, a metaphysics— whether it is called that or not is unimportant. The history of science, however, shows that there have been many such metaphysics and that shows that such a metaphysics cannot be given an *a priori* foundation. What can be justified in that way, what Kant calls a proper or true metaphysics, provides at most the form of a scientific metaphysics.

> But all true metaphysics is taken from the essential nature of the thinking faculty itself, and therefore in nowise invented, since it is not borrowed from experience, but contains the pure operations of thought, that is, conceptions and principles *a priori*, which the manifold of empirical presentations first of all brings into legitimate connection, by which it can become empirical knowledge, i.e., experience. These mathematical physicists were thus quite unable to dispense with such metaphysical principles, and amongst them, not even with that which makes the conception of their own special subject, namely, matter, available a priori, in its application to external experience (as the conception of motion, of the filling of space, of inertia, etc.). But to allow merely empirical principles to obtain in such a question, they rightly held as quite unsuited to the apodictic certainty they desired to give to

---

136 Ibid., p. vi.

their natural laws, and hence they preferred to postulate such, without investigating their sources a priori.[137]

To experience something here means: to know it empirically. Experience, so understood, aims fundamentally at truth.

What are the conditions that make such a knowing and not only thinking possible? Kant thought he had provided the demanded metaphysics with a transcendental foundation drawn only from "the essential nature of the thinking faculty itself," a foundation that he took to include pure intuitions of time and of space. That foundation was to be shaken by the discovery of non-Euclidean geometry by Carl Friedrich Gauss, János Bolyai, and Nikolai Lobachevsky. But that does not challenge Kant's ideal of science as a discipline supported by principles that are given it *a priori*, i e., drawn only from "the essential nature of the thinking faculty itself," even if we no longer can claim to possess a pure intuition of space as Euclidean, and thus of Euclidean space as constitutive of nature. The essence of space and time has proven more elusive than Kant had thought. But this does not call into question Kant's ideal of the mathematical nature of natural science.

The step from Kant and Schopenhauer to Hertz and Wittgenstein is not very great. Consider the way Hertz, without appealing to the concept of force, in the development of his mechanics requires only the concepts of space, time, and mass. They are presupposed. A presupposition of his mechanics is thus a metaphysics of nature. That metaphysics can appeal to Kant's *The Metaphysical Foundations of Natural Science*. Kant understood space and time as pure intuitions, presupposed by every experience of nature, matter as "what is movable in space."[138] In thinking space and time as joined the concept of matter is given. Kant thus thought that his transcendental idealism could provide the metaphysics of nature with a firm foundation.

From this transcendental part of metaphysics Kant distinguishes a special or particular part.

> What may be called natural science proper presupposes a metaphysics of nature; for laws, i.e., principles of the necessity of that which belongs to the existence of a thing, are occupied with a conception which does not admit of construction, because its existence cannot be presented in any *a priori* intuition; natural science proper, therefore, presupposes metaphysics. Now this must indeed always contain exclusively principles of a non-empirical origin (for, for this reason it bears the name of metaphysics); but it may be either without ref-

---

137 Ibid., p. xiii.
138 Ibid., p. 1.

erence to any definite object of experience, and therefore undetermined as regards the nature of this or that thing of the sense-world, and treat of the laws rendering possible the conception of nature in general, in which case it is the transcendental portion of the metaphysics of nature; or it may occupy itself with the particular nature of this or that kind of thing, of which an empirical conception is given, in such wise, that except what lies in this conception, no other empirical principle will be required for its cognition. For instance: it lays the empirical conception of a matter, or of a thinking entity, at its foundation, and searches the range of the cognition of which the reason is *a priori* capable respecting these objects; and thus, though such a science must always be termed a metaphysic of nature (namely, of corporeal or thinking nature), it is then not a universal but a particular metaphysical natural science (physics and psychology), in which the above transcendental principles are applied to the two species of sense-objects.[139]

A particular metaphysics has thus an empirical component. This raises the question: how is this particular metaphysics related to the transcendental. At bottom this is the question: to what extent does mathematics determine the form of every science? For a pure science, and just this distinguishes it from logic, has to draw its content from what is given *a priori*. But what is given *a priori* are, according to Kant, the pure intuitions, space and time. Space Kant understands "as nothing other than the mere form of appearances of the outer senses, that is the subjective condition of sensibility, by which alone outer intuition is possible for us,"[140] time as "the formal condition of all appearances whatsoever."[141] In both apodictic synthetic proposition are said to find their foundation, in the pure intuition of space the propositions of geometry, in the pure intuition of time the propositions of arithmetic. The discovery that Euclidean space is but one possible construction of the intuition of space presupposed by our experience of nature forces us to modify Kant's claim. But it does not shake his conviction that the mathematical form of representation presents itself to the scientist as the only one that is truly scientific. The scientist seeks what "is valid for any human sense whatsoever" and leaves what "is valid only for a particular position or organization of this or that sense" behind.[142] That is to say, science has to replace what shows itself to our senses with its mathematical reconstructions of what is experienced. The objectivity demanded by science demands the mathematization of nature. But the chemistry of his day, Kant thought, let alone the

---

[139] Ibid., p vii-viii.
[140] Immanuel Kant, *Kritik der reinen Vernunft*; *The Critique of Pure Reason*, Paul Guyer, Allen W. Wood (Eds. and Trans.), (Cambridge: Cambridge University Press, 1999), A26/B42.
[141] Ibid., A34/B50.
[142] Ibid., A45/B62.

psychology, had not developed to a point that allowed its mathematization and thus hardly could lay claim to the title of a true science.

> But I maintain that in every special natural doctrine only so much science proper is to be met with as mathematics; for, in accordance with the foregoing, science proper, especially [science] of nature, requires a pure portion, lying at the foundation of the empirical, and based upon an *a priori* knowledge of natural things. Now to cognize anything *a priori* is to cognize it from its mere possibility; but the possibility of determinate natural things cannot be known from mere conceptions; for from these the possibility of the thought (that it does not contradict itself) can indeed be known, but not of the object, as natural thing which can be given (as existent) outside the thought. Hence, to the possibility of a determinate natural thing, and therefore to cognize it *a priori*, is further requisite that the intuition corresponding *a priori* to the conception should be given; in other words, that the conception should be constructed. But cognition of the reason through construction of conceptions is mathematical. A pure philosophy of nature in general, namely, one that only investigates what constitutes a nature in general, may thus be possible without mathematics; but a pure doctrine of nature respecting determinate natural things (corporeal doctrine and mental doctrine), is only possible by means of mathematics; and as in every natural doctrine only so much science proper is to be met with therein as there is cognition *a priori*, a doctrine of nature can only contain so much science proper as there is in it of applied mathematics.[143]

Kant's metaphysics of nature promises thus something like a foundation for the all-encompassing science demanded by Neurath:

> It may serve as a second ground for gauging this procedure, that in all that is called metaphysics the *absolute completeness* of the sciences may be hoped for, in such a manner as can be promised by no other species of knowledge, and therefore, just as in the metaphysics of nature generally, so here also, the completeness of corporeal nature may be confidently expected; the reason being, that in metaphysics the object is considered merely according to the universal laws of thought, but in other sciences as it must be presented according to data of intuition (empirical as well as pure).[144]

The conditions of the possibility of every experience laid out in the *Critique of Pure Reason* are considered sufficient to establish physics as the true science. This foundation is at the same time also "the limitation of the whole faculty of the pure Reason, and therefore of all metaphysics."[145]

---

[143] Immanuel Kant, *Metaphysische Anfangsgründe der Naturwissenschaft*, (Riga: Hartknoch, 1786), Ernest Belfort Bax (Trans.), *The Metaphysical Foundations of Natural Science*, CreateSpace Independent Publishing Platform (June 12, 2015), p. viii-ix.
[144] Ibid., p. xiv.
[145] Ibid, p. xv, *Anmerkung*.

But every such limitation invites us to think of what lies beyond these limits, even if access to this beyond is denied to us finite knowers. Of special significance in this connection is a passage towards the end of this Preface:

> For if it be permissible to indicate the boundaries of a science, not merely according to the construction of its object, and its specific kind of cognition, but also according to the aim that is kept in view as a further use of the science itself, and it is found that metaphysics has engaged so many heads, and will continue to engage them, not in order to extend natural knowledge (which could be done much more easily and certainly by observation, experiment, and the application of mathematics to external phenomena), but in order to attain to a knowledge of that which lies wholly beyond all the boundaries of experience, of God, Freedom, and Immortality; [in this case] one gains in the promotion of this object, if one liberates it from a shoot springing indeed from its own stem, but only detrimental to its regular growth, and plants this [shoot] apart, without thereby mistaking its origination, or ignoring its entire growth from the system of general metaphysics.[146]

Science cannot know anything of God, freedom, and immortality. And the same goes for values. And it should not burden itself with such questions. Here I have to agree with Kant's *Metaphysical Foundations of Natural Science*. I cannot agree with the Christian philosopher Alvin Plantinga when, divorcing science from the commitment to objectivity, he claims that "What the Christian community really needs is a science that takes into account what we know as Christians."[147] A Christian science is not what we need, is not what the Christian community needs. Science cannot let go of its commitment to objectivity. The Catholic philosopher Ernan McMullin is right to insist that "methodological naturalism [which refuses to consider supernatural causes] does not restrict our study of nature; it just lays down which sort of study qualifies as scientific. If someone wants to pursue another approach to nature—and there are many others—the methodological naturalist has no reason to object. Scientists have to proceed in this way."[148] A Christian science is an oxymoron. What we need today is something quite different: not a Christian science, but a critique of science that recognizes the legitimacy of science as well as its limits.

I want to conclude this chapter by returning to these already cited paragraphs from Wittgenstein's *Tractatus:*

> 6.41 The sense of the world must lie outside the world. In the world everything is as it is and happens as it does happen. In it there is no value—and if there were, it would be of no value.

---

146 Ibid., p. xxi-xxii.
147 Alvin Plantinga, "Methodological Naturalism?" *Origins & Design*, Winter 1997, p. 25.
148 Ibid.

> If there is a value which is of value, it must lie outside all happening and being-so. For all happening and being-so is accidental.
>
> What makes it non-accidental cannot lie in the world, for otherwise this would again be accidental.

The concept of nature that is a presupposition of our science forces us to accept this claim. On this Kant and the young Wittgenstein agree. But Kant, although he wants to free the metaphysics of nature of that part of traditional metaphysics, which would go beyond the limits of science and claim a knowledge of God, freedom, and immortality, recognizes the legitimacy of these concerns and suggests that both science and these concerns are best served when the tree of metaphysics is freed from its scientific offshoot. But this suggests that traditional metaphysics is worth saving and that there is still a soil in which it can flourish. And this in turn presupposes that the concept of nature that presides over our science does not exhaust nature, that science presupposes a narrowed concept of experience that does not coincide with what we ordinarily call experience. Do we not experience persons as responsible agents? And is there not experience of the beautiful, the good, and perhaps the divine? And though science cannot do justice to such experiences, they are part of our everyday existence.

VII Learning from Laputa

1 Metaphysics and Thinking

Kant had good reason to remark "that metaphysics has engaged so many heads, and will continue to engage them, not in order to extend natural knowledge (which could be done much more easily and certainly by observation, experiment, and the application of mathematics to external phenomena), but in order to attain to a knowledge of that which lies wholly beyond all the boundaries of experience, of God, Freedom, and Immortality."[149] So understood, metaphysics does not aim at a knowledge of nature but at a knowledge of what make our lives meaningful. The theodicy of Leibniz can serve as an example. But the proposed justification of the world cannot persuade in the face of so much evil in the world. Voltaire had good reason to ridicule such a view: God eludes our reason. What support can such a metaphysics claim? That the progress of science should have left metaphysics so understood behind ever more decisively is to be expected. Pure thinking has to lose all content and content itself with tautologies, which, to be sure, as opposed to contradictions that are always false, are always true, but precisely because of this devoid of meaning. Not that they are therefore senseless. As the young Wittgenstein remarks:

> 4.4611 Tautology and contradiction are, however, not nonsensical; they are part of the symbolism, in the same way that "0" is part of the symbolism of Arithmetic.

They show us the logic that is a presupposition of our world pictures:

> 6.22 The logic of the world which the propositions of logic show in tautologies, mathematics shows in equations.

But this is not to say that these equations and tautologies represent reality in some fashion?

The metaphysician, appealing to Kant, can object that even mathematics resists being limited in that way, that even here we meet with synthetic judgments that have their foundation in the pure intuitions of space and time and that therefore are not altogether without content or meaning. And do such intuitions,

---

[149] Immanuel Kant, *Metaphysische Anfangsgründe der Naturwissenschaft*, (Riga: Hartknoch, 1786), Ernest Belfort Bax (Trans.), *The Metaphysical Foundations of Natural Science*, CreateSpace Independent Publishing Platform (June 12, 2015), pp. xxi-xxii.

which according to Kant all possible experience has to presuppose, not allow us to give metaphysics a transcendental turn and thus to give it a new life?

But even if it should be possible to base metaphysical propositions on such intuitions, such a metaphysics would still have nothing to say about what we human beings ought to do, just because it claims to find its ground in something claimed to be a presupposition of all possible experience, such as Kant's pure intuitions of space and time. But if that should indeed be so, it would be in principle impossible for us human beings to experience or do anything that would not satisfy the transcendental conditions so understood. A metaphysics that claims to establish a transcendental foundation can in principle make no contribution to ethics or to what might render life meaningful. If there is a thinking that has something to say about freedom and duty, God and value, such thinking cannot be secured by a metaphysical foundation in that sense. And yet, with good reason Kant calls our attention to the fact that such thinking has its origin in metaphysics. But what support can we now give to what may well seem a relic of a past that cannot be recovered? In what soil can it still thrive?

We are given a pointer by Drew McDermott with his attempt to show "How Moral Absolutism Can Be True and False at the Same Time." With this we return to the theory of double truth. On one side we meet, if we follow McDermott, the truth that science claims to pursue. Its point of view is that of the third person. Presupposed is a certain distance of the subject from the objects to be thought and also from our interests and desires, also from the everyday and its "truths." Scientific thought demands objectivity. But when we feel free or experience ourselves as an enduring self or believe in absolute values that oblige us in some fashion, there can be no talk of objectivity. And yet we are right, according to McDermott, given the standpoint of the first person, to be convinced of the truth of what we believe in. Science, to be sure, has no room for such "truth." I take it this is why McDermott speaks of a non-phenomenological existentialism. Phenomenology, as McDermott, with Edmund Husserl, would seem to understand it, lays claim to being scientific. But a thinking such as that of Heidegger, e.g., cannot make this claim. This may be the reason why Heidegger, as he progressed on his path, came to understand his thinking increasingly as no longer philosophy, let alone as metaphysics, but as a different sort of thinking, *das andere Denken*. And yet McDermott claims to find in *Being and Time* a convincing representation of our being-in-the-world. Given the standpoint of the first person, i.e., of the human being engaged and acting in the world, this representation can claim "truth." Truth and "truth" thus confront each other.

Fichte's distinction between theoretical and practical reason, so obviously indebted to Kant, goes in the same direction. As did already Kant, Fichte, too, recognizes that a pure theoretical reason cannot know anything of freedom, value, or God. Such a reason leads, as Jacobi recognized, to nihilism. But nihilism contradicts the way we experience the world first of all and most of time, the way we act in it and feel the pull of obligations. As Fichte's I puts it:

> "Your vocation is not merely to know, but to act according to your knowledge"; this is loudly proclaimed in the innermost depths of my soul, as soon as I recollect myself for a moment and turn my observation inward upon my self. "You are here not for idle contemplation of yourself, or for brooding over devout sensations—no, you are here for action: your action, and your action alone, determines your worth."
>
> This voice leads me out from presentation, from mere knowing, to something that is beyond it and opposed to it—to something that is greater and higher than all knowledge, and that contains within itself the end and object of all knowledge (VM 83–84).

Only our practical reason is said here to let us experience something like meaning. And is this practical reason not more fundamental, because a presupposition of theoretical reason? Would human beings engage in the pursuit of science, were they not convinced of the significance of their work, that their work is not in vain—Hertz might say, that our spirit is in tune with nature and that the search for truth justifies itself? Such a faith is a presupposition of scientific work. Theoretical reason cannot justify it. But it proves itself in scientific practice.

> When I act, I doubtless know that I act, and how I act; nevertheless this knowledge is not the act itself, but only the observation of it. This voice thus announces to me precisely that which I sought; a something lying beyond mere knowledge, and, in its nature, wholly independent of knowledge (VM 84).

Here, too, an inner voice protests against the theoretical point of view ruling science. Theory does not know what to do with such a voice. Its point of view is that of the third person. Thus it knows neither an "I", nor an inner realm, let alone an inner voice. And yet even the purest theory remains a practice and as such presupposes a faith in a transcendent reality, i.e., hears an inner voice that speaks of something totally independent of our being.

> Shall I then refuse obedience to that inward voice? I will not do so. I will freely accept the vocation which this impulse assigns to me, and in this resolution I will lay hold at once of thought, in all its reality and truthfulness, and on the reality of all things which are presupposed therein. I will restrict myself to the position of natural thought in which this impulse places me, and cast from me all those overrefined and sophistical inquiries which alone could make me doubtful of its truth (VM 88).

In this opposition of theoretical and practical reason the Antinomy of Being finds expression. But theoretical reason resists being subordinated to practical reason. If the realms of theoretical and practical reason could be neatly separated, if their opposed truths could exist quite independently, no antinomy would arise. But our concrete being-in-the-world does not allow for such a separation. Again and again the truths of theoretical reason call into question the "truths" of "practical reason." In the *Introduction* to *The Critique of Judgment* Kant addresses the necessity of bridging the abyss that here opens up:

> Hence an immense gulf is fixed between the domain of the concept of nature, the sensible, and the domain of the concept of freedom, the supersensible, so that no transition from the sensible to the supersensible and by means of the theoretical use of reason is possible, just as if they were two different worlds, the first of which cannot have any influence on the second: and yet the second is to have an influence on the first, i.e., the concept of freedom is to actualize in the world of sense the purpose enjoined by its laws. Hence it must be possible to think of nature as being such that the lawfulness of its form will harmonize with at least the possibility of [achieving] the purposes that we are to achieve in nature according to laws of freedom.[150]

That the concept of nature presupposed by science cannot be neatly separated from the concept of freedom, or that McDermott makes things too easy for himself in his conviction that he can hold on to his faith in freedom of the will and absolute values, although as a scientist he has recognized their falseness, is shown by his observation that the progress of science had narrowed the realm of the basic intuitions demanded by the first person point of view, even if McDermott thinks it impossible to eliminate it altogether. That such a narrowing is even possible shows that theoretical and practical reason cannot be separated in such a way that the one need not concern oneself with the other. And that such a narrowing has in fact taken place cannot be denied: In the developed countries the majority of the population no longer believes in God. The United States is here, if we are to believe public opinion polls, the great exception. Here ca. 80 % of the population still claim to believe in God. But the statistic also makes one wonder: how robust is this faith? What content does the word "God" still possess? And McDermott's faith in absolute values has been called into question ever more decisively by the progress of reason. The words that Nietzsche put into the mouth of his madman are not easily dismissed:

> Have you heard of that madman who lit a lantern in the bright morning hours, ran to the market place, and cried incessantly, 'I seek God!' "Whither is God?' he cried. "I shall tell you. We have killed him – you and I. All of us are his murderers. But how have we done

---

150 Immanuel Kant, *Kritik der Urteilskraft*, *Critique of Judgment*, Axix-xx/Bxix-xx. Werner S. Pluhar (Trans.), (Indianapolis: Hackett, 1987).

this? How were we able to drink up the sea? Who gave us the sponge to wipe away the entire horizon? What did we do when we unchained this earth from its sun? Whither is it moving now? Away from all suns? Are we not plunging continually? Backward, sideward, forward, in all directions? Is there any up and down left? Are we not straying as through an infinite nothing? Do we not feel the breath of empty space? Has it not become colder? Is not night and more night coming on all the while? Must not lanterns be lit in the morning? Do we not hear anything yet of the gravediggers who are burying God? Do we not smell anything yet of God's decomposition. Gods, too, decompose. God is dead. God remains dead. And we have killed him. How shall we, the murderers of all murderers comfort ourselves? What was holiest and most powerful of all the world has yet owned has bled to death under our knives. Who will wipe this blood off us? What water is there for us to cleanse ourselves? What festivals of atonement, what sacred games shall we have to invent?[151]

Neither Fichte's practical reason, nor McDermott's "inescapable framework illusions' promise such consolation.

But what about absolute value? What about freedom?

2 The Age of God's Decomposition

Nietzsche's madman asks: "Do we not smell anything yet of God's decomposition?" The history of the last hundred years suggests that we must answer that question in the affirmative: We live in the age of God's decomposition. The fact that many today find it easier to profess faith in something vaguely divine or the Godhead is a sign that God is losing his essence, a process captured well by Nietzsche's talk of divine decomposition, *göttliche Verwesung*. Science has played a key part in this process. Our life-world cannot be neatly separated from the world picture of our science. For technology belongs to the very essence of our science and technology means also a practice that cannot be separated from its scientific presuppositions. That practice determines our world picture and carries the nihilism that inescapably accompanies science into our lifeworld. Lost in this process is not only the relation to God, but also the relation to the earth as more than meaningless material for our machinations. That holds also for our body: it, too, become ever more mere material, subject to our manipulations. In his essay "Nietzsche's Word 'God is dead'" Heidegger describes this process:

---

[151] Friedrich Nietzsche, *Die Fröhliche Wissenschaft*, III, 125, *Kritische Studienausgabe*, vol.3, pp. 480–481. *The Gay Science*, Walter Kaufmann (Trans.), (Random House, 1974).

> For the human being has risen [*aufgestanden*] into the subjectivity of the *ego cogito*. With this rise or revolt [*Aufstand*] all that is becomes object. As what is objective, all that is is absorbed into the immanence of subjectivity. The horizon no longer shines with its own light. It is only the point of view established in the will to power's positing of value (GA 5, 261).

The art historian Hans Sedlmayr spoke of the death of light, where he was thinking of Adalbert Stifter's description of a total solar eclipse, which he read as a metaphor of a darkening age. The human being becomes a stranger to himself, becomes a ghost.[152] Stifter's metaphor of the expiring sun corresponds to Chamisso's metaphor of the lost shadow. A related loss marks Heidegger's determination of our age as "The Age of the World-Picture (GA 5, 115).

The word *Weltbild*, World-Picture, invites thought. A picture, as Alberti would have us think it, is a representation. It invites us to look through the picture, a material object as if it were a window, a transparent medium—at what is represented in the picture, to which nothing real needs to correspond. Such a picture stands in an essential relation to the point of view of the observing subject. In the picture that subject is not to be found. In order to even see the picture, the subject must keep his distance from the picture.

The metaphor of the window we find in Alberti's *On Painting* and Heidegger's understanding of the modern world-picture does invite us to think of Alberti's conception of a properly executed painting. As did Descartes, in whom Heidegger finds a key to the modern world-picture, in *On Painting* Alberti found his Ariadne thread in mathematics. On the assumption of some point of view at some definite distance from the picture, the art of perspective, relying on a mathematical form of description, allows the painter to represent the reality that presents itself to his eyes or that he merely imagines, so convincingly that it may even let us mistake illusion for reality. In this sense the painter can be said to have learned to master the representation of appearances. Reason determines the form of representation to which the imagination must submit.

Alberti, unlike Descartes, is not concerned to understand nature; what concerns him is the painter's ability, given some definite point of view, to represent what appears so convincingly that the eye may be deceived, where we must not lose sight of the loss of reality that is the price of such representation: In order to keep his construction as simple as possible, Alberti presupposes a flat earth and a single eye at rest. Given these presuppositions the correctness of his construction is easily proven. Given the right conditions, the artful illusions created by the painter should let us forget their illusory character and conjure up a second

---

[152] Hans Sedlmayr, *Der Tod des Lichtes* (Salzburg: O. Müller, 1964), pp. 9–17.

reality. The artist is thus celebrated as a second God, who lets his own take the place of God's creation.

Even if 200 years separate Alberti and Descartes, the latter's method yet has its precursor in the *perspectiva artificialis* of the Renaissance and carries with it an analogous loss of reality. Alberti, to be sure, did not promise to render the master of his method the master and possessor of nature. More modest, he only promised to make the painter master and possessor of nature's visual appearances. But here, too, method makes the master. And here already the method subjects what appears to a human measure that in turn is subject to the demand for easily employed representation. The mathematical form of the *perspectiva artificialis* is a consequence of that demand. It provides the foundation for a practice of representing human beings and things so convincingly that his contemporaries thought of magic.

In analogous fashion Descartes' method and, following him, our science, subjects nature to a human measure that in turn responds to the demand for an easily managed form of representation. And science completes itself in technology. Here, too, method aims at a practice that promises to represent the things of this world, for instance a human heart, so convincingly that someday it should become possible to replace it with an artificial heart.

If Alberti's form of representation presupposes a single eye, placed at a definite distance before the picture and at rest, the Cartesian world-picture places the subject before the world, lets it in this sense fall out of the world. Just as the observer has no place in the observed picture, so the Cartesian *res cogitans*, the human subject, has no place in that nature whose essence Descartes determines to be *res extensa*. And thus our science knows nothing of such a subject. To be sure, it knows brain processes and computer-simulated intelligence, but of persons who as such demand our respect it cannot know anything. They have no pace in the scientific world-picture and demand a different understanding of reality. As Wittgenstein writes of himself:

> 5.631 ... If I wrote a book 'the world as I found it,' I should also have therein to report my body and say which members obey my will and which do not etc. This then would be a method of isolating the subject or rather of showing that in an important sense there is no subject: that is to say, of it alone in this book mention could not be made.
>
> 5.632 The subject does not belong to the world, but it is a limit of the world.

But this limit must be brought back into the world, if we are to find our way to the human being.

That Wittgenstein, too, should speak of a world-picture is not surprising (2.19). The subject, the person, has always already fallen out of this picture.

And this world-picture is presupposed by the demand for objectivity that presides over our science. In this sense the laboratory know nothing of persons as demanding respect as such, which of course is not to deny that the human being offers infinite material for experimentation.[153] But without the experience of freedom showing itself in the world, i.e., without the encounter with persons so understood, without the experience of a Thou, the experience of the second person, all ethics loses its foundation. This foundation can only be found if a window opens in the modern world-picture to something other, something that speaks to us, that makes demands of us.

With his method Descartes promised to make us human beings the masters and possessors of nature. A presupposition of this promise is an understanding of nature as mute matter that is endowed with meaning only by the subject. As the painter stands before his picture, so the scientist stands before nature. But with this not only the thinker, not only the scientist, but human beings threaten to lose their place in nature.

If the attempt to make human beings the masters and possessors of nature is frightening, even more frightening is the attempt to make ourselves the masters and possessors of our own nature. Today the possibility of becoming with the help of medicine someone else is more than just an idle dream. Has not our own nature, too, become material that with the help of medical technology we can manipulate as we see fit? But who is it who here attempts to become with the help of surgery and psychiatry another? Where does such an undertaking find measure and direction? Who or what here is the human being. That a human being who understands him- or herself as such a subject has lost his or her shadow requires no explanation.

3 The Goddess of Reason

Once more I want to return to the story of Peter Schlemihl. Chamisso lets his shadowless hero, who, thanks to his seven-league boots, has become a scientist, find something like a home in an Egyptian cave. Let us attempt to translate the story into our age! What today might take the place of Schlemihl's cave? Some dark attic, but filled with television and computer screens that would carry the world into his lonely abode? But would a more fitting home not be some sat-

---

[153] See Karsten Harries, "World-Picture and World-Theater: Wonder, Vision, Knowledge," *Laboratory, Theater. Scenes of Knowledge in the 17th Century*, Helmar Schramm, Ludger Schwarte, Jan Lazardzig (Eds.), (Berlin, New York: de Gruyter, 2005), pp. 507–525.

ellite? Such a space station would guarantee the necessary distance from human beings and at the same time would allow our scientist to observe heaven and earth.

There were of course no satellites in 1814. But there was already something like a fictional space station, the floating island of Laputa in the third book of Jonathan Swift's *Gulliver's Travels*, first published in 1726, another product of the Enlightenment, which here calls itself into question. Swift's description of this flying island and its inhabitants provides us with a prophetic caricature of our modern world. Even then the old world was shaking in its foundations. But it still stood, though Swift would seem to have recognized the threatening storm, which was to explode later in the century in the French revolution and was to place a pretty young ballerina on the altar of Notre Dame representing the Goddess of Reason, although the Church was more likely to see in her the whore of Babylon.

The Laputians, too, worship that goddess. To her they owe their flying island, which presupposes a technology that would have far exceeded everything that was then possible. Presupposition of such a technology is a highly developed science. Laputa thus gives us an image of an essentially mobile, i.e., rootless society which, thanks to its commitment to reason, has lifted itself not only above the earth, but also above the body, and now runs the risk of losing its relation to both.

But let me turn to the story. Gulliver first glimpses this air-born island when, after a hair-raising encounter with some pirates, he finds himself marooned on a rocky island. Suddenly he sees a huge shadow moving across the ground:

> I turned back, and perceived a vast opaque body between me and the sun, moving forwards towards the island: it seemed to be about two miles high, and hid the sun six or seven minutes.... I took out my pocket perspective and could plainly discover numbers of people moving up and down the sides of it, which appeared to be sloping....
>
> ...The reader can hardly conceive my astonishment to behold an island in the air, inhabited by men, who were able (as it should seem) to rise or sink, or put it into progressive motion as they pleased.[154]

Not only is the flying island, which allows its inhabitants to leave this messy earth beneath them, the work of prodigious engineers, but, as already with the first balloons, the power of flight is quickly put to military use: we learn

---

[154] Jonathan Swift, *Gulliver's Travels Into Several Remote Nations of the World*, Part III, Chapter. 1. The Project Gutenberg eBook, Release Date: June 15, 2009 [eBook #829] Transcribed from the 1892 George Bell and Sons edition by David Price.

that the Laputians are able to destroy whatever humans below might dare challenge their hegemony by raining destruction on them from above. Shock and awe would cow them into submission —another way in which the early 18th century here anticipated what was still to come.

But back to our story! Eventually Gulliver succeeds in communicating to the inhabitants of this floating island his plight and they lower a seat to raise him up, rather in the way Socrates in Aristophanes' *Clouds* is raised up in a basket from which he contemplates celestial matters and converses with the clouds, the presiding spirits of his school, surrounded by students engaged in all sorts of ridiculous pursuits, where Aristophanes singles out astronomy and geometry. Swift no doubt also had Aristophanes in mind when he wrote this third part of *Gulliver's Travels*. Both Aristophanes, with his description of Socrates' *Thoughtery*, and Swift, with his description of the island of Laputa, poke fun at a philosophy and a science that by raising itself above the world has lost touch with it.

Aristophanes' comedy suffers from the way it presents Socrates as little more than a buffoon. Plato was to be much kinder to Aristophanes when he caricatured him in the *Symposium*. But the image the conservative Aristophanes sketches of Socrates does raise some serious questions, questions that Nietzsche was later to repeat in *The Birth of Tragedy*. Indeed, we find in this comedy already an anticipation of the charges that were to be raised later against Socrates by the Athenians: Aristophanes' Socrates does not believe in Zeus, or for that matter in any gods. He is godless. And that lack of belief is said to have its foundation in the way Socrates, with his faith in the power of reason, allows his spirit to soar, to mingle with the clouds. This lets him think up new maxims that threaten the very foundation that had supported Athenian society. In the *Clouds* already this leads to the charge that Socrates is a corrupter of the young. The play ends with the burning of Socrates *Thoughtery*, described as a small and dingy building, by the enraged Strepsiades, whose son had learned all too well what Socrates had to teach.

Towards the beginning of the play there is a suggestion that Socrates, with his head in the clouds, had outdone even Thales, not only the first philosopher, but the first absent-minded philosopher, whose carelessness lets him fall into a well, to be mocked by a pretty Thracian servant girl, for whom he had no eyes. The flight of thought means inevitably also a kind of absent-mindedness.[155] Here we should recall that when Peter Schlemihl tried to explain how he came to lose

---

[155] Cf. Hans Blumenberg, *Das Lachen der Thrakerin: Eine Urgeschichte der Theorie* (Frankfurt am Main: Suhrkamp, 1987).

his shadow, he says it was because of a kind of carelessness. And indeed, he did not take adequate care of the whole human being. Nor did Socrates. Nor did Descartes. When human beings understand themselves as first of all thinking substances, they leave behind or perhaps better below them those caring beings we mortals are first of all and most of the time. The men of Laputa, too, understand themselves first of all as such thinking substances. Most of the time they are quite oblivious of their bodies.

In *The Birth of Tragedy* Nietzsche takes up the Aristophanic critique and finds in it a key to the essence of our modern culture. We know that Nietzsche at the time also took an interest in the Laputians.[156] It is to Socrates that we owe, according to Nietzsche "the unshakable faith that thought, using the thread of causality, can penetrate the deepest abysses of being, and that thought is capable not only of knowing being, but even of *correcting* it."[157] It was this faith that once placed the goddess of reason on the altar of Notre Dame and that has helped shape our modern world. Swift's caricature anticipates essential features.

It is hardly surprising that the Laputians should have a curious appearance and dress strangely:

> Their heads were all inclined, either to the right or to their left; one of their eyes turned inward, and the other directly up to the zenith. Their outward garments were adorned with the figures of suns, moons, and stars; interwoven with those of fiddles, flutes, harps, and trumpets, guitars, harpsichords and many other instruments of music, unknown to us in Europe.[158]

Note that our normal posture, which allows us to look ahead and also left and right, has been left behind. That posture does justice to our being on earth, to our having to watch out where we are going. The thinker purchases his freedom at the price of a certain self-forgetfulness—recall once more the story of the absent-minded Thales. Like Socrates and his students in the *Clouds,* like Thales, the Laputians are oriented towards what is above, towards some heavenly realm

---

[156] Friedrich Nietzsche, *Schopenhauer als Erzieher, Sämtliche Werke, Kritische Studienausgabe* in 15 vols. G. Colli and M. Montinari (Eds.), (München/ Berlin/ New York: Deutscher Taschenbuch Verlag and de Gruyter, 1980), vol.1, pp. 420–21.

[157] Friedrich Nietzsche, *Die Geburt der Tragödie 15, Kritische Studienausgabe*, vol. 1, p. 99. "*The Birth of Tragedy*" and "*The Case of Wagner*," Walter Kaufmann (Trans.), (New York: Vintage, 1967), p. 95.

[158] Jonathan Swift, *Gulliver's Travels Into Several Remote Nations of the World*, The Project Gutenberg eBook, Release Date: June 15, 2009 [eBook #829] Transcribed from the 1892 George Bell and Sons edition by David Price, Part III, Chapter 2.

rather than the earth. With one eye they are thus turned upward, to the zenith. But we should not forget their other eye, which is turned inward. Laputa is a society of introverts.

Like the Pythagoreans, the Laputians are great astronomers and great musicians. Remarkable is the way Swift has these astronomers anticipate the discovery of the two moons of Mars by Asaph Hall III in 1877 by151 years:

> They have likewise discovered two lesser stars, or satellites, which revolve about Mars; whereof the innermost is distant from the center of the primary planet exactly three of his diameters, and the outermost, five; the former revolves in the space of ten hours, and the latter in twenty-one and a half; so that the squares of their periodical times are very near in the same proportion with the cubes of their distance from the center of Mars; which evidently shows them to be governed by the same law of gravitation that influences the other heavenly bodies.[159]

And prophetic, too, is the high rank the Laputians gave to music, a ranking that came to be widely accepted in Europe only in the 19th century. Kant still considered music a somewhat questionable art. Only two decades later Schopenhauer was to place it above all the other arts. By then such a ranking no longer seemed questionable.

I pointed out that the Laputians join an extraordinary preoccupation with what is above, with the cosmos, to an equally extraordinary introversion. That finds expression in their bearing and in their style of dress. As Descartes shows us, pure theory and the turn to the self, belong together. It is precisely this inward turn, to which corresponds Descartes' retreat into a dingy little stove-heated room that allows his spirit to soar until reality itself threatens to lose its reality, as doubt takes hold of the philosopher. Such introversion means inevitably a loss of community. And so it is hardly surprising that the Laputians should have had trouble communicating with one another.

> I observed here and there, many in the habits of servants, with a blown bladder fastened like a flail to the end of a stick, which they carried in their hands. In each bladder was a small quantity of dried peas, or little pebbles, as I was afterwards informed. With these bladders they now and then flapped the mouths and ears of those who stood near them, of which practice I could not conceive the meaning. It seems that the minds of these people are so taken up with intense speculations, that they neither can speak, nor attend to the discourses of others, without being roused by some external action upon the organs of speech and hearing. [160]

---

159 Ibid., Part III, Chapter 3.
160 Ibid., Part III, Chapter 2.

The thinker's freedom of thought is bought at the price of a certain absence from himself as an embodied self, existing as member of a community of such selves. In this respect the Laputians are not unlike the man without a shadow.

> This flapper is likewise employed diligently to attend his master in his walks, and upon occasion to give him a soft slap on his eyes; because he is always so wrapped up in cogitation, that he is in manifest danger of falling down every precipice, and bouncing his head against every post; and in the streets, of justling others, or being justled himself into the kennel.[161]

Think of individuals preoccupied with their cell-phones and quite oblivious of those around them. Nietzsche was led by these words to think of philosophers, who, so lost "in such deep thoughts," that they were "in constant danger or running with their head at every beam," now had found in the form of natural scientists and historians the flappers they so desperately needed to call them back to reality.[162]

Later Gulliver is joined for dinner by four courtiers, to discover to his astonishment that a shoulder of mutton had been cut into an equilateral triangle, a piece of beef into a rhomboid, and a pudding into a cycloid. And as food is subjected to the rule of geometry, so is clothing. A love of geometry defined the being of the Laputians. We can assume that they would have loved Cubist paintings. The analogy that links these three, taste in food, taste in clothing, and taste in painting and building, was to be exploited later by Adolf Loos in his characterization of modernity. All are expressions of the same ruling ethos. That the Laputians should want to dress themselves in the image of the heavens stands to reason. This then is a logocentric society that seeks to subject whatever its members encounter to their logos.

> Their ideas are perpetually conversant in lines and figures. If they would, for example, praise the beauty of a woman, or any other animal, they describe it by rhombs, circles, parallelograms, ellipses, and other geometrical terms, or by words of art drawn from music, needless here to repeat.[163]

---

161 Ibid., Part III, Chapter 2.
162 Friedrich Nietzsche, *Schopenhauer als Erzieher*, Sämtliche Werke, *Kritische Studienausgabe* in 15 vols. G. Colli and M. Montinari (Eds.), (München/ Berlin/ New York: Deutscher Taschenbuch Verlag and de Gruyter, 1980), vol. 1, pp. 420–21.
Jonathan Swift, *Gulliver's Travels Into Several Remote Nations of the World*, The Project Gutenberg eBook, Release Date: June 15, 2009 [eBook #829] Transcribed from the 1892 George Bell and Sons edition by David Price, Part III, chapter 2.

As this quote shows, these logocentrists are misogynists. Women are included among animals. That the Laputians should neglect their wives is to be expected.

One can infer that the art of such a literally rootless people, each person lost in himself, would have to be geometric and abstract. In their aesthetic sensibility, too, they were modernists before their time. That the art historian Hans Sedlmayr should have found in Swift's description of the Laputians an anticipation of the aesthetic sensibility that has presided over modern art is not surprising.[164]

4 The Whore of Babylon

Somewhat surprisingly, while shut up in their separate private worlds, the Laputians have yet an extraordinary interest in public affairs and passionately dispute every inch of a party opinion even though it has little relevance to their lives. In this respect, too, they resemble us. The Laputians would have loved television and the ways it brings public affairs close to each one of us. And they would have made great pundits on today's talk shows: our pundits, too, are all too often unable to listen and I think our television stations should consider hiring flappers to hit some of these pundits on their ears when they interrupt and don't listen, preoccupied as they are with their own thoughts.

I should also mention that Gulliver speculates about the etymology of Laputa, which he takes to mean a flying or floating island. According to one etymology, which he finds too contrived, it means high governor, suggesting dreams of mastery. He then offers a learned conjecture of his own, which would have Laputa derive from "quasi *lap outed: lap* signifying properly the dancing of the sunbeams in the sea, and *outed* a wing: which, however, I shall not obtrude, but submit to the judicious reader."[165] This etymology suggests dreams of flying. Both suggestions deserve our consideration. Although absent-minded, the Laputians yet know very well, as I mentioned, how to use their flying island to dominate the subjected humanity quite literally below them, by denying them, if necessary, sunlight and rain by placing their island above them or, if that should not help, by bombing them.

---

164 Hans Sedlmayr, *Die Revolution der modernen Kunst* (Hamburg: Rowohlt, 1955), p. 102. Sedlmayr, "Das große Reale und das große Abstrakte," *Der Tod des Lichtes*, (Salzburg: O. Müller, 1964), p. 23.
165 Jonathan Swift, *Gulliver's Travels Into Several Remote Nations of the World*, The Project Gutenberg eBook, Release Date: June 15, 2009 [eBook #829] Transcribed from the 1892 George Bell and Sons edition by David Price, Part III, Chapter 2.

The true etymology Gulliver tells us he could never learn. We are told, however, that the language of the Laputians sounds rather like Italian. In Spanish *La puta* is the harlot, raising the question why this floating abode of logocentrists who have distanced themselves from their bodies should bear just that name. Recall that in the Bible Babylon is called a harlot, the city that has turned its back on God. And God does not seem to have a place in the life of the Laputians. Laputa figures the modern Babylon, raised by reason above the earth.

Not that their reason gives the Laputians a sense of security. As expert astronomers they know very well that life on this earth must come to an end sooner or later. Could some comet not turn our earth to ashes? And will the sun always shine as benignly as it shines for us today? Their reason does not let the Laputians look confidently into the future. Quite the opposite. They know that their reason is insufficient to ward off the catastrophes that frighten them. Such concerns prevent them from sleeping well. But thoughts of such catastrophes also entertain and give life a content. Gulliver thus likens the Laputians to children that listen with the greatest pleasure to stories of goblins and ghosts that fill them with such fear that they are unable to go to bed.

I said the Laputians had lost contact with their bodies and with the earth. But why not say that they had elevated themselves above their earth-bound existence? And is such a self-elevation not a presupposition of genuine freedom and of scientific objectivity? What need is there still for God? Is Nietzsche's madman not mad precisely because he clings to something that has lost its meaning for us? Only someone who knows of the former life of God and has to struggle with what has been lost can speak of the decomposition of God. A truly enlightened humanity will find it difficult to make much sense of such talk.

5 The Two Faces of Curiosity

We should not over-emphasize the extent to which the Laputians have lost touch with reality. As already pointed out, the creation of their floating island presupposes an extraordinarily advanced science and technology. And science and technology translate into very real power. Not that it is such power that the Laputians are most interested in. Their love of geometric forms is pure: they love such forms for their own sake. They want to know just in order to know. This helps to explain what Gulliver finds difficult to understand: the Laputians extraordinary interest in politics and current affairs:

> But what I chiefly admired, and thought altogether unaccountable, was the strong disposition I observed in them towards news and politics, perpetually inquiring into public affairs,

giving their judgments in matters of state, and passionately disputing every inch of a party opinion. I have indeed observed the same disposition among most of the mathematicians I have known in Europe, although I could never discover the least analogy between the two sciences; unless those people suppose, that because the smallest circle has as many degrees as the largest, therefore the regulation and management of the world require no more abilities than the handling and turning of a globe; but I rather take this quality to spring from a very common infirmity of human nature, inclining us to be most curious and conceited in matters where we have least concern, and for which we are least adapted by study or nature.[166]

What did the stars matter to the Laputians? What did they matter to Thales? How should we understand the insatiable and yet at bottom unconcerned interest in sad events and horrifying news to which newspapers and television owe much of their existence? St. Augustine already knew about and lamented such curiosity:

> For what pleasure is there to see, in a lacerated corpse, that which makes you shudder? And yet if it lie near, we flock there, to be made sad, and to turn pale. Even in sleep they fear lest they should see it. Just as if when awake any one compelled them to go and see it, or any report of its beauty had attracted them! Thus also is it with the other senses, which it were tedious to pursue. From this malady of curiosity are all those strange sights exhibited in the theatre. Hence do we proceed to search out the secret powers of nature (which is beside our end), which to know profits not, and wherein men desire nothing but to know. Hence, too, with that same end of perverted knowledge we consult magical arts. Hence, again, even in religion itself, is God tempted, when signs and wonders are eagerly asked of Him – not desired for any saving end, but to make trial only.[167]

Was it not curiosity that once let Adam and Eve lose paradise? Again and again curiosity will let us lose some paradise or other. Concealed in the snake's promise that by eating the fateful apple Adam and Eve would become like God, a promise that led us human beings to lose our place in the order of nature and made us into essentially restless, never quite contented animals, is our reason's claim to truth and autonomy.

But why condemn our curiosity as lust of the eyes? Isn't it precisely the loss of paradise that is the other side of that liberation from our subjection to nature that is constitutive of full humanity? This is how Aristotle understood the desire

---

166 Jonathan Swift, *Gulliver's Travels Into Several Remote Nations of the World*, The Project Gutenberg eBook, Release Date: June 15, 2009 [eBook #829] Transcribed from the 1892 George Bell and Sons edition by David Price, Part III, Chapter 2.
167 St. Augustine, *Confessions*, Edward B. Pusey (Trans.), (New York: Modern Library, 1949), Book X, 55.

to see just in order to see, which he placed at the very origin of our philosophy and science.

In rather the same spirit Ortega y Gasset addressed an audience of mostly architects at the same *Darmstädter Gespräch* where Heidegger gave his lecture "Building Dwelling Thinking." Ortega spoke on "The Myth of the Man Behind Technology," spoke about the human being as the being that had fallen out of nature, that had lost its place in nature, the discontented misfit, the animal that had no home in nature, ever seeking things it had never had. This restless discontent Ortega compared to a love without the beloved, with a "pain, that we feel in limbs that we never had."[168] And this discontent Ortega called what is highest in the human being, just because it is a discontent, because it desires things it has never had.[169] Technology has its origin in such discontent, which demands a new world "because the real world does not fit us, because it has made us sick. This new world of technology is for us like a gigantic orthopedic apparatus, which you [he was addressing the architects present] want to create; and all of technology has this wonderful, but—as everything about man—dramatic dynamism and quality of being a fabulous, immense orthopedic creation."[170]

Heidegger spoke the next morning, offering the audience his example of an 18th century Black Forest farmhouse, to which, to be sure—Heidegger knew this and underscored it—we cannot ever return, but which is yet supposed to show how "a dwelling that has been" once was able to build, showing us how building "receives its nature from dwelling."[171] Heidegger invites us to repeat this "dwelling that has been" in a manner in keeping with our own age, to "repeat" it in the sense of *Being and Time* as a resolute appropriation of our history. "Building Dwelling Thinking" seeks to provide us with a pointer how such a repetition might be thought. But does Heidegger's backward-looking determination of essential dwelling "as the fourfold preservation of the fourfold" not stand in the way of an understanding of the task of dwelling and building in keeping with our age? What is his fourfold of earth and sky, mortals and divinities to us?

Listening to Ortega, Heidegger may have thought not only of his Black Forest farmhouse, but also of Augustine's condemnation of curiosity, also of the way the Book of Genesis ascribes the invention of technology to the race of Cain, vainly hoping to regain the lost paradise by means of technology.

---

168 Otto Bartning, (Ed.), 2. *Darmstädter Gespräch 1951. Mensch und Raum* (Darmstadt: Neue Darmstädter Verlags-Anstalt. 1952), p. 116.
169 Ibid., p. 117.
170 Ibid., p. 117.
171 Ibid., p. 83.

As Ortega and Heidegger in this *Darmstädter Gespräch* called each other into question with their contributions, so our longing for the distant and unknown and the longing for home, *Fernweh* and *Heimweh*, call each other into question.

I would like to conclude this chapter with a few verses by Hölderlin that Heidegger liked to cite:[172]

> For at home is the spirit
> Not in the beginning, not at the source. Home wears on him.
> Colony loves, and brave forgetting the spirit.[173]

To find itself, the spirit must leave home, has to find its home abroad. Thus in his interpretation of Hölderlin's hymn "Der Ister" Heidegger calls the law of not being at home the law of coming to be at home.[174] There is a sense in which to become ourselves we must leave home. And yet home wears on us, does not leave us. And thus the sting of home stays with us, lets us seek, even abroad, in foreign parts, home. Is this not at bottom the same insight that let Ortega y Gasset compare technology to a fabulous orthopedic apparatus and demand of the architect, too, similar creations? We should not forget that the creation of such an orthopedic apparatus presupposes not only that dissatisfaction with our in so many ways less than perfect bodies, emphasized by Ortega, but also knows about the body's indispensability. And similarly the spirit knows about the many imperfections, but also about the indispensability of home, knows about both. This is why it loves home even in the strange and unfamiliar, why it loves colony, the repetition of home in the foreign, but loves also the unexpected and never before seen that it is encountering in the new world it has now entered, knows that clinging to home stands in the way of such love and for this reason the spirit loves also brave forgetting. In this sense Heidegger can say that it is that home we have left behind and which yet does not let go of us, which calls us mortals into our dwelling. Centrifugal and centripetal tendencies war and compete in us human beings, in our dwelling—should war and compete also in our building. Human beings would lose themselves were they not to remain on the way, in search of home.

---

172 Martin Heidegger, GA53, pp. 156–170.
173 Friedrich Beissner, *Hölderlins Übersetzungen aus dem Griechischen* (Stuttgart; Metzler, 1933), p. 147.
174 Martin Heidegger, GA53, p. 166.

VIII Abysmal Freedom and the Antinomy of Space

1 Freedom and the Infinite Cosmos

In his valedictory oration to the professors at Wittenberg in 1588 Giordano Bruno pleaded for *philosophica libertas,* for philosophical freedom, that is the freedom to pursue his ideas wherever his reason might lead him. Perhaps he was the first to do so explicitly. It was a concept that was eagerly picked up by others. Tommaso Campanella argued in his *Apologia pro Galileo* of 1622 at some length for the freedom to philosophize as one pleases. In his *Theology* he was to insist *sapientia quaerit libertatem animi,* wisdom seeks liberty of the mind. A few years before that Galileo had insisted that philosophizing needs to be free.[175]

This theme, too, has an Aristotelian root: Aristotle explicitly links freedom and truth. But in what sense does the pursuit of truth demand freedom of thought? Keep in mind that the very word religion is, according to a widely accepted, if probably false, etymology tied to binding: must religion not bind freedom? This raises the question: must our freedom not perhaps be bound in some way, as religion insists? That our reason alone should bind freedom is of course the position of the Enlightenment. Think of Kant's understanding of autonomy. But is reason sufficient to bind freedom?

Today Bruno is perhaps best known as someone who not only denied the earth its long taken for granted central position in the cosmos, but went far beyond Copernicus by calling the very concept of such a center into question, insisting on the infinity of the universe. Here is how Arthur Lovejoy in *The Great Chain of Being* describes Bruno's significance, a description explicitly endorsed by Alexandre Koyré:

> Though the elements of the new cosmography had, then, found earlier expression in several quarters, it is Giordano Bruno who must be regarded as the principal representative of the doctrine of the decentralized, infinite, and infinitely populous universe; for he not only preached it throughout western Europe with the fervor of an evangelist, but also first gave a thorough statement of the grounds on which it was to gain acceptance from the general public.[176]

---

[175] See John M. Headley, *Tommaso Campanella and the Transformation of the World* (Princeton: Princeton University Press, 1997), pp. 172–173, n. 109.
[176] Quoted by Alexandre Koyré, *From the Closed World to the Infinite Universe* (New York: Harper Torchbook, 1958), p. 39.

Even that brief description suggests why the Church would have been concerned. There is first of all the challenge Bruno posed to the geocentric worldview presupposed by the Bible. That challenge is compounded when the cosmos is said to be infinite both in space and in time and infinitely many stars are said to be populated. We might speak here of the principle of cosmic homogeneity as opposed to the medieval Aristotelian principle of cosmic heterogeneity, which placed the earth at the center of the cosmos and opposed an ever changing sublunar realm to an unchanging superlunar realm. That the principle of cosmic homogeneity makes it difficult to make sense, not just of the Christian creation account, but more importantly, of the Christian salvation account, of the unique significance of Christ, is evident: how did that account relate to the populations of other planets and stars? Bruno's understanding of an infinite cosmos is incompatible with the conviction that there are uniquely significant places and times. The new cosmology and central dogmas of the Church appeared impossible to reconcile and the latter mattered more to the Church than the former.

Bruno has come to be cited as perhaps the first martyr that the Copernican revolution produced: on account of his denial of geocentrism and his teachings about the infinity of the cosmos, the Inquisition is said to have tried him for heresy. Found guilty, he was burned at the stake. So understood he appears as a more courageous, but just because of his courage less fortunate, precursor of Galileo. Such an edifying interpretation of his gruesome end is, however, somewhat difficult to reconcile with the available facts. First of all there is the fact that it took the Church quite some time to place Copernicus' *De Revolutionibus* on the index of forbidden books. That only happened in 1616, in response to the teachings of Galileo. Copernicus' main work was thus placed on the index only sixteen years after the execution of Bruno. And we should note that there were many other Copernicans in the Church who did not meet with Bruno's fate. There must have been other factors that led the Church to single him out.

More than any other of his many works, it was the *The Ash Wednesday Supper* that established Giordano Bruno's reputation as a leading Copernican. But why should a work so often and with good reason cited as a defense of the Copernican system be given a title that invites us to think of communion? And the content of the work makes it quite clear: Bruno here is indeed as concerned with the Lord's Supper, which he parodies, as he is with Copernicus. But what is the connection? Even a cursory reading of the *Ash Wednesday Supper*[177] suggests that any interpretation of Bruno as the first martyr of the Copernican cause

---

[177] Giordano Bruno, *The Ash Wednesday Supper*, Edward A. Gosselin and Lawrence S. Lerner (Ed. and Trans.), (Hamden: Archon, 1977).

fails to do justice to the complexity of his life and thought. Such an interpretation also fails to do justice to the way he died. Bruno was executed on February 17, 1600, the day after Ash Wednesday.[178] He was then fifty-two. Early that morning he was led from the dungeon by the Friars of the Company of St. John the Beheaded, "dedicated to the comfort and conversion of condemned prisoners."[179] Bruno, however, unrepentant, made a point of ridiculing his executioners, averting his eyes from the crucifix offered to him. His tongue was spiked and the heretic burnt at the stake.

Why did the Church feel it had to execute Bruno in such gruesome fashion? It has long been recognized that the Church connected Bruno with another Copernican of sorts, the already mentioned Tommaso Campanella, who at the time was in a prison in Naples. Both were thought to represent related threats to the established order. Campanella saw himself as the Messiah of a new age, inspiring Calabrian peasants with his dreams of a communist, democratic, God-centered republic, based on the community of goods and wives. In the year 1600, relying on the authority of Joachim of Fiore and supported by his own astrological observations, Campanella expected the advent of the Age of the Holy Spirit. Such expectation led him to incite the peasants of Calabria to revolt against the Spanish authorities in 1598 and 1599.[180] As Frances Yates suggests, it is difficult not to see a connection between Campanella's imprisonment and torture in Naples and his fellow Dominican's execution in Rome.

And yet there is also a profound difference between the two. Campanella escaped execution, although not torture and 27 years in prison, even though politically he had been much more active than Bruno. And Campanella was in fact never a committed Copernican. He did defend Galileo, but he was quite willing to waffle on the Copernican issue, at least in public. Copernicus does not seem to have been all that much of a concern. Columbus and his discovery of a new world seemed more important. Campanella was, however, a committed millenarian. This revolutionary impulse does link him to Bruno, who also longed for and

---

178 V. Spampanato, *Vita di Giordano Bruno, Con documenti edite e inedite*, vol. 1 (Messina: Principato, 1921), pp. 579–597. See also Bruno , Giordano, *The Ash Wednesday Supper*, Edward A. Gosselin and Lawrence S. Lerner (Ed. and Trans.), (Hamden: Archon, 1977), pp. 11–53; and Hans Blumenberg, *Die Legitimität der Neuzeit* (Frankfurt am Main: Suhrkamp, 1966). Robert M. Wallace (Trans.), *The Legitimacy of the Modern Age* (Cambridge, MA: MIT Press, 1983), pp. 416–454.
179 Bruno, The Ash Wednesday Supper, p. 22; V. Spampanato, *Vita di Giordano Bruno, Con documenti edite e inedite*, vol. 1 (Messina: Principato, 1921), pp. 582–583.
180 John M. Headley, *Tommaso Campanella and the Transformation of the World* (Princeton: Princeton University Press, 1997), p. 3. See also Frances A. Yates, *Giordano Bruno and the Hermetic Tradition* (Chicago and London: The University of Chicago Press, 1979), pp. 360–397.

hoped to help bring about a new political order based on freedom of thought and reason. But Bruno's own understanding of infinite space and time makes it difficult to speak of the age whose coming he awaited so impatiently as the millennium that would mean the end of history.

Millennial thinking thinks of a succession of ages culminating in a final and golden age in which history attains its telos and comes to a glorious end. Such millennial ideas were common in the Middle Ages. Joachim of Fiore (1135–1202), whose thought Campanella appropriated, thus thought history in terms of three ages, the age of the Father, the Son, and the Holy Spirit, as a history of the progressive descent of the divine into the human which means also the progress of freedom. Mediated by Lessing, Hegel's understanding of the progress of history still owes a great deal to this milllennial schema, as does the thinking of Marx. But such a schema requires that there is a sense in which history does progress towards an end state. Just this Bruno's understanding of both the infinite cosmos and of history as without beginning or end denied.

Eschatological ideas have resurfaced again and again.[181] They flourished especially in the years just preceding 1600, thought to "be particularly important, owing to the numerological significance of nine and seven, the sum of which is sixteen. In the coming dispensation there will be established a better religious cult and better moral laws, both based on nature and natural religion."[182]

But Bruno's thinking is much more pagan than that of Campanella. As we have seen, for Bruno, as for Aristotle, the cosmos has no beginning. There can therefore not be a progress covering the whole of history. Bruno thus does not anticipate Hegel, who would have us understand Descartes as the sailor who finally reaches *terra firma*. According to Bruno there can be no *terra firma* in that sense. That is true of the cosmos and it remains true when the thought is extended to history. With this, however, the promise of a final golden age is ruled out and, just as there is something terrifying about the infinite cosmos, so there is something terrifying about this vision of history, which only knows the unending and therefore finally pointless succession of dark and light.

Bruno invites us thus to think perspectival illusion not just with respect to particular places, but also with respect to particular times. We can thus speak of the Copernican revolution being raised to a higher level, or perhaps being transposed into a different key. This is true not just of the vision of the cosmos that Bruno gives us; it is also true of the historical vision of which we get glimp-

---

[181] See Norman Cohn, *The Pursuit of the Millennium*, 2nd edition (New York: Harper Torchbooks, 1961).
[182] Frances A. Yates, *Giordano Bruno and the Hermetic Tradition* (Chicago and London: The University of Chicago Press, 1979), p. 364.

ses. We can say: just as the eye is subjected to its spatial location, so reason is subjected to its temporal location. Bruno invites us to struggle against both. But there can be no final victory of truth. Darkness will return.

Bruno did think that the long night of the Christian Middle Ages was finally ending. Copernicus, who denied the earth its place at the center of the cosmos, yet retained the idea of such a center, is thus likened to the dawn that announces the coming day that Bruno associated with himself. That day would not only lead to a changed understanding of our place in the cosmos, but also bring about a transformation of the established religious and political order. Freedom of thought and reason would reign once again. The Church had good reason to be concerned.

In an announcement published on February 19, 1600 in the *Avvisi Romani* we find an account of Bruno's execution. We read there that surrendering to his capricious fantasy, the obstinate heretic refused to renounce the dogmas he had formed against the Catholic faith, particularly against the Virgin and the saints. No mention is made of his Copernicanism. The report also says that he wanted to die a martyr for his conviction. If we are to believe this contemporary account, what was found most offensive was Bruno's rejection of central doctrines of the Church, doctrines that at first blush would seem to have little to do with the Copernican revolution. Bruno, to be sure, thought them inseparably linked.

Bruno was first jailed in Venice on May 23, 1592. He was moved to Rome in January 1593. As the record of his interrogations shows, the main charges concerned key dogmas; cosmological issues were given much less weight by his judges; and there is hardly any mention of Copernicus in the entire record. Among the condemned theses is that of the eternity of the world, but that is not a Copernican, but an Aristotelian thesis. The Copernican issue is raised by Bruno, not by his interrogators, when he says of the *Ash-Wednesday Supper* that in this work he wanted to ridicule the geocentric views of some doctors.[183] The interrogators seem quite uninterested; they respond with a question that leads in a quite different direction: have you ever praised heretical princes?[184] There were good reasons for this question: in the *Ash Wednesday Supper* Bruno celebrates Queen Elizabeth as the ideal monarch, who would realize Bruno's political vision of a Europe that would have become unified and overcome the division between Protestants and Catholics that was tearing it apart, granting religious freedom to all. Before that Bruno had celebrated the French King Henry

---

[183] *Documenti veneti* XIII June 3, 1592, V. Spampanato, *Vita di Giordano Bruno, Con documenti edite e inedite*, vol. 1 (Messina: Principato, 1921) p. 733.

[184] Hans Blumenberg, *Die Legitimität der Neuzeit* (Frankfurt am Main: Suhrkamp, 1966). Robert M. Wallace (Trans.), *The Legitimacy of the Modern Age* (Cambridge, MA: MIT Press, 1983), p. 326.

III as a peace-loving prince, who, not at all "pleased with the noisy uproar of martial instruments," with his justice and sanctity would reconcile Protestants and Catholics.[185] And after he became disenchanted with Queen Elizabeth, he expected that transformation of the Catholic faith of which he dreamed from the Calvinist King of Navarre, who had just converted to Catholicism in order to ascend to the French throne as Henry IV, but stood for religious freedom. The King of Navarre had been engaged in a religious war that was to end only in 1598, when the king issued the Edict of Nantes, granting freedom of worship to Protestants, the same freedom Bruno claimed for himself.

In an earlier session Bruno had offered the inquisitors a summary of his understanding of nature, underscoring his conviction that the universe was infinite in both time and space, the inevitable outpouring of the infinite divine power, which had to express itself in an infinite space, in which could be found worlds without number, similar to our earth.[186] We still sense something of the enthusiasm with which, even in these dire circumstances, Bruno, citing the *Wisdom of Solomon*, Virgil's *Aeneid*, and *Ecclesiastes*, seized on this topic. The inquisitors showed little interest. They wanted to know about his denial of the Trinity.

In Bruno's mind his plea for freedom and his vision of an infinite cosmos were intimately linked. The freedom of thought does not tolerate walls and boundaries, does thus not tolerate a finite, bounded cosmos. Imagine that boundary: will our thoughts not turn to what lies beyond that supposed boundary? The freedom of thought demands infinite space and infinite space denies us the thought of a center of the cosmos and of privileged places. Bruno saw an intimate connection between the finite, hierarchically ordered cosmos of the Middle Ages and a hierarchical social and religious order that assigned individuals their proper places. Both he opposed with extraordinary zeal.

But while Bruno exulted in the universe he described, following Nicolaus Cusanus, as an infinite sphere, "seventy years later," Borges observes, "there was no reflection of that fervor left and men felt lost in space and time.... The absolute space that meant liberation for Bruno, became a labyrinth and an abyss for Pascal."[187] Nature had "become a fearful sphere, whose center is everywhere and whose circumference is nowhere." Before Pascal, Kepler had remarked on the way the infinity of space threatens to plunge us into a cognitive labyrinth. To

---

[185] Frances A. Yates, *Giordano Bruno and the Hermetic Tradition* (Chicago and London: The University of Chicago Press, 1979), p. 181, quoting Bruno's *Spaccio della bestia trionfante*.
[186] *Documentri veneti* XI, V. Spampanato, *Vita di Giordano Bruno, Con documenti edite e inedite*, vol. 1 (Messina: Principato, 1921), pp. 706–714.
[187] Jorge Luis Borges, "The Fearful Sphere of Pascal," *Labyrinths, Selected Stories and Other Writings* (New York: New Directions, 1964), pp. 189–192.

quote Kepler: "We shall show them [those who like Cusanus and Bruno hold that the universe is infinite] that by admitting the infinity of the fixed stars they become involved in inextricable labyrinths." And again: "This very cogitation [the thought of infinite space] carries with it I don't know what secret, hidden horror; indeed one finds oneself wandering in this immensity, to which are denied limits and center and therefore also all determinate places."[188] Kepler's observation can be generalized: on the reef of the infinite our comprehension founders. But our freedom draws us to the infinite.

Once the thought of the infinity of space has gotten hold of us there is no easy retreat to a place-assigning finite cosmos. There was good reason for Nietzsche to observe that since Copernicus, man "is slipping faster and faster away from the center into—what? into nothingness? into a *penetrating* sense of his own nothingness?"[189] If the Greek or the medieval cosmos assigned human beings their place near the center, the Copernican revolution would seem to have condemned us to an eccentric position. To be sure, Copernican eccentricity still presupposes a center. That is why Bruno considered him only the dawn of the age to come. Copernicus, as we should expect, given his place still on the threshold separating our modern from the medieval world, was himself only a half-hearted modernist and continued to hold on to the idea of a cosmic center, as he continued to invoke the idea of a divine architect and with it the idea of a bounded, well-ordered cosmos; he only denied the earth its central place, giving it instead to the sun. But of more fundamental importance than the shift from a geocentric to a heliocentric understanding of the cosmos proved to be a self-elevation that frees the thinking subject from any particular place and the associated perspective.

2 The Freedom of Thought

We should not place too much weight on Copernicus and the destruction of the medieval cosmos. The freedom of thought that refuses to be stopped by any boundary would seem to be inseparable from our human being. It brings to mind an old German folk song Pete Seeger made popular in this country:

---

[188] Alexander Koyré, *From the Closed World to the Infinite Universe* (New York: Harper Torchbook, 1958), p. 61.
[189] Friedrich Nietzsche, *On the Genealogy of Morals and Ecce Homo*, Walter Kaufmann and R. J. Hollingdale (Trans.), (New York: Vintage, 1989), p. 155.

1. Die Gedanken sind frei, wer kann sie erraten,
sie fliegen vorbei wie nächtliche Schatten.
Kein Mensch kann sie wissen, kein Jäger erschießen
mit Pulver und Blei: Die Gedanken sind frei!

1. Thoughts are free, who can guess them?
They fly by like nocturnal shadows.
No man can know them, no hunter can shoot them
with powder and lead: Thoughts are free!

3. Und sperrt man mich ein im finsteren Kerker,
das alles sind rein vergebliche Werke.
Denn meine Gedanken zerreißen die Schranken
und Mauern entzwei: Die Gedanken sind frei!

3. And if I am thrown into the darkest dungeon,
all these are futile works,
because my thoughts tear all gates
and walls apart: Thoughts are free![190]

The freedom of thought is here opposed to all walls that would imprison us. There is no architecture, built or conceived, that can imprison thought, another expression of the Antinomy of Being. The prehistory of the song can be traced back to the greatest of the German Minnesinger, Walther von der Vogelweide (1170–1230). Versions were sung at the time of the peasant wars, i.e., in the 16th century, and again in the early 19th century to protest the repressive restoration that followed the defeat of Napoleon, especially so at the time of the Revolution of 1848/49, when the song was forbidden, as it was again by the Nazis. Pete Seeger included it in his *Dangerous Songs* album (1966). But we meet with this sentiment already in Cicero: "Free are our thoughts," *Liberae sunt (...) nostrae cogitationes*, he said in a speech defending his friend Milo, who had been accused and subsequently was convicted of murder.[191] As a being of spirit I transcend myself as an embodied self. What limits are set to the freedom of thought?

I mentioned Walther von der Vogelweide. There were other Minnesinger at the time who expressed similar sentiments, such as Dietmar von Aist or Freidank, whose very name, no doubt a pseudonym, means "free thought." I find it of interest that such insistence on the freedom of the spirit is particularly characteristic of the beginning of what we can call the Gothic age. I am thinking es-

---

190 http://en.wikipedia.org/wiki/Die_Gedanken_sind_frei.
191 Cicero, *Pro Milone*, XXIX, 79.

pecially of the heresy of the Free Spirit against which orthodoxy then waged a relentless war.

A new sense of freedom developed at that time, especially in the developing larger cities, that could only frighten the establishment. One center of this awakening freedom were the convents in the large cities on the Rhine, especially Cologne and Strasbourg. Energies were set free that the Church found difficult or even impossible to control. The danger this new sense of freedom posed to the establishment is underscored by heresies such as that of the Free Spirit.[192]

Such heretics could cite in their support 2 Corinthians 3, 17: *Ubi autem spiritus domini, ibi libertas*, "Where the Spirit of the Lord is, there is freedom." The question is of course: how we are to understand this presence of the Lord? Does it mean that those in whom the Lord is truly present no longer have to feel bound by the laws of their society? Along with this new freedom went what we can call with Kierkegaard a teleological suspension of the ethical, where the ethical is suspended, however, not so much for the sake of Kierkegaard's abysmal God, as for the sake of an equally abysmal freedom.

Meister Eckhart gave striking expression to what the authorities found so objectionable. And that was even more true of some of his followers. Here a statement from a heretical treatise that was found in a hermit's cell near the Rhine:

> The divine essence is my essence and my essence is the divine essence. ... From eternity man was God in God.... From eternity the soul of man was in God and is God... Man was not begotten, but from eternity was wholly unbegettable; and he could not be begotten, so he is wholly immortal.[193]

The central thought is close to what some of the Arab philosophers had taught. Avicenna thus taught that when we transcend all sense experience in reflection and withdraw into the inner core of our consciousness, we also transcend ourselves as individuals and rejoin that soul in which all humanity is one. That is not so very different from the text I just read. The essence of the individual is here equated with the essence of God: in its essence the soul is nothing other

---

192 Cf. Eleanor McLaughlin, "The Heresy of the Free Spirit and Late Medieval Mysticism," *Medievalia et Humanistica*, n.s. 4 (1973).
193 Norman Cohn, *The Pursuit of the Millennium*, 2nd edition (New York: Harper Torchbooks, 1961), p. 181, citing Wilhelm Preger, *Beiträge zur Geschichte der religiösen Bewegung in den Niederlanden in der zweiten Hälfte des vierzehnten Jarhunderts, Abhandlungen der königlich bayerischen Akademie der Wissenschaften*_(Historische Classe), vol. XXI, Part 1 (Munich, 1984), pp. 62–63.

than God. How is this essence understood? Important here is the thought that the soul is not bound by the body.

The heresy of the Free Spirit insisted that the human power of self-transcendence allows the individual to achieve unity with God. Here a statement attributed to an unnamed woman associated with the order of the Free Spirit: "The soul is so vast that all the saints and angels would not fill it." This is to claim that everything finite, everything God has created, including saints and angels, is infinitely small compared to the vastness of the human soul. The followers of the Free Spirit thought themselves able to raise themselves above the sordidness of everyday reality, able to shed the burden of original sin, and not just occasionally, but for good. Such hubris is attributed by the mystic Ruysbroeck to his heretical counterpart. Here is what that heretic claims:

> When I dwelt in my original being and in my eternal essence there was no God for me. What I was I wished to be, and what I wished to be I was. It was by my own free will that I have emerged and become what I am. If I wished I need not have become anything and I would not now be a creature. For God can know, wish, do nothing without me. With God I have created all things and it is my hand that supports heaven and earth and all creatures... Without me nothing exists.[194]

The human power of self-transcendence is here pushed to a point where the boundary separating God and the self-transcending human being has to evaporate.

As Cohn points out, the mystic Ruysbroeck attributes these lines to a heretic. What he does not say is that Ruysbroeck must have considered Meister Eckhart that heretic, despite the fact that these two mystics, Ruysbroeck and Eckhart are often associated. One of Eckhart's sermons is clearly the source on which Ruysbroeck relies:

> When I stood in my first cause, I had no God and was cause of myself. I did not will or desire anything, for I was pure being, a knower of myself by divine truth. Then I wanted myself and nothing else. And what I wanted I was and what I was I wanted, and thus existed untrammelled by God or anything else. But when I parted from my free will and received my created being, then I had a God. For before there were no creatures, God was not God, but rather he was what he was. When creatures came to be and took on creaturely being, then God was no longer God as he is in himself, but God as he is with creatures.
>
> Now we say that God, in so far as he is only God, is not the highest goal of creation, nor is his fullness of being as great as that of the least of his creatures, themselves in God. And if a fly could have the intelligence by which to search the eternal abyss of divine being out of

---

194 Ibid., p. 184.

which it came, we should say that God, together with all that God is, could not give satisfaction to that fly. Therefore, we beg God that we may be rid of God, and take the truth and enjoy it eternally, where the highest angels and the fly and the soul are equal, there where I stood and was what I wanted. And so we say: if a person is to be poor in will, he must will and want as little as when he not yet was. This is how a person is poor, who wills nothing.[195]

Consider the self-understanding that speaks to us in this passage. An original state is contrasted with another: human being is said to have parted from its origin. In this latter state, a person understands him- or herself as a creature and thinks God from this creaturely perspective. But thought in that way, God depends on human being. He has no independent reality. God as He is can be found only when we transcend the entire dimension of the finite, of time, and of creatures. To free myself from my creaturely existence in this manner I also have to free myself from my creaturely needs and desires. It is easy to see why the atheist Schopenhauer should have had such high praise for Meister Eckhart.

The experience out of which such texts are written blurs the distinction between human and divine being. The human being identifies with his or her essential self, with the ground of her being, the womb from which she came, which radically transcends her time- and space-bound creaturely self. A clear distinction between this essential self and God is no longer possible. That origin from which we are said to have emerged is an infinite abyss that we may call God or that free will from which we departed when we assumed our creaturely being. But turning to this infinite ground does not help us to find our place in the world. Indeed, concern for that place would appear to be incompatible with the kind of poverty of which Eckhart is here speaking. The enlightened individual, it would seem, does not need to worry about what the world thinks important and values, about the standards it judges: does he or she not stand above that world's measure and law? To prove to himself his or her own enlightenment such an individual might even turn against the established order. Small wonder that such guardians of the establishment as the archbishop of Cologne were worried.

---

195 *"Beati pauperes spiritu, quia ipsorum est regnum coelorum,"* Quint 2: 492–494; Blakney (Trans.), pp. 228–229. Translation changed. Surprisingly Norman Cohn does not note this connection, indeed hardly mentions Eckhart in his *The Pursuit of the Millennium*. He does not appear in the index. Cohn does point out that *Schwester Katrei*, one of only two fragments (of what must have been a substantial literature produced by the adepts of the Free Spirit) to have survived the Inquisition's persecution, "was protected by being ascribed—quite wrongly—to the great Dominican mystic Meister Eckhart" (p. 151).

The threatened loss of the ethical dimension is particularly apparent in a text by the Rhenish mystic Heinrich Seuse (Suso), who had studied with Meister Eckhart in Cologne and courageously defended his master against the charges of heresy that had been brought against him, even when such a defense had become impolitic. Seuse tells us of a disciple, who, lost in meditation on a bright Sunday, sees an incorporeal image:

> He began to ask: where do you come from?
> It said: I did not come from anywhere.
> He said: Tell me, what are you?
> It said: I am nothing.
> He said: What do you will?
> It answered and said: I do not will.
> He, however, said: This is a miracle! What are you called?
> It said: I am called the wild that has no name (*daz namelos wilde*).
> The disciple said: You may rightly be called the wild, for your words and answers are indeed wild. Answer me now one question: What is the goal of your insight?
> It said: Unbound freedom.
> The disciple said: what do you call unbound freedom?
> It said: When a man lives entirely according to his own will, without anything other (*sunder anderheit*), without looking to before or after.[196]

To be sure, it is not *daz namelos wilde*, but the disciple who speaks for Seuse in Chapter Seven of *The Book of Truth*. This dialogue bears the title "What Those Men Lack, Who Live False Freedom" and ends with the disciple insisting that the person who becomes one with Christ, yet remains distinct from Him, and with an assertion of the importance of making proper distinctions. Crucial here is the difficult, but so important attempt to distinguish true from false freedom.

As Loris Sturlese has shown, *daz namelos wilde*, which here represents the brotherhood of the Free Spirit, is able to appeal to some of Eckhart's theses that had been condemned by the bull of John XXII, and just because of this proximity Seuse found it necessary to defend his master against what he considers a misinterpretation.[197] But this acknowledges that there is a strand in Eckhart's thought that invites such misinterpretation. The line that separates heretical from orthodox texts is indeed often difficult to draw.

---

[196] Heinrich Seuse, *Das Buch der Wahrheit, Daz buechli der warheit*, Loris Sturlese and Rüdiger Blumrich (Eds.), Loris Sturlese (Intro.), Rüdiger Blumrich (Trans.), Mittelhochdeutsch – Deutsch (Hamburg: Meiner, 1993), pp. 56–57. Cf. Cohn, p. 186.

[197] Heinrich Seuse, *Das Buch der Wahrheit, Daz buechli der warheit*, Introduction by Loris Sturlese, pp. xv – xxi.

Modernity, I want to suggest, has one origin in an understanding of God that places special emphasis on his infinity. That understanding opens an abyss: as all definite content is recognized to be profoundly incompatible with the divine, the divine comes to be thought of as "the wild that has no name." But a God who has become so indefinite threatens to evaporate altogether. God is transformed into an empty transcendence that cannot provide human beings with a measure. Experience of such a God cannot be distinguished from the experience of a freedom that, acknowledging no measure, has to degenerate into license. That is one reason why Thomas Aquinas and later Kant would have reason bind freedom. Only then, they insist, does freedom become true freedom. But as Kant also had to recognize and as Kierkegaard and Dostoevsky knew: human beings are capable of rejecting that bond. Kierkegaard spoke of a teleological suspension of the ethical. And such a suspension becomes dangerous when it descends from the spiritual or the ivory tower of learned academic discussions into this world, as it does when Abraham, obedient to his God, decides to sacrifice Isaac.

3 The Antinomy of Space

Bruno, as I pointed out, thought a bounded cosmos incompatible with the freedom of thought. Kepler thought an infinite cosmos incompatible with claims to truth. With their different responses to the thought of infinite space we have arrived at a version of Kant's first antinomy. We shall consider it in greater detail when we turn to time, in the tenth chapter. For the time being only the outline: The thesis of the First Antinomy claims that "The world has a beginning in time, and is also limited as regards space," the antithesis that "The world has no beginning, and no limits in space; it is infinite as regards both time and space" (A 427/B 455). The argument for the thesis rests on the claim that to really comprehend something we have to think it as a whole composed of parts, and that is to say as enclosed within limits. The comprehensibility of the world demands its constructability and that means its finitude.

But to think the world as such a constructed whole is not only to think the things that make up that whole as being in space, but also that whole as related to empty space. Such a space, however, is nothing. The thought of a limit of the world is the thought of a barrier that thought in its freedom inevitably leaps across. That also holds for the big bang with which our universe is supposed to have begun. But such a leap would be no leap at all were there not thoughts of the other side of that barrier. Neither a finite or an infinite world is fully intelligible and that for Kant meant that nature is at bottom incomprehensible. What science grasps is only its appearance, an appearance ruled by our reason's need to model reality with its constructions and architectures. At bottom the thought is as old as Zeno's paradoxes and Plato's *Timaeus*, and it continues to haunt the most recent cosmological speculations.

It also haunts every attempt to construct space. And with this I come to the title of this chapter: "Abysmal Freedom and the Antinomy of Space." Space cannot be thought of and never presents itself to us as a totally unstructured openness. Whenever we attempt to think space we turn to a construct. Think of Euclidean space with its three dimensions. But consider the phrase: "Space as Construct." That formulation suggests the possibility of also considering space in some other way, as more immediately apprehended, and opens up the possibility of other constructions. With Kant we may thus want to speak of this space as a pure intuition of something presupposed by all construction. But correcting Kant, we would have to add that Euclidean space, too, is such a construction, not a pure intuition.

"Space as Construct": in just what sense can space be constructed at all? Kant here points to the way the things that make up our world can be put in a certain order. This is here and has a particular shape, that over there and has a different shape. Geometrical construction determines the form of that order. Think of a line, of a point A on that line, of a second line perpendicular to the first through point A, of a third line, again through point A, but now perpendicular to both. Have I not invited you to construct three-dimensional Euclidean space? I can now place things in that space. But does every such construction of space, and it need not be Euclidean, not already presuppose an intuition of space? Kant speaks of a pure intuition, a *"reine Anschauung"*—"pure perception" may be a better translation. But *"reine Anschauung"* is a metaphor, itself a construction that threatens to obscure what is to be thought: for every *anschauen* already presupposes space. *Das Angeschaute*, what is perceived or intuited and the subject are separated by a "distance." The adjective *rein*, pure, is to guard against eliding what distinguishes the intuition of space from our ordinary intuitions. "I term all representations pure (in the transcendental sense) in which there is nothing that belongs to sensation" (A 20/B 34). But like the word *Anschauung*, *Vorstellung*, translated somewhat misleadingly as "representation," presupposes an experience of particular things in space. Kant's understanding of space as a *reine Anschauung* or *Vorstellung* is therefore itself not pure, but another kind of construction of space that attempts to domesticate what resists domestication.

But must we not domesticate space to render it comprehensible? Must we not domesticate space if we are to feel spiritually at home in it? In this sense the world is constructed and space domesticated by the demiurge in Plato's *Timaeus*. The Aristotelian cosmos represents an analogous domestication of space.

So does the homelike cosmos of the Middle Ages. The cosmos is thought here as a world building, a *Weltgebäude*. But every such construction is haunted by a space that is presupposed, but refuses to be domesticated. And our freedom keeps pulling us towards that space. Barriers want to be broken, shut doors invite us to open them, as fairy-tales teach us. Kant's first antinomy can thus be given an ethical expression: in human beings a desire for sheltering place is in inescapable tension with a desire for ever more open space, *Heimweh*, nostalgia, is in inesapable tension with *Fernweh*, a longing for an indefinite beyond.

4 Place and Space

Phenomenologists, following Aristotle, have insisted on a certain priority of place over space. They could point to the way our being is essentially a being-in-the world.[198] In *Being and Time* Heidegger thus analyzes space in terms of place (*Platz*) and region (*Gegend*). Regions are said to get their unity through activities: think of a workshop, a kitchen, a village as regions. Things have their proper places or are out of place in such a region.

> Equipment has its place [*Platz*], or else it "lies around"; this must be distinguished in principle from just occurring at random in some spatial position. When equipment for something or other has its place, this place defines itself as the place of this equipment—as one place of a whole totality of places directionally lined up with each other and belonging to the context of equipment that is environmentally ready-to-hand. Such a place and such a multiplicity of places are not to be interpreted as the "where" of some random Being-present-at-hand of Things. In each case the place is the definite 'there' or 'yonder' *["Dort" und "Das"]* of an item of equipment which *belongs somewhere* (GA2, 137; SZ, 102).

Here we are not at all dealing with the homogeneous space of Euclid or Descartes. Space is experienced here as heterogeneous, in terms of places.

> But in general the "whither" to which the totality of places for a context of equipment gets allotted, is the underlying condition which makes possible the belonging-somewhere of an equipmental totality as something that can be placed. This "whither," which makes it possible for equipment to belong somewhere, and which we circumspectively keep in view ahead of us in our concernful dealings, we call the "region" (GA2, 137; SZ, 103).

Aristotle is closer to such a regional understanding of space than, say, Descartes or Newton. Similarly a medieval *mappa mundi* is closer to such a regional under-

---

[198] See Edward S. Casey, *The Fate of Place. A Philosophical History* (Berkeley: University of California Press, 1997).

standing of space than, say, a modern map. Modern cosmology and cartography presuppose a reduction of experience and with it a homogenization of space. But "reduction" here cannot mean simply "loss." There is also a significant gain. Must we not say: a gain in truth?

The being that I am finds itself in the world by dealing with it, using tools, etc. To deal with the world is to get in touch with it in some way or other. A tendency towards nearness is thus said by Heidegger to be constitutive of Dasein.

> We use the expression "deseverance" [*Ent-fernung*] in a signification that is both active and transitive. It stands for a constitutive state of Dasein's being—a state with regard to which removing something in the sense of putting it away is only a determinate factical mode. "De-severing" amounts to making the farness vanish—that is making the remoteness of something disappear, bringing it close. Dasein is essentially de-severant: it lets any entity be encountered close by as the entity which it is. De-severance discovers remoteness (GA2, 140; SZ, 105).

As old as humanity is this desire to bring things close. Revolutions in transportation and communication have meant an ever progressing loss of both distance and proximity. Think of the way radio, television, and computers have brought things ever closer. Heidegger calls the consequences of this development *noch nicht übersehbar* (GA2, 141; SZ, 105): we are unable to foresee what brave new world is awaiting us. One thing deseverance would seem to entail is a loss of genuine intimacy.

The second term Heidegger uses to characterize the spatiality of Dasein is *Ausrichtung*, which suggests both orientation and directionality.

> Out of this directionality arise the fixed directions of right and left. Dasein constantly takes these directions along with it, just as it does its de-severances. Dasein's spatializtion in its 'bodily nature' is likewise marked out in accordance with these directions. (This 'bodily nature' hides a whole problematic of its own, though we shall not treat it here.) Thus things which are ready-to-hand and used for the body—like gloves, for example, which are to move with the hands—must be given directionality towards right and left (GA2, 145; SZ, 108–109).

We may well wonder: Why does the body not figure more in *Being and Time*? It seems to deserve a much more prominent place in the discussion. And there is the question of how deseverance relates to this problematic of the body. Is there a sense in which our bodies have become less important to us moderns?

There is a related question: how dependent on a particular culture is Heidegger's analysis? Would such an analysis look different in the computer age?

To be in the world is to be placed, placed by the body, here and now, at this time, on this earth and under this sky. Such placement brings with it a certain orientation, up and down, right and left, front and back carry meanings not captured by the x, y, and z axes of Euclidean space. There is a sense in which our body provides us with a natural, if moving, center. And it is not only our body that places us. We can also speak of our spiritual situation. A specific history has provided every one of us with an orientation that orders our possibilities.

But the orientation provided by our bodies and histories is challenged ever more insistently by our essential mobility, where I am thinking not only of the possibility of literally moving from this place to another, but of a spiritual mobility that knows no limits. Such mobility is inseparable from our freedom, which resists firm placement. Freedom demands open space. The problem of space is inescapably entangled with the problem of freedom.

5 Elusive Space

In English we distinguish between "space" and "room." "Space" signifies an open expanse in which things exist and move. "Room," on the other hand, suggests part of a building or a space thought in relation to possible occupation. The German *Raum* obscures that distinction. Where German speaks of the *Weltraum*, English speaks simply of space, as when we call this the space age, or speak of cosmic space. There is reason for the blurring that characterizes the German expressions. As discussed earlier, can we think space except as in some way already structured, Heidegger might say, *eingeräumt*, i.e., as made room-like?

In ordinary German the word *einräumen* means first of all to concede or admit something, e.g., to concede a point or to grant some person the space or time needed to complete a certain task. But it can also mean to put things in their proper places, e.g., when we furnish a house or an apartment. The *Einräumen* of an apartment makes it livable or *wohnlich*.

In this sense we can speak of an *Einräumendes Denken* or *Bauen*, i.e., of a thinking or building that, so to speak, furnishes the world and thus allows us to feel at home in it, to dwell in Heidegger's sense. But *einräumen*, as I pointed out, also means to grant something to some other person, to accommodate him, to give him or her the necessary space. Such accommodation builds bridges to others and thus founds community. In this respect, too, the *Einräumen* of the world make it more livable.

I make these references to the German since the word *einräumen* plays such an important role in Heidegger's *Being and Time*, in "Building Dwelling Thinking," and in the essay *"Kunst und Raum,"* "Art and Space."

According to Heidegger *Einräumen* happens "in the twofold manner of letting-be and of furnishing":

For one, *Einräumen* admits something, lets it be. It allows openness to hold sway, which among other things allows the appearance of present things to which human dwelling is directed.

For another, *Einräumen* grants things the possibility of belonging to their respective places and from these to one another.[199]

So understood it is only *Einräumen* that establishes the spaces that allows things to be for us. As we have seen, Heidegger understands the essence of language in similar fashion. Language and building, both refer to the origin that lets beings be. With language and building human history begins.

Heidegger calls *Einräumen* the fundamental character of all *Räumen*. *Räumen* "means: *Roden*, to clear the wilderness. *Räumen* produces the clear (*das Freie*), the open space for a settling and dwelling of human beings" (GA13, 206). *Räumen*, thought as a freeing (*Freigabe*) or granting (*Gewähren*) of locations (*Orten*) and things, gives human beings the necessary space.

> *Raum*, *Rum* means a place cleared or free for settlement and lodging. A space (*Raum*) is something that has been made room for, something that is cleared and free, namely within a boundary, Greek *péras*. A boundary is not that at which something stops, but, as the Greeks recognized, the boundary is that from which something *begins its presencing*. This is why there is the concept *horismos*, i.e. boundary. Space is in essence that for which room has been made, that which is let into bounds. What is thus bounded is always granted and thus put together, i.e. gathered, by means of a location (*Ort*), i.e. through a thing such as a bridge..... Accordingly spaces receive their being from locations, not from space.[200]

The building, here in "Building Dwelling Thinking" a bridge, establishes room. In similar fashion Heidegger says in "Kunst und Raum" of a sculpture that it is "the embodiment of locations, which, opening and preserving a region (*Gegend*) gather a clearing (*Freies*) around itself that grants to the several things an abiding presence and to human beings a dwelling in the midst of things" (GA13, 208).So understood, a space or room (*Raum*) is essentially livable (*wohnlich*). In such a space we are always already in some sense at home.

But this granting of space or room is difficult to understand. *Raum*, so it seems, cannot be understood here as a presupposition of the things and places that we can meet with, for the building of a bridge and the raising of a sculpture always already presupposes some suitable space. What then can Heidegger mean when he claims: only the liberating *Einräumen* gives *Raum*? "The location (*Ort*) is

---

199 "Die Kunst und der Raum," GA13, 207.
200 "Bauen Wohnen Denken," GA7, 56; "Building Dwelling Thinking,"*Poetry, Language, Thought*, Albert Hofstadter (Trans. and Intro.), (New York: Harper and Row, 1971), p. 154.

not in a pregiven space of the sort of the physical-technological space. This space unfolds itself only from the presencing (*Walten*) of locations (*Orten*) of a region (*Gegend*)"(GA13, 208). But the bridge that is said to give space was built by human beings, who already were at home in their world. This again presupposes an understanding of space. Every space granting *Einräumen* thus presupposes space in a different sense. And if the bridge builders owed that space to an antecedent *Einräumen*, every such *Einräumen* presupposes some differently understood space.

Two conceptions of space here collide: one has its foundation in our everyday being-in-the world and the associated understanding of space. What discloses space thus is first of all the way we encounter and deal with persons and things. So understood, some space or other always lets us belong somewhere. First of all and most of the time we are at home in our world. World is *Umwelt*, environment, *Raum* is *Umraum*, which discloses to us possibilities of acting, circumscribes and limits them. In this sense Heidegger takes *Einräumen* to be a structure constitutive of human being, or, as he puts it, an existentiale. Space has always disclosed itself to us in some fashion, but initially not as a free open expanse, but as already structured in some way and thus by assigning to things and persons their proper places as always in some fashion orienting and binding us. Only "on the basis of spatiality thus discovered," Heidegger claims, "space itself becomes accessible to knowing" (GA2, 149; SZ, 111).

"Space itself," *der Raum selbst*, with this we arrive at a different conception of space. The path that leads us from one to the other conception is a path of the ever more decisive liberation from place and the perspectives with which our embodied being-in-the-world, bound by place and time, nature and society, but also by our reason's constructs, conditions our seeing and understanding. Activities like the construction of dwellings, building in that sense, and agriculture are here first steps. They call for a surveying of the chosen site. The origin of geometry should probably be sought in such surveying.

> Such thematization of the spatiality of the environment is still predominantly an act of circumspection by which space in itself already comes into view in a certain way. The space which thus shows itself can be studied purely by looking at it, if one gives up what was formerly the only possible access to it—circumspective calculation. When space is 'intuited formally', the pure possibilities of spatial relations are discovered. Here one may go through a series of stages in laying bare pure homogeneous space, passing from the pure morphology of spatial shapes to *analysis situs* and finally to the purely theoretical science of space (GA2, 149; SZ, 112).

Heidegger speaks of a *Stufenfolge der Freilegung des reinen, homogenen Raumes*, steps that progressively uncover pure, homogeneous space.

Dasein, Heidegger insists, is not in space. It is itself spatial.

> And because Dasein is spatial in the way we have described, space shows itself as *a priori*. This term does not mean anything like previously belonging to a subject which is proximally still worldless and which emits a space out of itself. Here "*apriority*" means the previousness with which space has been encountered (as a region) whenever the ready-to-hand is encountered environmentally (GA2, 149; SZ, 111).

But is a liberation from all that could limit our seeing and understanding, from the various perspectives that distort our vision, not a demand raised by the pursuit of truth? Even a seeing that just wants to see is liberating. Here already the human being no longer is limited by the world of his everyday concerns. No longer bound to the work-world, circumspection is freed. Thus liberated, the human being is pulled towards what is distant and unknown. Curiosity, the desire to see just to see or what Augustine condemns as the lust of the eyes, the desire to understand just to understand that Aristotle understood as the beginning of all theory and science, gives the spirit wings, lets us raise ourselves above the world that environs us and dream of other worlds. Curiosity, freedom and the loss of home belong together.

Every attempt to comprehend space will structure it in some way. Heidegger speaks of *einräumen*. But the space thus structured or *eingeräumt* presupposes a space that eludes comprehension.

IX The Antinomy of Freedom

1 Introduction

Autonomy signifies, as the word already suggests, a binding of freedom, not by some foreign authority, but by a law of which we ourselves are the author, and for Kant that means a law that we are given by our own reason. True autonomy would thus reconcile what freedom demands and the claims of reason. Such a reconciliation would be the mark of a truly positive freedom. But that dream threatens to fall apart; and it threatens to fall apart in two quite different ways.

On one hand theoretical reason threatens to leave no room for a robust sense of freedom. That led Jacobi to reject Spinoza and all philosophy, committed as Jacobi thought it had to be to the principle of sufficient reason. And our science would seem to be a branch of philosophy so understood. McDermott thus, as we saw, called freedom an inescapable framework illusion. As he recognizes, this cannot shake our subjective first person conviction that we are free. McDermott is even willing to admit that subjectively we experience freedom as an absolute truth. As Fichte shows in the first part of the *Vocation of Man*, to which I shall return presently, something in us refuses to accept the scientific world picture, rational though it may be.

But if the dream of autonomy is called into question by theoretical reason, again and again freedom and irrational desire will challenge the rule of practical reason. Kant sought in this rebellion the root of evil. But such a determination does not silence the voice of unfettered freedom; it does not silence its appeal, which finds expression in the protest of Dostoevsky's man from the underground:

> Twice-two-makes-four is, in my humble opinion, nothing but a piece of impudence. Twice-two-makes-four is a farcical, dressed-up fellow who stands across your path with arms akimbo and spits at you. Mind you, I quite agree that twice-two-makes-four is a most excellent thing; but if we are to give everything its due, then twice-two-makes-five is sometimes a most charming little thing, too."[201]

In twice-two-makes-five a freedom that tolerates no authority that would bind it finds a refuge. Can we make sense of such a freedom? In the preceding chapter I suggested that we meet with such an understanding of freedom in the heresy of the free spirit. As free beings, we are capable of transcending ourselves as beings

---

[201] Fyodor Dostoevsky, *The Best Short Stories*, D. Magarshack (Trans.), (New York: Random House, 1955), p. 139.

bound to a particular time and space, limited by particular perspectives. In thought I can transcend myself as thus limited. The concept of freedom is inseparably bound up with that of the infinite, as Descartes points out in his fourth *Meditation:* "It is only the will, or freedom of choice, which I experience within me to be so great that the idea of any greater faculty is beyond my grasp; so much so that it is above all in virtue of the will that I understand myself to bear in some way the image and likeness of God."[202] That such an understanding of myself is incompatible with an understanding of human beings as just parts of nature is something Descartes recognizes, as does Kant, and as does Fichte to whom I now want to return.

2 Fichte: Freedom and Necessity

The issue of how to reconcile a scientific determinism and freedom is one with which Fichte, following Kant, wrestles in *The Vocation of Man*. The question the book attempts to answer is: "what am I myself, and what is my vocation?" (VM 5). The word "vocation" suggests a calling. What are we human beings and to what have we been called? Have we been called at all? If so, who or what has called us? What are we supposed to be? These questions intertwine with one with which we are already familiar: Can reason tell us what constitutes a meaningful life?

The first thing we human beings confront is nature. Everything in nature is something, a concrete entity that seems determined in every respect. It is what it is. But not only that: it has become this something. Nature is a ceaseless process of becoming. And we are parts of nature and as such part of this process.

We can add to this a third statement: Nature is governed by causality:

> Nature proceeds throughout the whole infinite series of her possible determinations without pause; and the succession of these changes is not arbitrary, but follows strict and unalterable laws. Whatever exists in Nature, necessarily exists as it does exist, and it is absolutely impossible that it could be otherwise. I enter within an unbroken chain of phenomena, in which every link is determined by that which has preceded it, and in its turn determines the next; so that, were I able to trace into the past the causes through which alone any given moment could have come into actual existence, and to follow out in the future the consequences which must necessarily flow from it, then, at that moment, and by means of thought alone, I could discover all possible conditions of the universe, both past and future —past, by explaining the given moment; future, by predicting its con-

---

[202] René Descartes, *The Philosophical Writings of Descartes*, 2 vols., John Cottingham, Robert Stoothoff, Dugald Murdoch (Trans.), (Cambridge: Cambridge University Press, 1985), vol 2, p. 40.

sequences. In every part experience the whole, for *only* through the whole is each part what it is; but through this it is *necessarily* what it is (VM 9–10).

Fichte insists that if I could know anything precisely and completely I would know everything about the universe, its past and its future. Everything is absolutely determined.

> A spirit who could look through the innermost secrets of Nature, would, from knowing one single man, be able distinctly to declare what men had formerly existed, and what men would exist at any future moment; in one individual he would discern *all* individuals. It is this, my interconnection with the whole system of Nature, which determines what I have been, what I am, and what I shall be. From any possible moment of my existence the same spirit could deduce infallibly what I had previously been, and what I was afterwards to become. All that, at any time, I am and shall be of absolute necessity; and it is impossible that I should be anything else (VM 18).

Fourteen years after Fichte's *Vocation of Man* appeared, Pierre-Simon Laplace was to conjure up his demon, arguing that if someone knows the precise location and momentum of every atom in the universe the laws of classical mechanics allow us to reconstruct the past and to predict the future.

> We ought then to regard the present state of the universe as the effect of its anterior state and as the cause of the one which is to follow. Given for one instant an intelligence which could comprehend all the forces by which nature is animated and the respective situation of the beings who compose it, an intelligence sufficiently vast to submit these data to analysis, it would embrace in the same formula the movements of the greatest bodies of the universe and those of the lightest atom; for it, nothing would be uncertain and the future, as the past, would be present to its eyes. The human mind offers, in the perfection which it has been able to give to astronomy, a feeble idea of this intelligence. Its discoveries in mechanics and geometry, added to that of universal gravity, have enabled it to comprehend in the same analytical expressions the past and future states of the system of the world. Applying the same method to some other objects of its knowledge, it has succeeded in referring to general laws observed phenomena and in foreseeing those which given circumstances ought to produce. All these efforts in the search for truth tend to lead it back continually to the vast intelligence which we have just mentioned, but from which it will always remain infinitely removed.[203]

Something of the sort would indeed seem to have been a cardinal tenet of all science ever since Galileo and Descartes. Some 50 years before Laplace, Roger Joseph Boscovich, whom Nietzsche placed besides Copernicus as "the greatest and

---

[203] Pierre Simon, Marquis de Laplace, *A Philosophical Essay on Probabilities*, Frederick Wilson Truscott and Frederick Lincoln Emory (Trans.), (New York: Wiley, 1902), p. 4.

most victorious opponent of visual appearance," had thus already imagined such an intelligence.[204] Kant, whom Fichte here follows, thought he had proved something of the sort with respect to phenomena, although he would have underscored and called into question the specified condition: "if someone knows the precise location and momentum of every atom in the universe." He would have insisted that nature resists being known as such a whole and that means also that our knowledge of any particular thing will never be complete. That, as we shall see, is the lesson of the antinomies. But as a regulative ideal some such view continues to preside over our science.

To be sure, categories have become a bit softer in our day. Causality is no longer the hard and fast relation that it was in classical physics. Entropy and quantum physics have thus been said to have defeated Laplace's demon.[205] Still, everything happens according to a cause and it is legitimate to ask for this cause. Probability does not change this. The very fact that we can expect nature to behave according to our probability calculations presupposes regularity.

But what happens to the human being on such a view? I myself am a link in this chain. I am part of nature and as such can be an object for scientific investigation as any other part of nature. Is psychology not in principle as much a science as physics, although the complexity of the human phenomenon caused psychology to operate with far less precision? Am I in principle more than a very complicated robot with an even more complicated computer brain? Is this not what cognitive science tells us? This is what fills Fichte's "I" with dread.

Such an understanding of human being, Fichte suggests, must rob man of all freedom and thus of responsibility. Take the example of someone who committed a crime. A social scientist is called in by the court and points out all the circumstances that caused this unfortunate individual to stray. If this causation is so strict as not to permit the individual any choice, with what right do we punish him at all? Punishment seems appropriate only when the person judged is in some sense responsible for his or her actions. But such responsibility can be only where there is freedom. In the absence of freedom, the only thing left is correction of what is considered an undesirable state of affairs. Corrective rather than punitive legislation and action seems called for. But are they more humane? I want to leave that question open, but in considering it, keep in mind the different understanding of human being that is presupposed in each case. What kind of beings are we? Are we human beings totally the product of forces

---

[204] Boris Kožnjak, "Who let the demon out? Laplace and Boscovich on determinism," *Studies in History and Philosophy of Science* (2015), Part A 51, pp. 42–52.
[205] See Wikipedia article "Laplace's demon," https://en.wikipedia.org/wiki/Laplace%27s_demon

beyond our control, or is there a sense in which we must judge ourselves free and responsible for our actions?

That freedom is an unscientific conception we must grant. Science cannot make sense of it; where it confronts so-called freedom of the will it will always try to uncover hidden causes. Should it fail in this, it will have to be content to call what happens an accident. There is no freedom in the world known by science.

And yet, as someone who, like McDermott, is committed to the scientific world view has to grant: I am conscious of myself as a free agent:

> I am, indeed, conscious of myself as an independent, and, in many occurrences of my life, a free being; but this consciousness may easily be explained on the principles already laid down, and may be thoroughly reconciled with the conclusions which have been drawn. My immediate consciousness, my proper perception, cannot go beyond myself and the modes of my own being. I have immediate knowledge of myself alone: whatever I may know more than this, I know only by inference, in the same way in which I have inferred the existence of original powers of Nature, which yet do not lie within the circle of my perceptions. But I myself—that which I call *me*, my personality—am not the same as Nature's power of producing a human being; I am only one of the manifestations of this power. And in being conscious of myself, I am conscious only of this manifestation and not of that power whose existence I infer when I try to explain my own (VM 18–19).

How then would a scientist account for my sense of freedom? The scientist, too, would try to explain it in terms of natural causes, but might insist, that where there is a sense of freedom these causes are internal to the organism.

> Bestow consciousness on a tree [where we should ask ourselves whether consciousness can be thought apart from freedom, and if not, whether the thought of such a bestowal has any place in the scientific world picture] and let it grow, spread out its branches, and bring forth leaves and buds, blossoms and fruits, after its kind, without hindrance or obstruction—it will perceive no limitation to its existence in being only a tree, and a tree of this particular species, and this particular individual of the species; it will feel itself perfectly *free*, because, in all those manifestations, it will do nothing but what its nature requires; and it will desire to do nothing else, because it can only desire what that nature requires (VM 19).

Spinoza said something very much like that of a stone in flight: supposing it had consciousness, it would think itself free. We have to distinguish metaphysical freedom from freedom from external causes. The latter freedom is perfectly compatible with science, while science can make no sense of the former. The human being, the scientist might say, is the place where nature becomes conscious of herself (VM 21).

> In each individual, Nature beholds herself from a particular point of view. I refer to myself as *I*, and to you as *you*. You call yourself *I* and me *you*; I exist beyond you, as you exist beyond me. Of what there is beyond me, I comprehend first those things which touch me most nearly; you, those which touch you most nearly—from these points we each proceed to the next step; but we traverse very different paths, which may here and there intersect each other, but never run parallel. There is an infinite variety of possible individuals, and hence also an infinite variety of possible starting points of consciousness. This consciousness of all individuals, taken together, constitutes the complete consciousness of the universe; and there is no other, for only in the individual is there definite completeness and reality (VM 22).

Why does Fichte's "I" find this description of the human condition unsatisfactory? His aspirations, he tells us, are denied by that view. What are these aspirations? For one, we want to think of ourselves as free in a stronger sense. We want to feel responsible, take credit and blame for our actions.

> My actions shall be the result of this will; without it I shall not act at all, since there shall be no other power over my actions but this will. Then my powers, determined by, and subject to the dominion of, my will, will affect the external world. I shall be the lord of Nature, and she shall be my servant. I will influence her according to the measure of my capacity, but she shall have no influence on me.
> This, then, is the substance of my wishes and aspirations (VM 28).

But there is a second demand I make. I want this world to make sense. I demand that there be such a thing as good and evil, that without that concrete subject that I am there be some standard by which I can measure my actions or which I can perversely deny. One can be good only if one is open to the temptation of evil. If one cannot be anything but good, is one still good, or if one cannot be anything but evil, is one still evil? Thus I demand both, freedom and a supreme authority, perhaps a God. But if the latter, God here would mean not so much the Biblical God, but more generally, any principle that furnishes human beings and their actions with a measure. According to Kant, practical reason provides such a principle. The two positions that here confront each other are that of human autonomy, where the individual is his own author, or heteronomy. The former demands that our thoughts be the sources of our actions, the latter takes these thoughts to be just epiphenomena of natural processes, having their place in the chain of natural events.

In the First Book of the *Vocation* the view that we human beings are autonomous remains unsupported. It has only been stated as a view that we would like to be true. The contrary view is said to be certainly true in its place: the question is: can our sense of freedom be reduced to a manifestation of nature subject to her law?

> Which of these two opinions shall I adopt? Am I free and independent or am I nothing in myself, and merely the manifestation of a foreign power? It is clear to me that neither of the two doctrines is sufficiently supported. For the first, there is no other recommendation than the mere fact that it is conceivable; for the latter, I extend a principle which is perfectly true in its own place, beyond its proper and natural application. If intelligence is merely the manifestation of a power of Nature, then I do quite right to extend this principle to it: but the very question at issue is whether intelligence is such a manifestation. And this is a question which is not to be answered by deducing a one-sided assumption, which I have made at the start of my inquiry; the question must be answered by reference to other premises. In short, it would seem that neither of the two opinions can be established by appeal to proofs (VM 31).

Where Fichte's own sympathies lie is clear:

> The system of freedom satisfies my heart; the opposite system destroys and annihilates it. To stand, cold and unmoved, amid the current of events, a passive mirror of fugitive and passing phenomena—this existence is insupportable to me; I scorn and detest it. I will love; I will lose myself in sympathy; I will know the joy and the grief of life (VM 31).

Does the scientific world view allow for love? Love presupposes that the individual who loves is in possession of himself. To love is to make a gift of oneself. But to make such a gift, must we not possess ourselves?

So where does the end of Book One of the *Vocation of Man* leave us? As the chapter's title "Doubt" suggests, it leaves us somewhat uncertainly between the positions sketched. The hold that the scientific world picture has on us is rooted in the world we live in, a world shaped ever more decisively by technology and thus by science and its presuppositions. And yet there is the resistance to that worldview to which Fichte gives voice: The scientific world-picture has no place for a vocation of man, as it has no place for freedom.

3 Kant: The Third Antinomy – The Thesis

Fichte's statement of the collision of the scientific world view and our sense of freedom is of course indebted to Kant, who deals with the problem of causality and freedom in the Third Antinomy of the *Critique of Pure Reason*. Kant, too, is concerned with the way the understanding of nature presupposed by science leaves no room for meaning or value:

> In nature the understanding can cognize only *what exists*, or has been, or will be. It is impossible that something in it *ought to be* other than what, in all these time-relations, it in fact is; indeed, the ought, if one has merely the course of nature before one's eyes, has no

significance whatever. We cannot ask at all what ought to happen in nature, any more than we can ask what properties a circle ought to have; but we must rather ask what happens in nature, or what properties the circle has (A547/B575).

The Third Antinomy attempts to show that such an understanding of nature is inadequate. Consider once more the claim that everything about the world can in principle be known. That presupposes an understanding of the world as "the totality of all facts." This is how Wittgenstein defines the world in the *Tractatus* (proposition 2). Note that some such view would seem to be entailed by an insistence on God's omniscience. It poses a similar threat to human freedom: If God knows what I am going to do even before I do it, am I still free?

Kant takes this understanding of the world as the totality of facts to be a construct of our reason that every attempt to explain the world must presuppose. But we cannot claim that this construct captures some existing thing in itself. Still, we cannot help but project it. Using McDermott's term, we may want to speak of an inescapable framework illusion. McDermott, to be sure, would not want to consider it an illusion. Our reason bids us understand what and why something is. While it does not seem necessary that, say, the things in this room are just as they happen to be, are there not reasons for why they are here? Usually we settle for less than full explanations. But are there not always fuller explanations and must there not be, in principle at least, a full or sufficient explanation of why something is just the thing it is? In this sense the principle of sufficient reason presides as a regulative ideal over the way our reason operates (A498/B526-A500/B528). Our reason would have us think that everything can in principle be explained.

But what justifies such confidence? What justifies faith in the principle of sufficient reason? Kant insists not only that the principle of sufficient reason, considered as constitutive of reality, cannot be justified, but that it is false. It is false because it contradicts itself. As proof he offers his antinomies. Here we are concerned with the third:

Let me return to the thesis.

> Causality according to the laws of nature, is not the only causality operating to originate the phenomena of the world. A causality of freedom is also necessary to account fully for these phenomena.
>
> PROOF.
> Let it be supposed, that there is no other kind of causality than that according to the laws of nature. Consequently, everything that happens presupposes a previous condition, which it follows with absolute certainty, in conformity with a rule. But this previous condition must itself be something that has happened (that has arisen in time, as it did not exist before), for, if it has always been in existence, its consequence or effect would not thus originate for

the first time, but would likewise have always existed. The causality, therefore, of a cause, whereby something happens, is itself a thing that has happened. Now this again presupposes, in conformity with the law of nature, a previous condition and its causality, and this another anterior to the former, and so on. If, then, everything happens solely in accordance with the laws of nature, there cannot be any real first beginning of things, but only a subaltern or comparative beginning. There cannot, therefore, be a completeness of series on the side of the causes which originate the one from the other. But the law of nature is that nothing can happen without a sufficient *a priori* determined cause. The proposition therefore—if all causality is possible only in accordance with the laws of nature—is, when stated in this unlimited and general manner, self-contradictory. It follows that this cannot be the only kind of causality.

From what has been said, it follows that a causality must be admitted, by means of which something happens, without its cause being determined according to necessary laws by some other cause preceding. That is to say, there must exist an absolute spontaneity of cause, which of itself originates a series of phenomena which proceeds according to natural laws—consequently transcendental freedom, without which even in the course of nature the succession of phenomena on the side of causes is never complete (A445/B473-A446/B474).

We should note that freedom here is not to be equated with what we ordinarily understand freedom to mean. It is given a more formal and thus emptier, but also more encompassing significance. As Kant explains:

The transcendental idea of freedom is far from constituting the entire content of the psychological conception so termed, which is for the most part empirical. It merely presents us with the conception of spontaneity of action, as the proper ground for imputing freedom to the cause of a certain class of objects. It is, however, the true stumbling-stone to philosophy, which meets with unconquerable difficulties in the way of its admitting this kind of unconditioned causality. That element in the question of the freedom of the will, which has for so long a time placed speculative reason in such perplexity, is properly only transcendental, and concerns the question, whether there must be held to exist a faculty of spontaneous origination of a series of successive things or states. How such a faculty is possible is not a necessary inquiry; for in the case of natural causality itself, we are obliged to content ourselves with the *a priori* knowledge that such a causality must be presupposed, although we are quite incapable of comprehending how the being of one thing is possible through the being of another, but must for this information look entirely to experience. Now we have demonstrated this necessity of a free first beginning of a series of phenomena, only in so far as it is required for the comprehension of an origin of the world, all following states being regarded as a succession according to laws of nature alone. But, as there has thus been proved the existence of a faculty which can of itself originate a series in time—although we are unable to explain how it can exist—we feel ourselves authorized to admit, even in the midst of the natural course of events, a beginning, as regards causality, of different successions of phenomena, and at the same time to attribute to all substances a faculty of free action (A448/B 476-A450/B478).

"The transcendental idea of freedom" thus covers not only human, but divine freedom or events that happen without any reason at all. One might want to think of the big bang as such an event. But reason resists such appeals to spontaneous generation and it is not at all clear that it captures what we usually mean by a free act. Suppose my arm suddenly shoots up for no reason at all. We would not want to call that a free act. A nervous twitch perhaps. Is not every truly free act done for some reason and as such determined. I can ask: why did you do this? What was your motive? Kant would appeal to practical reason, which can present us with hypothetical or categorical imperatives.

But why then call such an act free? Why does whatever reason we have in mind not determine the action? But if so, why do we not always act in accord with what practical reason commands? Is it obvious that freedom is more compatible with indeterminism than with determinism? Kant grants that were we purely intelligible beings, our will would indeed be determined by the moral law. But we are of course also sensible beings and pulled by our sensible desires away from moral action. Only because of that conflict within do we experience what pure practical reason commands as an "ought." But given that conflict within the self, what determines its resolution? Is that determination again ruled by some reason? Here something inexplicable would seem to come into play.

4 Kant: The Third Antinomy – The Antithesis

The Antithesis states that there is no freedom. "There is no such thing as freedom, but everything in the world happens solely according to the laws of nature" (A445/B473). The proof begins with the assumption that there is such a thing as transcendental freedom in order to demonstrate its untenability:

> Granted, that there does exist freedom in the transcendental sense, as a peculiar kind of causality, operating to produce events in the world—a faculty, that is to say, of originating a state, and consequently a series of consequences from that state. In this case, not only the series originated by this spontaneity, but the determination of this spontaneity itself to the production of the series, that is to say, the causality itself must have an absolute commencement, such that nothing can precede to determine this action according to unvarying laws. But every beginning of action presupposes in the acting cause a state of inaction; and a dynamically primal beginning of action presupposes a state, which has no connection—as regards causality—with the preceding state of the cause—which does not, that is, in any wise result from it. Transcendental freedom is therefore opposed to the natural law of cause and effect, and such a conjunction of successive states in effective causes is destructive of the possibility of unity in experience and for that reason not to be found in experience—is consequently a mere fiction of thought.

> We have, therefore, nothing but nature to which we must look for connection and order in cosmic events. Freedom—independence of the laws of nature—is certainly a deliverance from restraint, but it is also a relinquishing of the guidance of law and rule. For it cannot be alleged that, instead of the laws of nature, laws of freedom may be introduced into the causality of the course of nature. For, if freedom were determined according to laws, it would be no longer freedom, but merely nature. Nature, therefore, and transcendental freedom are distinguishable as conformity to law and lawlessness. The former imposes upon understanding the difficulty of seeking the origin of events ever higher and higher in the series of causes, inasmuch as causality is always conditioned thereby; while it compensates this labor by the guarantee of a unity complete and in conformity with law. The latter, on the contrary, holds out to the understanding the promise of a point of rest in the chain of causes, by conducting it to an unconditioned causality, which professes to have the power of spontaneous origination, but which, in its own utter blindness, deprives it of the guidance of rules, by which alone a completely connected experience is possible (A446-B474-A447/B475).

A power of absolutely beginning a state cannot be thought, according to Kant, because contrary to the causal law. We face that difficulty in trying to think the big bang. Transcendental freedom cannot be experienced. So considered, it is an empty thought. This is essentially McDermott's position, who nevertheless also wants to hold on to the thesis, but subordinate it to the antithesis. Freedom is subjectively real.

5 The Objective Reality of Freedom

In the *Critique of Judgment* Kant was to claim that our experience of persons allows us to claim not just the subjective, but the objective reality of freedom. Of special interest is the following passage:

> What always remains very remarkable about this is that among the three pure ideas of reason, *God*, *freedom*, and *immortality*, that of freedom is the only concept of the supersensible which (by means of the causality that we think in it) proves in nature that it has objective reality, by the effects it can produce in it. It is this that makes it possible to connect the other two ideas with nature, and to connect all three with one another to form a religion. Therefore, we have in us a principle that can determine the idea of the supersensible within us, and through this also the idea of the supersensible outside us, so as to give rise to cognition [of them], even though one that is possible only from a practical point of view; and that is something of which merely speculative philosophy (which could provide also merely a negative concept of freedom) had to despair.[206]

---

[206] Immanuel Kant, *Kritik der Urteilskraft*, A461/B467–468; *The Critique of Judgment*, Werner S. Pluhar (Trans.) (Indianapolis: Hackett, 1987). p. 368.

5 The Objective Reality of Freedom — 159

Freedom, by its effects, opens a window in nature to the supersensible. And we should note that here Kant asserts that it proves that the supersensible has objective reality, albeit "only from a practical point of view."

Kant does think that we experience human beings as persons demanding our respect, although he gives us no developed account of how we are to think such an experience. But if there is indeed such an experience, this presupposes that the concept of a person is a concept of the understanding.

> If I determine the causality of man, in view of certain products that are explicable only [as arising] through an intentional purposiveness, by thinking this causality as an understanding in man, then I need not stop there [i.e. at the mere thought] but can attribute this predicate to him as a very familiar property of his and cognize him through it. For I know that intuitions are given to the concept and hence under a rule. I know that this concept contains only the common characteristic[s] (and omits the particular) and hence is discursive, and that the rules for bringing given presentations under a consciousness as such are given by the understanding even prior to those intuitions, etc. Hence I attribute this property to man as a property through which I *cognize* him. Now if I want to think a supersensible being (God) as an intelligence, then for a certain point of view in my use of reason this is not only permitted but also unavoidable. But I am in no way entitled to flatter myself that I [can] attribute [an] understanding to this being and cognize this being through it as through a property.[207]

As Kant tells us in the *Introduction:* key to the *Critique of Judgment* is the project of finding the bond that prevents nature and morality from being separated by an abyss that cannot be bridged. Beauty promises such a bridge, even if it does not build such a bridge in a way that would allow us to claim for what transcends nature as understood by science what Kant calls objective reality. But our experience of persons, Kant claims, does build this bridge in a way that allows us to claim objective reality for what we experience as persons deserving our respect.

Kant's way out of the antinomy is transcendental idealism. Without it, he insists,

> A human being would be a puppet [*Marionette*] or a Vaucansonian automaton[208] built and wound up by the master of all artificial devices; and although self-consciousness would turn the automaton into a thinking one, yet the automaton's consciousness of its spontane-

---

[207] Ibid., A475/B481; trans, p. 379.
[208] Jacques de Vaucanson (1709–1782) was a creator of automata, much discussed in the 18th century.

ity, if regarded as freedom, would be mere delusion, because this spontaneity deserves to be called freedom only comparatively.[209]

This raises the question whether we can even think self-consciousness without freedom.

6 The Condemnation of 1277: Divine Freedom

To show that the problem with which Kant wrestles in his third antinomy is a perennial one, I would like to conclude this chapter by taking another brief look at the Condemnation of 1277. What prompted the Condemnation was the collision of Christian wisdom, as represented by St. Augustine, and Greek, especially Aristotle's thought, mediated by such Arab philosophers as Avicenna and Averroes, which appeared to deny both divine and human freedom. The main culprit here was "Siger the Great," as he was called, a much admired, but controversial teacher at the University of Paris[210] At issue was the threat rational, scientific inquiry poses to freedom in both senses, Kant might have said to transcendental freedom.

Let me turn first to divine freedom. The authors of the Condemnation wanted to make sure that the faithful not limit God's freedom by subjecting it to supposed philosophical necessities or laws of nature. Thus they objected to the claim "27. That the first cause cannot make more than one world."[211] Thomas Aquinas may have been one of the targets here. If God is omnipotent, all-knowing, and good, must he not, as Leibniz thought, have created the best of all possible worlds? In Neo-Platonism everything emanates from the One, a view Christian theology appropriated. The order of the world was thought to stem from this. Divine wisdom tends towards unity. The power of God should not be divorced from his wisdom. That such convictions could easily lead one to agree with the condemned proposition is evident. The condemnation of 1277, on the other hand, invites us to understand the uniqueness of this world as a contingent fact. Given God's infinite power, how can there be a limit to the number of worlds He could have created, had He chosen to do so? Aren't there countless possible worlds? The condemnation thus invites a voluntaristic conception of God, which

---

[209] Immanuel Kant, *The Critique of Practical Reason*, Werner S. Pluhar (Trans.), (Indianapolis: Hackett, 2002), p. 128.
[210] Friedrich Heer, *Europäische Geistesgeschichte* (Stuttgart: Kohlhammer, 1953), p. 162.
[211] "Condemnation of 219 Propositions" in Arthur Hyman and James J. Walsh (Eds.), *Philosophy in the Middle Ages* (Indianapolis: Hackett, 1973). Numbers in the text refer to this edition.

uncouples God's unfathomable will from what our reason demands and is able to grasp.

Of particular interest are the propositions dealing with God's will. Consider, e.g., "17. That what is impossible absolutely speaking cannot be brought about by God or by another agent. – This is erroneous if we mean what is impossible according to nature." The Condemnation insists on the distinction between *impossibile simpliciter* and *impossibile secundum naturam*, between logical and natural impossibility. Even God cannot make a contradiction be true, nor can God commit suicide, which would violate his own being. But he can of course create miracles.

The concern to safeguard divine freedom is evident in "20. That God of necessity makes whatever comes immediately from Him. – This is erroneous whether we speak of the necessity of coercion, which destroys liberty, or of the necessity of immutability, which implies the inability to do otherwise." Once more the point is to safeguard the free will of God. The condemned Neo-Platonic view threatens such freedom. Is it not evident that, in his omnipotence, God could have created quite a different world or even worlds?

Quite a number of the condemned propositions presuppose a view of nature as a hierarchical order, where I would like to underscore both "hierarchical" and "order." An attempt is made to subordinate the freedom of God to the regularity suggested by Aristotle's *Physics* or for that matter by Neo-Platonic thought. To save the omnipotence and freedom of God, the Condemnation challenges both the insistence on hierarchy and on order. Thus it condemns the following proposition: "22. That God cannot be the cause of a newly-made thing and cannot produce anything new." The denial of God's power to create anything new is incompatible both with the creation account and with miracles. According to the condemned proposition God is bound by the laws of nature. To challenge this is to shake the foundation of Aristotle's physics. And such a challenge is also implicit in the condemnation of "23. That God cannot move anything irregularly, that is, in a manner other than that in which He does, because there is no diversity of will in Him." The condemned proposition insists on absolute regularity. This would rule out miracles. That a medieval Christian thinker should want to reject such a proposition is to be expected. And this rejection inevitably leads to another thought: the world cannot be just as Aristotle describes it. God's freedom may not be imprisoned in Aristotle's philosophy. That invites thoughts of alternative cosmologies.

7 The Condemnation of 1277: Human Freedom

The authors of the Condemnation were concerned not only to save the free will of God, but also to create room for human freedom. Let us consider some of the propositions that address human freedom: "151. That the soul wills nothing unless it is moved by another. Hence the following proposition is false: the soul wills by itself. – This is erroneous if what is meant is that the soul is moved by another, namely by something desirable or an object in such a way that the desirable thing or object is the whole reason for the movement of the will itself." The condemned proposition would deny human freedom and thus responsibility. The condemnation insists that while natural desire does play a significant part in determining our choices, it is not sufficient to explain how the individual chooses. We can resist our desires.

Freedom of the will is also at issue in the following propositions: "157. That when two goods are proposed, the stronger moves more strongly. – This is erroneous unless one is speaking from the standpoint of the good that moves." Once again the Condemnation rejects all determinism and insists on human freedom. To be sure, the good that moves me moves me. That is a tautology. But I am not determined in my actions by the strength of some pre-given good.

Thus the following condemned propositions deny:

> 158. That in all his actions man follows his appetite and always the greater appetite. – This is erroneous if what is meant is the greater in moving power.
>
> 159. That the appetite is necessarily moved by a desirable object if all obstacles are removed. – This is erroneous in the case of the intellectual appetite.
>
> 160. That it is impossible for the will not to will when it is in the disposition where it is natural for it to be moved and when that which by nature moves remains so disposed.

All the condemned propositions challenge freedom by subjecting our actions to appetite.

The following, also condemned, attempt to preserve freedom while subjecting freedom to reason lets us think of Kant: "163. That the will necessarily pursues what is firmly held by reason and that it cannot abstain from that which reason dictates. This necessitation, however, is not compulsion but the nature of the will." We are not free to believe that 2+2 = 5. Reason necessarily binds freedom, but such binding is not compulsion, Thomas Aquinas insists that it is indeed true freedom. You are truly free when bound by knowledge of what is truly good. The authors of the condemnation are concerned that by subjecting the will in this way to reason, freedom is once again lost. Thus they have to condemn "164. That man's will is necessitated by his knowledge, just as the appetite of a brute [animal is]."

The following condemned propositions develop this theme. "165. That after a conclusion has been reached about something to be done, the will does not remain free, and that punishments are provided by law only for the correction of ignorance and in order that the correction may be a source of knowledge for others."

Jeremy Bentham might be taken as a much later representative of the position being condemned here. But according to Plato, too, it would seem that those who act badly do so only because they are ignorant about what is in their best interest, where Bentham and Plato would of course disagree about how "best interest" is to be understood. Sin, the authors of the condemnation insist, is not just a matter of faulty reasoning. And so they have to condemn "166. That if reason is rectified, the will is also rectified.—This is erroneous because contrary to Augustine's gloss on this verse from the *Psalms:* My soul has coveted too long, and so on [Psalms 118:20], and because according to this, grace would not be necessary for the rectitude of will but only science, which is the error of Pelagius".

Once again Thomas Aquinas is close to the condemned view.

Nor is sin to be explained in terms of bodily desires overwhelming the intellect: "167. That there can be no sin in the higher powers of the soul. And thus sin comes from passion and not from the will." That a Christian would have to reject this seems evident. And a Christian would also have to reject "168. That a man acting from passion acts from compulsion." Especially amorous passions were said to enslave the will. The Condemnation rejects such views, rejects thus the claim "169. That as long as passion and particular science are present in act, the will cannot go against them." The particular judgment, according to Thomas Aquinas, is practical and itself an expression of the will, which thus cannot go against it. At issue is once again the close tie between reason and freedom on which Thomas insists, both in the case of God and in the case of man, and which the Condemnation calls into question. Both divine and human freedom are said to transcend reason. An abyss opens up that is a presupposition of evil as it is a presupposition of grace and forgiveness. Kant touches on this abyss with his conception of radical evil.[212]

---

212 Immanuel Kant, *Die Religion innerhalb der Grenzen der blossen Vernunft*, A32/B35.

X The Antinomy of Time

1 Kant's First Antinomy Reconsidered

Although inseparable from experience, like Being, time resists comprehension. Kant calls it a pure intuition, a *reine Anschauung*, to indicate with the word "pure" that it is given *a priori*, before all experience. And we can grant Kant, time is presupposed by all experience. But it is never given apart from experience. Experience is never pure. Nor is our experience of time. As pointed out above with reference to space,[213] *reine Anschauung* is a metaphor whose vehicle is provided by sight and which is thus tied to sensibility. The word *rein* or pure is meant to sever that tie. But with this the meaning of the term threatens to slip away. A *reine Anschauung* would seem to be a wooden iron.

The difficulty of thinking time haunts Kant's First Antinomy, which considers the question of the world's beginning in space and time. The Thesis states that the world has a beginning in time and space. Here I am interested in time, although the argument is easily transferred to space (A427/B455).

Once again the proof of the thesis begins by assuming the opposite, that the world has no beginning, that it is infinite. This means that an infinite number of events has taken place. But we cannot think the completion of an infinite series of events. The thought is contradictory. Therefore, the world must have a beginning.

Presupposed here is an understanding of time, and also of space, as a limitless pre-given empty container, a position held by Newton (A430–34/B458–63). Here is Newton's account of absolute time:

> Absolute, true and mathematical time, of itself, and from its own nature flows equably without regard to anything external, and by another name is called duration: relative, apparent and common time, is some sensible and external (whether accurate or unequable) measure of duration by the means of motion, which is commonly used instead of true time....[214]

Two conceptions of time are here juxtaposed: "absolute, true, and mathematical" and "apparent and common time." The former would seem to be what Kant has in mind when he speaks of a pure intuition of time.

---

[213] See chapter VIII, 3 above.
[214] Scholium to the Definitions in *Philosophiae Naturalis Principia Mathematica*, Bk. 1 (1689); Andrew Motte (Trans.), (1729), rev. Florian Cajori, (Berkeley: University of California Press, 1934), pp. 6–12.

The definition of common time seems sensible enough. But I have difficulty understanding absolute time, difficulty thinking of a flow as not some sort of motion. How are we to think of what here is supposed to move equably? "True time" seems to elude our understanding.

But let me return to Kant: The Antithesis states that "The world has no beginning and no bounds in space, but is infinite with regard to both time and space" (A427/B455). Once again the proof begins by assuming the opposite, that the world has a beginning in time. This presupposes a preceding, empty time in which the world did not yet exist. But what would prompt something to come into existence, given such an empty time? There would be no reason for it to come into existence when it did. We cannot make sense of the world having a beginning in time. Therefore, the world is infinite as far as time is concerned.

Is the statement that the world has no beginning equivalent to the statement that it is infinite as far as time is concerned? Kant seems to suggest this here. Descartes would have raised a question: Descartes distinguishes between the "indefinite" and the "infinite." Only God can be called truly infinite, where the thought of such an infinite God can be figured by the thought of a maximum or absolute number and poses analogous difficulties. To the maximum number nothing can be added, but that is incompatible with the very concept of number to which something can always be added. The concept of a maximum number would seem to be a contradiction in terms. And must the same not be said of God understood as an infinite whole? Sartre had good reason to declare the idea of God a contradiction.[215] And does an analogous difficulty not present itself when we try to make sense of Kant's pure intuitions of space and time? We cannot think an infinite whole made up of parts. As Leibniz writes in the *New Essays*, we should thus not try to suppose an absolute space to be such a whole. "There is no such thing: it is a notion which implies a contradiction... the true infinite, strictly speaking, is only in the *absolute* [God], which precedes all composition."[216]

> Descartes and his followers, in making the world out to be indefinite so that we cannot conceive of any end to it, have said that matter has no limits. They have some reason for replacing the term 'infinite' by 'indefinite', for there is never an infinite whole in the world,

---

215 Jean-Paul Sartre, *Being and Nothingness*, Hazel E. Barnes (Trans. and Intro.), (New York: Philosophical Library, 1956), p. 615.
216 G.W. Leibniz, *New Essays on Human Understanding*, Peter Remnant and Jonathan Bennett (Eds.) (Cambridge: Cambridge University Press, 1981), p. 157 f. See Omri Boehm, *Kant's Critique of Spinoza* (New York: Oxford University Press, 2014), pp. 73–74.

though there are always wholes greater than others *ad infinitum*. As I have shown elsewhere, the universe itself cannot be considered to be a whole.[217]

The distinction between the infinite and the indefinite played already a crucial role in the philosophy of Nicolaus Cusanus, who figured God with the concept of the maximum number and thus sought a key to the divine in the coincidence of opposites. As pointed out, the thought of a number implies the possibility of always adding 1. The number sequence is therefore endless. That thought is readily transferred to time and space. The infinite, however, is to be thought as a whole. It is not composed of parts. Just because it is composed of parts, the world cannot be infinite, but only indefinite. Cusanus thus, like Descartes and Leibniz after him, already denied the world's infinity. But that means that the world cannot finally be comprehended, for such comprehension would have to grasp it as an infinite whole.

Key to understanding the first antinomy is Kant's notion of the infinite as a whole, a notion that Cusanus, Descartes, and Leibniz would have insisted, fits only God. Would Kant have disagreed? Kant, while insisting that an infinite whole cannot be understood or comprehended, refuses to deny it being. Crucial is his insistence that infinity need not be thought of as made up of infinite parts. Kant thus writes in the *Critique of Pure Reason* that even if the infinite "whole of nature" is "spread before us," there could be no experience of it. It would be impossible to have "consciousness of its absolute totality" (A482f/B510f).

In the *Critique of Judgment* Kant makes essentially the same point in his discussion of the sublime. Kant here speaks of mathematical infinity, which always allows for the addition of an additional unit *ad infinitum*. But from this we must distinguish true infinity. The former consists in negating the finite (the possibility of enlarging any given series) and it remains essentially abstract. Judging the size of anything actual requires a material measure. But reason demands totality.

> The mind listens to the voice of reason within itself, which demands totality for all given magnitudes, even those that we can never apprehend in their entirety [...] and it exempts from this demand not even the infinite (space and time). Rather, reason makes us unavoid-

---

[217] G.W. Leibniz, *New Essays on Human Understanding*, Peter Remnant and Jonathan Bennett (Eds.) (Cambridge: Cambridge University Press, 1981), p. 151. See Omri Boehm, *Kant's Critique of Spinoza* (New York: Oxford University Press, 2014), p. 104, fn. 15: "Indeed Leibniz is not as consistent as Descartes in distinguishing between the *terms* infinite and indefinite; yet he does not consider the universe to be a completed whole—that is, he considers it to be indefinite and not infinite. Hence, even when speaking of an 'infinity' of monads, the implication is an endless number of monads (hence, indefinite number) but *not* a completed infinity, which, as the passages above make clear, Leibniz strictly denies."

ably think of the infinite (in common reason's judgment) as given in its entirety (in its totality).[218]

This suggests that the pure intuitions of space and time are in fact not so much intuitions as ideas of reason, to which experience necessarily leads us. And similarly it leads us necessarily to the notion of the cosmos as a complete whole:

> If the human mind is nonetheless to *be able to think* the given infinite without contradiction, it must have within itself a power that is supersensible, whose idea of a noumenon cannot be intuited but can yet be regarded as the substrate underlying what is mere appearance, namely, our intuition of the world.[219]

This recalls the position rejected by the thesis of the first antinomy. But Kant is thinking here not of the phenomenal world, but of its noumenal substrate. Implied is the incomprehensible idea of time as a complete whole.

Can we make sense of this notion of the infinite? What evidence can be cited in its support? Clearly it eludes comprehension. No ordinary experience can support it. There is, however, Kant claims, an experience that we can appeal to: the experience of the sublime.

2 The Sublime

The experience of the sublime is not an experience of something objective. Science knows nothing of the sublime. Kant's definition of the sublime as what is *schlechthin groß* (*absolute non comparative magnum*), i.e., what is great, not in comparison with some other thing, but absolutely,[220] recalls what Nicolaus Cusanus had said of the maximum number that he offers as a metaphor of the infinite God, who, like the world He created, transcends our finite understanding, bound as that is to comparison.[221] Whenever our finite understanding attempts to comprehend the infinite it suffers shipwreck. The coincidence of opposites, illustrated by Cusanus with the coincidence of our understanding of number, to which one can always be added, and the idea of a maximum, a plenitude to which

---

218 Immanuel Kant, *Kritik der Urteilskraft*, A 90–91/B91–92; *The Critique of Judgment*, Werner S. Pluhar (Trans.), (Indianapolis: Hackett, 1987), p. 111.
219 Ibid, A 90–91/B91–92; trans), p. 111.
220 Ibid, A 80/B 81; trans. p. 103.
221 See Jasper Hopkins, *Nicholas of Cusa on Learned Ignorance. A translation and appraisal of De docta ignorantia* (Minneapolis: Banning Press, 1981), pp. 50–55.

nothing can be added, in the essentially elusive thought of the absolute number, marks the site of this shipwreck. So does the thought of the coincidence of a circle with both tangents and secants when the circle's radius is stretched to infinity; so stretched square and circle coincide. And so does the impossible attempt to square the circle, i.e., to construct a square with the same area as a given circle using only compass and straightedge, an attempt taken by Dante to figure the impossibility of understanding paradise. [222] But that shipwreck of our human reason is thought by Cusanus to open a window to what is higher than what we can comprehend. Something analogous can be said of the sublime. Here Kant's explication:

> That is sublime in comparison with which everything else is small. We can easily see here that nothing in nature can be given, however large we may judge it, that could not, when considered in a different relation, be degraded all the way to the infinitely small, nor conversely anything so small that it could not, when compared with still smaller standards, be expanded for our imagination all the way to the magnitude of a world; telescopes have provided us with a wealth of material in support of the first point, microscopes in support of the second. Hence, considered on this basis, nothing that can be an object of the senses is to be called sublime. [What happens is that] our imagination strives to progress towards infinity, while our reason demands absolute totality as a real idea, and so [the imagination,] our power of estimating the magnitude of things in the world of sense, is inadequate to that idea. Yet this inadequacy itself is the arousal in us of the feeling that we have within us a supersensible power; and what is absolutely large is not an object of sense, but is the use that judgment makes naturally of certain objects so as to [arouse] this (feeling), and in contrast with that use any other use is small. Hence what is to be called sublime is not the object, but the attunement that the intellect [gets] through a certain presentation that occupies reflective judgment.
>
> Hence we may supplement the formulas already given by another one: Sublime is what even to be able to think proves that the mind has a power surpassing any standard of sense.[223]

Sublime nature transcends our ability to comprehend it. The imagination (*Einbildungskraft*) cannot hold on to it and take its measure as if it were a beautiful bounded picture. The sublime floods every frame. But precisely this inadequacy raises a feeling that awakens a faculty in us, namely reason, which is not bound to the finite and comprehensible.

---

222 Dante, *Paradiso*, Canto 33, 133–141.
223 Immanuel Kant, *Kritik der Urteilskraft*, A 84/B 85; *The Critique of Judgment*, Werner S. Pluhar (Trans.), (Indianapolis: Hackett, 1987), pp. 105–106.

Significant in this context is what Kant has to say about the mathematically sublime: We call sublime, Kant tells us, what is absolutely large or great.[224] Such absolute greatness can be given a spatial and a temporal expression: in the first case it would be incommensurable with any bounded space, in the latter with any given stretch of time. Such incommensurability defines what Kant calls "Absolutely Large," akin to the maximum number Cusanus offers us as a figure of the incomprehensible infinity of God. But in what sense can we be said to experience the "Absolutely Large?" When I call something large I compare it to other things of the same or a similar type. The judgment is based on comparison. But the sublime resists such comparison: "That is sublime in comparison with which everything else is small."[225] Think once more of the maximum number. Just as there can be no such number, the absolutely large is not something that is objectively large. Rather the experience of the sublime is also the shipwreck of our ability to comprehend something. Thus, if what confronts us, i.e., what we apprehend, is so complex that when our attention passes from one aspect of the phenomenon to another it loses as much as it gains, then this proves that the imagination's ability to apprehend what it confronts has been stretched to its limits. The phenomenon confronting us no longer can be comprehended as a whole.

> In order to take in a quantum intuitively, so that we can then use it as a measure or unity in estimating magnitude, the imagination must perform two acts: apprehension (*apprehensio*) and comprehension (*comprehensio aesthetica*). Apprehension involves no problem, for it may progress to infinity. But comprehension becomes more and more difficult, the further apprehension progresses, and it soon reaches its maximum, namely the aesthetically largest basic measure for an estimation of magnitude. For when apprehension has reached the point where the partial presentations of sensible intuition that were first apprehended are already beginning to be extinguished in the imagination, as it proceeds to apprehend further ones, the imagination then loses as much on the one side as it gains on the other; and so there is a maximum in comprehension that it cannot exceed.[226]

Although the phenomenon confronting us cannot be given to us as a whole, it still can be thought as a whole, and just in this respect reason exhibits itself as of wider scope than understanding and imagination.

The very notion of the mathematically sublime invites us to think it against the background of the mathematical estimation of magnitude, i.e., of measuring. The logical estimation of magnitude, Kant suggests, "progresses without hin-

---

[224] Ibid., A80/B81; trans., p. 103.
[225] Ibid., A 83/B84; trans. p. 105.
[226] Ibid., A86/B87; trans. p. 108.

drance to infinity."²²⁷ But reason demands that the infinite be presented as a totality. In every experience, and may it be just a blade of grass, lurks thus the thought of absolute space and time, the thought of something infinite, inviting reason to think it. But reason can think space and time only as infinite wholes. In this ability to think the infinite as a whole, the human being's power to transcend itself as a embodied being, limited in space and time, manifests itself, even as our understanding suffers shipwreck on the reef of the infinite.

> To be able even to think the infinite as a whole indicates a mental power that surpasses any standard of sense. For thinking the infinite as a whole while using a standard of sense would require a comprehension yielding a standard that would have a determinate relation to the infinite, one that could be stated in numbers, and this is impossible. If the human mind is nonetheless to be able even to think the given infinite without contradiction, it must have within itself a power that is supersensible, whose ideas of a noumenon cannot be intuited, but can yet be regarded as the substrate underlying what is mere appearance, namely, our intuition of the world.²²⁸

The passage suggests the possibility of distinguishing between a negative and a positive sublime, between the sublime as an epiphany of freedom, and the sublime as an epiphany of the noumenon understood as the substrate of the world.

What Kant judges to be sublime is first of all nature, which Kant calls sublime "in those of its appearances whose intuition carries with it the idea of their infinity."²²⁹ Kant is thinking of the starry sky, which carries with it the idea of the infinite cosmos. But must something of the sort not be said even of a blade of grass, which we have no difficulty describing and which yet, as this unique thing transcends every description, no matter how long. So understood, does this blade of grass not carry with it the idea of its infinity? Indeed, is this not part of our experience of the reality of things, of their thingliness? Kant, to be sure, is not thinking here of particular things but of nature.

> Now the proper unchangeable basic measure of nature is the absolute whole of nature, which, in the case of nature as appearance, is infinity comprehended. This basic measure, however, is a self-contradictory concept (because an absolute totality of an endless progression is impossible). Hence that magnitude of a natural object to which the imagination fruitlessly applies its entire ability to comprehend must lead the concept of nature to a supersensible substrate (which underlies both nature and our ability to think), a substrate that is large beyond any standard of sense and hence makes us judge as sublime not so

---

227 Ibid., A84/B 85; trans, p. 105.
228 Ibid., A91/B92; trans. p. 111.
229 Ibid., A92/B93; trans. p. 112.

much the object as the mental attunement in which we find ourselves when we estimate the object.[230]

The sublime, Kant tells us, fills us with respect.[231] But such respect, according to Kant, has its object not in nature, but in our human being and in our high destination as free autonomous actors. In respect to the understanding the sublime is said to be simply unpleasant, since nature here presents itself in a way that eludes our efforts to grasp it. But reason delights in this shipwreck of the understanding.

The passage that links the sublime to a feeling of respect, however, also demands to be applied to our experience of other persons as moral agents: Such an experience, too, must fill us with respect. It is indeed a presupposition of all morality. Kant's categorical imperative would idle were there not an experience of persons as deserving our respect. Were I able to totally comprehend the other, I would be able to reconstruct her or him, i.e., I would find it impossible to distinguish in principle a person from a robot with a computer brain. But such a robot is not deserving of our respect. Our ability to fully comprehend the other must suffer shipwreck if we are to experience the other as a person. It is an experience of something one might perhaps call intensive infinity that leads reason to the concept of a person. The experience of persons must be understood as an experience of the positive sublime.

The moral significance of the experience of the sublime had indeed been recognized by Kant already in the *Critique of Practical Reason*, albeit with reference to the subject as moral agent:

> Two things fill the mind with ever new and increasing admiration and reverence, the more frequently and persistently one's meditation deals with them: *the starry sky above me and the moral law within me*.... The first thing starts from the place that I occupy in the external world of sense and expands the connection in which I stand into the immensely large, with worlds upon worlds and systems of systems, and also into boundless times of their periodic motion, the beginning and continuance thereof. The second thing starts from my invisible self, my personality, and exhibits me in a world that has true infinity but that is discernible only to the understanding, and with that world (but thereby simultaneously also with all those visible worlds) I cognize myself not, as in the first case, in a merely contingent connection, but in a universal and necessary one. The first sight, of a countless multitude of worlds, annihilates, as it were, my importance as an *animal creature* that, after having for a short time been provided (one knows not how) with vital force, must give back again to the planet (a mere dot in the universe) the matter from which it came. The second sight, on the contrary, elevates infinitely my worth as that of an *intelligence* by my person-

---

230 Ibid., A93/B94; trans. p. 112.
231 Ibid., A95/B96; trans. p. 114.

ality, in which the moral law reveals to me a life independent of animality and even of the entire world of sense, at least as far as can be gleaned from the purposive determination of my existence by this law, a determination that is not restricted to conditions and boundaries of this life but proceeds to infinity.[232]

The experience of the sublime awakens me to something in me that transcends my animality. So understood the sublime is egocentric, as emphasized already by Edmund Burke. But the moral law presupposes the respect I feel when I meet another person, presupposes an experience of that person as transcending the world of phenomena. In that world such experience opens a window to what is higher.

3 The Time of the Everyday

Let me return to the difficulty of comprehending time. How do we think of time? Newton's scholium distinguishes absolute from common time. The latter does indeed seem to capture time as we experience it first of all and most of the time. Clocks allow us to measure time, where the sun provides us with the most obvious natural clock. We think of events as taking time; we tell people not to waste time; we have time on our hands; we do not have enough time. Time appears in all these cases as an entity of sorts that we encounter and deal with, almost as if it were a strange kind of equipment. Here Heidegger's statement of the everyday understanding of time:

> Everyday Dasein, the Dasein which takes time, comes across time proximally in what it encounters within-the-world as ready-to-hand and present-at-hand. The time which it has thus 'experienced' is understood within the horizon of that way of understanding Being which is the closest for Dasein; that is, it is understood as something which is itself somehow present-at-hand. How and why Dasein comes to develop the ordinary conceptions of time, must be clarified in terms of its state-of-Being as concerning itself with time—a state-of-Being with a temporal foundation. The ordinary conception of time owes its origin to a way in which primordial time has been leveled off. By demonstrating that this is the source of the ordinary conception, we shall justify our earlier interpretation of temporality as *primordial time* (GA2, 535; SZ, 405).

Heidegger goes on to point out that in the theoretical unfolding of the vulgar conception of time there has been a remarkable vacillation between subjective and

---

[232] Immanuel Kant, *Kritik der praktischen Vernunft*, A288; *The Critique of Practical Reason*, Werner S. Pluhar (Trans.), (Indianapolis: Hackett, 2002), p. 203.

objective interpretations of time: "Where time is taken as being in itself, it gets allotted primarily to the 'soul' notwithstanding. And where it has the character which belongs to 'consciousness', it still functions 'objectively'" (GA2, 535–536; SZ, 405).

Is time to be understood as somehow being in itself? Is it to be linked to consciousness?

Heidegger, too, distinguishes what he calls primordial time from the ordinary conception. The latter is said to be marked by its privileging of the present: back then, when I was younger; let us meet in an hour. The past here is understood as what is no longer, and similarly the future as what is not yet. Heidegger's claim that the time of fallen everyday being-with-others gives primacy to the present seems unproblematic, even if elusive, as this present is marked by negativity, the evanescent threshold between a not yet and a no longer. Schopenhauer gave striking expression to what Heidegger calls the ordinary conception of time: "In time each moment is, only in so far as it has effaced its father the preceding moment, to be effaced just as quickly itself. Past and future (apart from the consequences of their content) are as empty and unreal as any dream; but present is only the boundary between the two, having neither extension nor duration."[233]

Heidegger next turns to another related structure: we fix time with respect to a time scale, a calendar or something of the sort; back when…; I will see you at 5; it is just about noon. We date events. Heidegger thus speaks of their *Datierbarkeit*, their datability. In this connection we may want to think about the significance of being up to date, of having a date; also about the significance of a certain resistance today to the term "dating."

The datability of events has its foundation in the priority of the ready-to-hand and its temporality. How much time do I have to catch the train; it is almost time to start; time for a break. In this connection Heidegger speaks of a time span:

> Not only does the 'during' have a span; but every 'now', 'then', and 'on that former occasion' has, with its datability structure, its own spanned character, with the width of the span varying: 'now'—in the intermission, while one is eating, in the evening, in summer; 'then'—at breakfast, when one is taking a climb, and so forth (GA2, 541; SZ, 409).

---

[233] Arthur Schopenhauer, *Die Welt als Wille und Vorstellung*, 2 vols. (Wiesbaden: Brockhaus, 1965). E. F. J. Payne (Trans.), *The World as Will and Representation*, 2 vols. (New York: Dover, 1966), vol. 1, p. 7.

Thought provoking is Heidegger's suggestion that saying "I have no time" betrays an inauthentic mode of existence:

> He who is irresolute understands himself in terms of those very closest events and befallings which he encounters in such a making-present and which thrust themselves upon him in varying ways. Busily losing himself in the object of his concern, he loses his time in it too. Hence his characteristic way of talking—'I have no time'. But just as he who exists inauthentically is constantly losing time and never 'has' any, the temporality of authentic existence remains distinctive in that such existence, in its resoluteness, never loses time and 'always has time' (GA2, 542; SZ, 410).

What allows Heidegger to say this? In inauthentic existence the individual reckons with time as something other, rather like an object to be dealt with. Time here appears as something I can have, lack, or perhaps lose altogether. But is time something I can possess or lose? Is time not constitutive of my being. What kind of a self-understanding is presupposed by the locution "I have [no, too little, enough, always] time?"

A further aspect to which Heidegger calls our attention is the publicness of everyday time. Time is first of all not my time, but a time that has its foundation in the community of which I am part. We have to use the time with which one reckons. Don't take so much time! It is in this public time that we encounter things ready-to-hand and present-at-hand: the train is leaving at …; the morning light is falling into my room —it is time to get up. Time is initially time to…

The last example points to what Heidegger calls the most natural measure of time:

> In terms of this dating arises the 'most natural' measure of time – the day. And because the temporality of that Dasein which must take its time is finite, its days are already numbered. Concernful awaiting takes precaution to define the 'thens' with which it is to concern itself — that is, to divide up the day. And the 'during-the-daytime' makes this possible. This dividing up, in turn, is done with regard to that by which time is dated – the journeying sun. Sunset and midday, like the sunrise itself, are distinctive 'places' which this heavenly body occupies. Its regularly recurring passage is something which Dasein, as thrown into the world and giving itself time temporalizingly, takes into its reckoning. Dasein historizes from day to day by reason of its way of interpreting time by dating it – a way which is adumbrated in its thrownness into the "there" (GA2, 545; SZ, 413).

The very word "everyday" points to the significance of this measure. Part of the way we find ourselves in and understand our world are the temporal orders in which we always already have been placed: time to go to bed; time to get up; time to work. We measure time. And a public time requires a shared measure. This public time is the *Weltzeit*, the world-time, where world is to be thought of not as a collection of entities, but as a way of relating to the persons and things that surround us, as we do when we speak of the world of the Middle Ages.

> As the 'time-for-something', the time which has made itself public has essentially a world-character. Hence the time which makes itself public in the temporalizing of temporality is what we designate as "*world-time*". And we designate it thus not because it is *present-at-hand* as an entity *within-the-world* (which it can never be), but because it belongs *to the world* [*zur Welt*] in the sense which we have interpreted existential-ontologically (GA2, 547–548; SZ, 414).

In this connection we should consider the history of time-keeping devices, from sun dials to water, mechanical, and atomic clocks, from public time keeping devises such as obelisks and clocks on church towers to small watches to be carried in a pocket or on a wrist. What is the significance of the shift from natural time to clock time? Of ever more accurate time keeping?

A homogenization of time corresponds to the homogenization of space. Both are linked. Both are founded in the human power of self-transcendence, which demands an objectification of time, as it demands an objectification of space and the world. The other side of the resulting progress is a loss of place. Can we also speak of an analogous loss of time. Is there not a sense in which time is lost when we come to think of it as a dimension?

Is time subjective or objective? The question is related to the question "is the world subjective or objective?" Given that human being is essentially a being-in-the-world, this "or" must be challenged. Heidegger thus insists that there is a sense in which time is both more objective than any object and more subjective than any subject:

> The time 'in which' the present-at-hand is in motion or at rest is not 'Objective', if what we mean by that is the Being-present-at-hand-in-itself of entities encountered within-the-world. But just as little is time 'subjective' if by this we understand "Being-present-at-hand and occurring in a subject'. *World-time is 'more Objective' than any possible Object, because, with the disclosedness of the world, it already becomes 'Objectified' in an ecstatico-horizonal manner as the condition for the possibility of entities within-the-world.* Thus contrary to Kant's opinion, one comes across world-time just as immediately in the physical as in the psychical, and not just roundabout by way of the psychical (GA2, 553–554; SZ, 419).

And time is also more subjective than any possible subject: "*World-time, moreover, is also 'more subjective' that any possible subject; for it is what first makes possible the Being of the factually existing Self – that being which, as is now well understood, is the meaning of care*" (GA2, 554; SZ, 419). It is in this way, as world-time, that time gets understood first of all and most of the time:

think of the sun's movement across the sky, or of the moving hands of a clock, which is said to have blocked a more fundamental understanding of time.

But how are we to arrive at this more fundamental understanding? How does time show itself? Consider once more the clock: The hands turning around: now here, now here. It is this understanding of time that seems to be captured well by the Aristotelian definition: "For time is just this – a number of motion in respect to 'before' and 'after'" (*Physics*, Delta 11, 219 b; GA 2, 525; SZ, 421). The definition seems both questionable, indeed question begging, and obvious, questionable in that by presupposing motion it would seem to presuppose time in a sense different from that defined; obvious in that it captures very well the way we reckon with time. Not surprising then that subsequent discussions of time should have moved within the orbit of Aristotle's definition.

> Ever since Aristotle all discussions of the concept of time have clung in principle to the Aristotelian definition; that is, in taking time as their theme, they have taken it as it shows itself in circumspective concern. Time is what is 'counted'; that is to say, it is what is expressed and what we have in view, even if unthematically, when the traveling pointer (or the shadow) is made present. When one makes present what is moved in this movement, one says 'now here, now here, and so on. The "nows" are what gets counted. And these show themselves 'in every 'now' as "nows" which will 'forthwith' be 'no-longer-now' and "nows" which have 'just been not-yet-now'. The world-time which is 'sighted' in this manner in the use of clocks, we call the "now-time" [*Jetzt-Zeit*] (GA2, 556–557; SZ, 421).

This "now-time" expresses the ordinary understanding of time:

> Thus for the ordinary understanding of time, time shows itself as a sequence of "nows" which are constantly 'present-at-hand', simultaneously passing away and coming along. Time is understood as a succession, as a 'flowing stream' of "nows", as 'the course of time'. *What is implied by such an interpretation of world-time with which we concern ourselves?* (GA2, SZ, 422).

Although rooted in world-time, this now-time also involves a leveling of the former:

> In the ordinary interpretation of time as a sequence of "nows", both datability and significance are *missing*. These two structures are *not* permitted 'to come to the fore' when time is characterized as a pure succession. The ordinary interpretation of time *covers them up*. When these are covered up, the ecstatico-horizonal constitution of temporality, in which the datability and significance of the "now" are grounded, gets *leveled off*. The "nows" get shorn of these relations, as it were; and, as thus shorn, they simply range themselves along after one another so as to make up the succession (GA2, 557–558; SZ, 422).

3 The Time of the Everyday — 177

We speak, as Newton did, of the flow of time: time passes. In every now another now has perished and yet: do this now that is now and the now that just was share this: their participation in the self-same "now?" Something of the sort finds expression in the passage from the *Timaeus* Heidegger cites: "Wherefore he resolved to have a moving image of eternity, and when he set in order the heaven, he made this image eternal, but moving according to number, while eternity rests in unity; and this image we call time." (*Timaeus*, 37 d; GA2, 559; SZ, 423). Plato's locution of eternity resting in unity invites comparison with the time of absolute time as an infinite whole. But so understood absolute time would seem to be far removed from what Heidegger calls primordial time. Plato's understanding of time as the moving image of eternity betrays a desire to keep time. But time of course, despite all our time keeping devices, refuses to be kept. In this desire to ground time in eternity and unity, in something eternally at rest, which does not pass away, something like a tendency to flee from what Heidegger considers primordial time betrays itself. An understanding of this primordial time is implicit in the saying: *Die Zeit lässt sich nicht halten*—"time will not be kept." This awareness of a time that will not be kept, that time passes—and Heidegger insists on the remarkable priority which time passes has over time arises —is inseparable from our self-awareness as mortals.

> *Dasein knows fugitive time in terms of its 'fugitive' knowledge about its death.* In the kind of talk which emphasizes time's passing away, the finite futurity of Dasein's temporality is publicly reflected. And because even in talk about time's passing away, death can remain covered up, time shows itself as a passing-away 'in itself'... But even in now-time this primordial time manifests itself as the irreversibility of time" (GA2, 562; SZ, 425).

There is no human experience without an awareness of self, no awareness of self without an awareness of fugitive time. Even the everyday understanding of time as world-time recognizes its special relationship to something like soul or spirit. Once again Heidegger cites Aristotle: "But if nothing but soul, and in soul reason is qualified to count, there would be no time unless there were soul" (*Physics*, Delta 14. 225 a 25; GA 2, 564; SZ, 427).

Must we not insist that there is movement and thus time of some sort even without soul? That question intertwines with the question with which I began: can we make Being dependent on human being? Must we not insist that the being of beings does not depend on human beings? But what meaning can we here give to Being? And what meaning can we give to time apart from time-keeping and thus from soul?

To support the intimate connection between soul and time Heidegger adds a quote from Augustine's *Confessions:* "Hence it seemed to me that time is nothing else than an extendedness; but of what sort of thing it is an extendedness, I do not know; and it would be surprising if it were not an extendedness of the soul itself" (*Conf.* XI, 26; GA2, 564; SZ, 427). But this only serves to underscore the riddle of time, which is inseparably bound up with what I have called the Antinomy of Being.

4 Saving and Spending Time

Let me conclude with an extreme example of what Heidegger would consider an inauthentic understanding of time. In Rilke's "The Notebooks of Malte Laurids Brigge" we read of a strange person who thinks he has still much time left and therefore considers himself very rich.[234] Don't we say, time is money. This Nikolaj Kusmitsch at any rate counts time as he counts money, which one should not spend thoughtlessly. And do we not count time similarly when we think we have enough or too little time, as if time were some sort of material of which one can have enough or not enough? Don't lose so much time! And we make plans for whatever time we expect is left to us. Kusmitsch thinks he has about 50 years left, counted in seconds an enormous sum. And again: is not time money? Nikolaj Kusmitsch would seem to have good reason to consider himself rich. But money one can waste or lose. And is the same not true of time? Kusmitsch thus decides to carefully watch the time belonging to him, to save time, only to have to make the discovery that on Sunday there was no saved time. So he feels himself cheated.

Kusmitsch counts with time as with a scarce resource that one must use thoughtfully. But can the human being distance himself from time without distancing himself from himself? Does time not belong so essentially to us that it is impossible to waste, let alone to lose time? That is why Heidegger can say in *Being and Time* that it is a distinguishing mark of an authentic existence that it never loses time and "always has time" (GA2, 542; SZ, 410). Inauthentic existence deals differently with time. First of all and most of the time we reckon with time, that is to say, we count years, days, minutes or seconds and thus subject time to reason. The time that we can lose or waste is an always already measured time. To this so understood measured time, which is inseparable from our everyday dealings with persons and things, Heidegger opposes a more primor-

---

[234] Rainer Maria Rilke, *Die Aufzeichnungen des Malte Laurids Brigge, Werke in 3 Bänden*, Band 3. Frankfurt am Main: Insel, 1966), pp. 265–270. English translation by William Needham: https://archive.org/stream/TheNotebooksOfMalteLauridsBrigge/TheNotebooksOfMalteLauridsBrigge_djvu.txt

dially understood time: what he understands as authentic time. Authentic time cannot be measured.

Two concepts of time collide here. This collision presents itself to us already in the first definitions of time that philosophy has given us, definitions that still shape the way we think time. In the *Timaeus*, as I pointed out, Plato takes time to be the numerically ordered, moving image of eternity, related to the passing moments, as unity is related to the different numbers. So defined time has been subjected to number, has been measured. But this definition presupposes time in a different sense, as a medium that allows for such measuring.

In similar fashion, as we saw, Aristotle understand time as "the number of motion with respect to its 'before' and 'after,'" This definition, too, spatializes time and subjects it to number. With time thus measured one can reckon. But a presupposition of all such reckoning is a more primordial understanding of time.

Fascinated by the possibility of so reckoning with time, Nikolaj Kusmitsch blurs the difference between time and money. Soon to be sure, he has to discover that in that way we do not do justice to time.

> I've been getting myself into a mess, he told himself. It's just that I don't understand a thing about numbers. But clearly they shouldn't be granted too much importance; they are, so to speak, only some arrangement introduced by the government. Yet no one has ever seen them anywhere except on paper. In a group of people it was impossible to meet, for example, a seven or a twenty-five. There simply aren't any. And that was how this slight mix-up had come about through sheer absent-mindedness: time and money, as if you couldn't tell them apart.[235]

We cannot reckon with time as with money. Time cannot be saved. Our life-time is limited. But time cannot end. It is infinite and cannot be counted.

Nikolaj Kusmitsch has, as he says, gotten himself into a mess by getting preoccupied with numbers. A presupposition of reckoning with time is a certain distance from time to which corresponds a certain self-alienation. An authentic existence cannot thus distance itself from time. And so Kusmitsch does not succeed, after confusing time with money because of a certain absent-mindedness, as he puts it, simply to leave that confusion behind: he has become too used to counting time. Like a draft of wind a more primordial time suddenly touches him, passes by in front of him.

> Something peculiar happened. It suddenly wafted across his face, it passed by his ears, he felt it on his hands. He opened his eyes wide. The window was closed tight. And as he sat

---

235 Ibid., p. 268. Translation by William Needham.

there in the dark room with his eyes wide open he began to understand that what he was feeling now was real time passing. He actually recognised all these seconds, all tepid, uniform, but fast, fast. Heaven only knew what they still intended to do. Why did it have to be him in particular, to whom every sort of wind felt like an insult? He would now sit there and it would go on blowing ceaselessly his whole life long. He could foresee all the attacks of neuralgia he'd get; he was beside himself with rage.[236]

A presupposition of this uncomprehending recognition of the quickly passing seconds is something like a falling out of time, which now becomes a terrifying other that cannot be grasped, terrifying because we sense that we cannot step out of time and that our life has to end. No reckoning with time can help. Time will not be kept. Nor will reality. That is one lesson of the Antinomy of Being.

---

[236] Ibid., p. 269. English translation by William Needham.

XI The Rediscovery of the Earth

1 The Terror of Time and Space

I introduced you to Rilke's Nikolaj Kusmitsch, who is terrified by the endless flow of time. To the terror of time corresponds the terror of boundless space. To the windy draft of time corresponds the draft of space that threatens every supposedly firm standpoint and causes it to sway and slide. And so Nikolaj Kusmitsch, immediately after his unsettling experience with time, has the following unpleasant experience with space:

> He jumped up, but the surprises weren't yet finished. Under his very feet there was something like a movement, not just one but several strange movements interlocking confusedly. He was rigid with terror: could it be the earth? Certainly, it was the earth. Yes of course it moved. He'd heard about it at school, but the topic had been dealt with rather cursorily and later it had been readily hushed up as it wasn't considered suitable for discussion. But now that he'd grown more sensitive he could even feel it. Did the others feel it? Possibly, but they gave no indication of it. Perhaps, being sailors, they didn't mind. Of all people Nikolai Kusmitsch was somewhat sensitive on this point, he avoided even the trams. He staggered about in his room as if he were on deck and needed to hold on right and left. Unfortunately he recalled something else about the tilt of the earth's axis. No, he couldn't bear all these movements. He felt ill.[237]

That the earth moves has been, of course, ever since Copernicus, a generally known fact, hardly worth mention. But we also know that this is not how we experience the earth. First of all and most of the time the earth remains firm ground. Sun and moon still rise and set. The geocentric world picture of an Aristotle or of the Middle Ages better agrees with our everyday experience than the modern world picture. To grant that the earth moves, is not to say that we experience that motion. That Rilke's Nikolaj Kusmitsch claims to experience it, lets us consider him slightly insane. Once again it is his calculating reason that has caused him to fall out of his life-world. For us normal human beings the earth would seem to remain the center of our world.

But does our life really remain untouched by our knowledge that the earth moves? Has this knowledge no impact on the way we conduct our lives? Have

---

[237] Rainer Maria Rilke, *Die Aufzeichnungen des Malte Laurids Brigge, Werke in 3 Bänden* (Frankfurt am Main: Insel, 1966), vol. 3, . 268. English translation by William Needham: https://archive.org/stream/TheNotebooksOfMalteLauridsBrigge/TheNotebooksOfMalteLauridsBrigge_djvu.txt

we indeed covered up the knowledge that we do not stand on firm ground, where the loss of this center becomes a metaphor for other and weightier losses? Or must we recognize here, too, something like a double truth, where in our everyday dealings with persons and things the subjective truth retains its primacy, even though we know that objectively considered what this subjective truth tells us is a lie? The earth after all does move. But once again the boundary supposed to separate objective and subjective truth threatens to blur. Nietzsche had good reason to claim that "Since Copernicus, man seems to have got himself on an inclined plane—now he is slipping faster and faster away from the center into —what? into nothingness? into a penetrating sense of his own nothingness?" But how has the discovery that what was once thought to furnish firm ground really moves affected our lives? To be sure, we have no difficulty understanding talk of our earth as a spaceship, floating aimlessly in the immensity of the universe. The metaphor of a sea-journey for our life is familiar, as is the metaphor of a ship for our earth.[238] Have we not all become at bottom sailors? But how adequate are these metaphors? Do they describe how we experience the world? Do we share Nietzsche's sense that we are "slipping faster and faster away from the center?"

2 July 20, 1969

Let me accompany the quotation from Rilke's *The Notebooks of Malte Laurids Brigge* with a suggestion that Al Gore, then vice-president of the United States, made in the spring of 1998. Gore suggested that we send a satellite into space that would continuously beam back images of our earth, reminding us of its majesty and fragility. Making that suggestion, Gore invoked Socrates who, according to Gore, had said already some 2400 years ago that human beings would have to raise themselves above the earth in order to really understand the earth that is our home.[239] I do not know where or when or in what spirit Socrates is supposed to have said such a thing, but understood as a metaphor it is not difficult to reconcile Gore's invocation of Socrates with the Platonic Socrates' teaching of the forms. But perhaps Gore was also thinking of the *Clouds* of Aristophanes, where Socrates, pulled up in a basket by his disciples, looks down at what is below him.

---

238 Cf. Hans Blumenberg, *Schiffbruch mit Zuschauer* (Frankfurt am Main: Suhrkamp, 1979).
239 *New York Times*, March 14, 1998, A7.

What is important to me here is not the invocation of Socrates, but the suggestion that we should leave the earth, rise above it, in order to return to it, but with greater insight, more open eyes. Can this not be understood also as a metaphor for what makes our human lives truly worth living? Must we not raise ourselves above our bodily, place- and time-bound existence, above the earth, but only to return to it with more open eyes, guided by our now educated reason? As Plato already recognized, such a self-elevation is inseparable from the pursuit of truth. It thus provides the key to Cartesian method, which helped lay the foundation of our modern world-picture, as it provides the key to Kant's *Critiques of Pure* and *Practical Reason*. Kant demands such self-elevation both of those who would lay claim to truth and of those who would do what practical reason commands. But both the pursuit of truth and that of the moral life must return to the earth if they are not to idle. If Kant is clear both about the need to raise ourselves in reflection above our time- and space-bound perspectives and prejudices, and about the necessity of a return, he fails to provide us with a sufficiently developed account of the latter. Thus, in the *Critique of Pure Reason*, in his discussion of the schematism, Kant pays insufficient attention to the need and requirements for an empirical schematism, to the way we have to descend from what Kant took to be the categories, the pure concepts of the understanding, to such empirical concepts as "rose" or "hedgehog." Only with his discussion of the reflective judgment in the *Critique of Judgment* does Kant begin to address that lacuna. In the *Critique of Practical Reason* Kant does not see a need for a schematism at all, let alone the need for an empirical schematism, an omission that generated countless critiques of the categorical imperative for its inhuman abstract formalism.[240] In both *Critiques* the contribution made by the concrete and particular, the role of the imagination in what Kant calls reflective judgments, demands more careful attention.

Let me return to Gore's pronouncement. Only astronautics has made it possible for us to literally leave the earth, to observe it from above, say from a satellite or from the moon. It was in 1957 that the Russians sent their sputnik circling around the earth. Its merry peeping frightened the West: Had the progress of Soviet astronautics not literally left us in earthly dust?[241] Only four

---

[240] I was alerted to the need for an empirical schematism, especially in the *Critique of Practical Reason*, in the course of extended discussions with George A. Schrader in the sixties and seventies. See George A. Schrader, "Basic Problems of Philosophical Ethics. On Lewis White Beck: *A Commentary on Kant's Critique of Practical Reason* [Zur Diskussion], in: *Archiv für Geschichte der Philosophie* 46, 1964, p. 102.

[241] See Hans Blumenberg, *Die Vollzähligkeit der Sterne*, 2nd ed (Frankfurt am Main: Suhrkamp, 1997), pp. 547–548.

years later, in 1961, Juri Gagarin became the first human being to circle the earth in a satellite and to observe it from above. To be sure, such a research deficit could not be tolerated by the United States: Less than a year later John Glenn circled the earth as the first American.

Gore thought that the view of the earth from space would remind us of its beauty and fragility. In his office in the West Wing of the White House he thus displayed the *Blue Marble*, the famous photograph of the earth taken by Apollo 17 astronauts on their way to the moon. Widely reproduced, this unforgettable image of our blue planet floating in black space gave support to the environmental movement. The fact that 1962, the year that John Glenn circled the earth, also saw the publication of *Silent Spring* invites reflection. With that book Rachel Carson showed the world how thoughtlessly we human beings have dealt with our earth, how fragile our planet is, how much in need of our care and protection. That Al Gore should have mentioned satellite technology and environmental protection in one breath should not surprise us. And yet, the two developments would seem to go in opposite directions: one centrifugal, leaving the earth behind, the other centripetal, calling on us to care for this endangered earth.

In 1969 Neil Armstrong and Buzz Aldrin landed as the first human beings on the moon. Three years later the sixth, and for the time being last, moon landing followed. Why have there been no further flights, not to speak of visits to Mars? Were the lunar rocks that our astronauts brought home not worth the effort? Were our lunar flights worth the time and resources invested in them? Has astronautics changed our understanding of our place in the cosmos in any fundamental way? If so, how? Did humanity make a giant leap, as Neil Armstrong proclaimed.

I still remember where I was when I saw the first television images of the first moon landing on July 20, 1969. We were in Maine at the time. We awakened the children so that they would not miss this momentous event. They were too sleepy to show much interest. Our seven-year old son kept staring at our then still black and white television screen and finally said: "Look at all those green people!" We sent him back to bed. What we saw was not nearly as interesting. Popular comparisons of what had just happened to the discovery of America were no more than wishful thinking: No new world opened itself to us; despite Armstrong's famous words, humanity did not take a giant leap. What Armstrong and Aldrin had to tell us was not nearly as exciting as the stories brought home by a Columbus or even by explorers of what was then still called the dark continent in the 19th century. There were no real surprises. The moon turned out to be much as our science had led us to expect. Not only did the astronauts not see God out there, they did not even see little green men, only mute matter. As a result of the moon landings, space lost another part of the aura with which it has so long been invested—think of Stanley Kubrick's film *2001: Space Odyssey*, released just a year before the first moon landing. As that film showed once again, the aura of space had from the very beginning been supported by two contradictory desires: on the one hand the desire for the sublime, the longing for the excitement of encountering something totally other, an excitement born of a gnostic longing for a reality beyond and altogether different from this all too familiar world; on the other hand the desire for the beautiful, the longing to encounter out there intelligent beings much like ourselves, but hopefully much wiser, kinder, somehow more divine, so that, instead of feeling lost in space, we could once more feel at home, not alone in this now so greatly enlarged cosmos. Neither the one nor the other desire was satisfied.

Human beings have always sought to increase their mobility, to make distance less important. Such a lessening of the power of distance went along with an increase in freedom. That flying machines such as balloons and airplanes should have been immediately understood as symbols of liberation is hardly surprising. In this connection the enthusiasm that greeted the first balloon flights in the 1780's deserves our special attention. This was the decade that issued in the French revolution.

The brothers Joseph Michel and Jacques Étienne Montgolfier staged the first balloon flight on June 4, 1783 in front of a group of assorted dignitaries. It covered 2 km, lasted 10 minutes, and rose to a height of about a mile, but was unmanned, indeed did not carry anything. On September 19 a basket attached to a balloon carried a sheep, a duck and a rooster to test the reaction of animals to such a flight, which this time took place at the royal palace of Versailles. A larger balloon, with one of the brothers, Étienne, and another enthusiast, the chemistry and physics teacher Jean-François Pilâtre de Rozier aboard, was tested in tethered flights later in 1783 on October 15, 17, and 19. It was de Rozier, who on 21 November 1783 made the first manned free flight in history, accompanied by the Marquis d'Arlandes. It lasted 25 minutes and covered 12 kilometers, rising to a height of 3000 feet. How much the idea was in the air is shown by the fact that less than two weeks later the French physicist Jacques Charles (1746–1823) and Nicolas Robert (1758–1820) made the first untethered ascension with a gas hydrogen balloon on December 1, 1783. Their technology won out over the hot air balloon. Half of Paris came to watch. De Rozier, by the way, died when he attempted to cross the English Channel and his balloon, relying on a mixture of hot air and hydrogen, suddenly deflated and crashed on June 15, 1785. He and his companion, Pierre Romain, became thus the first known victims of an air crash.

As the crowds that came to watch these events demonstrate, the first flights attracted enormous interest and attention. Balloons promised human beings the power of flight and thus an altogether new freedom and changed relationship to space: finally humans would be able to realize the old dream of raising themselves above the earth, of flying like birds, like Icarus, flying across whatever boundaries and false walls separated human beings. The balloon promised a godlike freedom from the tyranny of place.

Here is what the philosopher and social historian Helmut Reinicke wrote of the first balloons: heralds of a freer, more genuinely humane, because truly cosmopolitan world, "these balls of air are the first invention linked to the concept of world revolution. The balloon rises into the sky, — as a sign that reason on earth is extending its sway. Such a revolution (we are still in the year 1786!) has this subjective aspect that human beings want to find themselves, want to give themselves a human countenance."[242] This raises the question: just what does it mean for human beings to truly find themselves, "to give themselves a human countenance?" The quoted passage presupposes an understanding of what makes us truly human that invites question. In this particular case the assumption is that what we are is determined most fundamentally by freedom. Dreams of freedom do indeed preside over the progress of humanity. The balloon invites thus to be understood as an expression of human self-assertion, of emancipation, both presumption — human beings cannot fly like angels or birds — and liberation. And, as so often, liberating technologies very quickly are put in the service of destruction — think of Swift's Laputians. Benjamin Franklin thus recognized the military potential of the balloon as soon as it first rose into the sky. And he was hardly alone. On June 2, 1794 Marie-Joseph Coutelle, a French officer who had been put in command of the French army's first balloon unit, rose in the balloon *Entreprenant* to conduct the first aerial surveillance. The results proved decisive in helping the French win the battle of Fleurus against the Austrians.

With such inventions the way our bodies bind us to the earth seemed to have lost some of its power. Suddenly not only our thoughts were free, as it says in the German folksong I cited earlier. As did Daedalus, the new technology gave us human beings wings. To be sure, part of the story of Daedalus is the fall of Icarus and from the very beginning the history of human flight is also a story of death and disaster: recall the sad end of Jean-François Pilâtre de Rozier. The warning communicated by the Icarus story will not be dismissed: pride comes before the fall. Is this the fate that unfettered freedom has in store for us? Is freedom, when

---

[242] Helmut Reinicke, *Aufstieg und Revolution. Über die Beförderung irdischer Freiheitsneigungen durch Ballonfahrt und Luftschwimmkunst* (Berlin: Transit, 1988), pp. 76–77.

it leaves all constraints behind, bound to destroy itself in the end, as all content is lost?

3 "The Spirit Loves Colony and Brave Forgetting"

In what matters most fundamentally the progress of astronautics would seem to have left us at home; and that is also true of the astronauts, who knew that their home was here on earth. No new world was discovered; no colony was founded on some distant planet. To be sure, that may change some day: the visionary billionaire and space enthusiast Elon Musk presents us with this either/or: "I think there are really two fundamental paths. History is going to bifurcate along two directions. One path is we stay on Earth forever, and then there will be some eventual extinction event. I do not have an immediate doomsday prophecy, but eventually, history suggests, there will be some doomsday event. The alternative is to become a space-bearing civilization and a multi-planetary species, which I hope you would agree is the right way to go. So how do we figure out how to take you to Mars and create a self-sustaining city—a city that is not merely an outpost but which can become a planet in its own right, allowing us to become a truly multi-planetary species?"[243] That humanity, if it continues on it present course, is headed for disaster is difficult to deny. Think of population growth, climate change and, not unrelated, the likelihood of evermore destructive wars. But is Musk's alternative, his dream of a city of a million to be raised on Mars even before the end of this century, at all realistic? Is the establishment of such a city something that, as Musk suggests, any right thinking person will support? I do not think the founding of such a colony on Mars, let alone on some other heavenly body, at all likely in the foreseeable future. But if that should indeed be the case, if Musk's dreams of a large Martian city should prove to be just that, mere dreams, should we regret this? There is something seductive, perhaps consoling, about thoughts of leaving this small increasingly stressed planet for some other hopefully more welcoming star. There is also something very sad about thoughts of such a leave-taking.

For the time being there would seem to be no alternative to the earth. And would the inhabitants of Musk's Martian city ever be able to feel really at home on Mars? Or would the need for something deserving to be called home perhaps have disappeared?

---

[243] Elon Musk, "Making Humans a Multi-Planetary Species," *New Space*, Vol. 5, No. 2, Commentary, Published Online:1 Jun 2017https://doi.org/10.1089/space.2017.29009.emu

Heidegger liked to quote a line by the poet Hölderlin that we discussed in an earlier chapter: *"Kolonie liebt und tapfer Vergessen der Geist,"* "the spirit loves colony and brave forgetting."[244] The poet touches here not only on the importance, but also on the difficulty of forgetting what was left behind. Only such difficulty lets the poet call such forgetting "brave." We find it difficult to let go of the past; is it not our past that provides needed orientation and an idea of home? In the poet's saying nostalgia and a desire to forget intersect. A presupposition of the founding of a colony is that what once was home left those venturing into the unknown somehow dissatisfied. The founders wanted a different life. And yet the home that left them dissatisfied nevertheless continued to claim them. That Musk envisions pizza joints in his Martian city is telling. Again and again, colonies have sought to translate the image of the home left behind into the new environment, enacting a contest between nostalgia and the need to forget. Nostalgia shows us thus two faces, one oriented to the past, the other to the future; one seeks to return home, the other is content to leave home a beautiful memory to be regained more splendidly in the future.

Dreams of leaving what was once home, to leave the place that nature and society have assigned to us behind, to establish in some other place a newer more humane mode of dwelling, to discover a new home, are as old as dreams of freedom. Is there perhaps a sense in which we all have to first leave home to establish our true home? But the latter will bear nevertheless many of the features of the home that was left behind. Think of paradise lost and regained.

The hyperbolic version of utopian dreams of some regained paradise, which yet bears many of the features of the paradise lost and left behind, is the gnostic understanding of this all too familiar earth as only seemingly our home, in truth a prison that denies us what we most profoundly desire: a more complete freedom. And does our technology not allow us, as his wings allowed Daedalus, to escape this labyrinth, this prison. We meet with a trace of such gnostic yearning in Musk's desire to make humanity into "a truly multi-planetary species." The dream of a redemption from this earth, of a return to an altogether different sort of existence, answers to the gnostic caricature of this world as a prison and we can speak today of a postmodern Gnosticism. It has found an extreme expression in more or less fantastic dreams of an escape from this world. Some of these dreams have led to self-destructive insanity: Might it not be possible to discover our true home somewhere out there, perhaps in the form of a spaceship hidden in the tale of a comet, as not too many years ago, a sect

---

[244] Cf. Martin Heidegger, *"Andenken," Erläuterungen zu Hölderlins Dichtung*, GA4, pp. 89–94; *Hölderlins Hymne "Andenken,"* GA 52, pp. 189–191; *Hölderlins Hymne "Der Ister,"* pp. 156–170.

with the seductive name "Heaven's Gate" believed. Unshaken in their faith in beneficent UFO's, these cult members were willing to sacrifice their lives on earth to the illusory promise of heavenly bliss. On March 26, 1997, when the comet Hale Bopp was as its brightest, the police discovered 39 bodies of members of this cult who had committed suicide in the expectation of a better life. Unfortunately this sort of fanaticism is more common than one would like. Think of the Anabaptists of Münster (1534–1535), who expected their city to become the Heavenly Jerusalem, only to be annihilated by the world they would leave behind.

But given the way this earth is becoming ever less homelike, in good part because of the demands an ever more demanding and still increasing humanity has placed on it, isn't it time to think of founding colonies in space, one of Elon Musk's stated goals, whose company SpaceX is supposed to facilitate such colonization and to "help humanity establish a permanent, self-sustaining colony on [Mars] within the next 50 to 100 years."[245]

Long before astronautics became a reality, when it was little more than a fantasy in the heads of a few astronoetic dreamers,—I owe the word "astronoetic" to Hans Blumenberg, to whom I shall turn in our next chapter—dreamers who rely on their reason and imagination to carry them through space while they remain safely ensconced at home, the progress of astronomy and more generally of science has called into question the aura the earth once enjoyed as the unique center of our lives. Consider yet one more time Nietzsche's questioning lament that ever since Copernicus "The self-diminution of man, his will to self-diminution," seems to be "in an unstoppable progress." This statement is from the *Genealogy of Morals*, where Nietzsche also writes that "Since Copernicus, man seems to have got himself on an inclined plane – now he is slipping faster and faster away from the center into – what? into nothingness? into a penetrating sense of his own nothingness?"[246] Essentially the same thought returns in the posthumous notes later fashioned into the book *Will to Power*.

But is that loss of the center only a loss? Is it not also a gain, a gain in freedom? We may be enthralled by the place-establishing *genius loci* of some old-world community. But would we really want to live in such a place? What kind of a homecoming can do justice to our desire for freedom?

---

[245] Wikipedia article "Colonization of Mars," https://en.wikipedia.org/wiki/Colonization_of_Mars

[246] Friedrich Nietzsche, *On the Genealogy of Morals and Ecce Homo*, Walter Kaufmann and R. J. Hollingdale (Trans.), (New York: Vintage, 1989), p. 155.

4 Looking at the Stars

Earlier I mentioned the story of Thales, who, looking up in wonder at the stars above, falls into a well. Hans Blumenberg calls it the "*Urgeschichte der Theorie,*" a story that illuminates the very origin of theory.[247] The philosopher's mind is not in the place he happens to occupy. It is in some other place. Was that Thracian maid for whom Thales no eyes not right to mock him for his absent-mindedness? What could Thales hope to find up there in that starry realm the Greeks thought inaccessible? What did the stars matter to Thales? What do they matter to us?

Vitruvius may also have thought of the story about Thales when in his account of the origin of building he comes to speak of what distinguishes his proto-humans from such building animals as ants and bees, swallows and badgers. What he mentions in first place is not their extraordinary ability to use their hands, nor their capacity to imitate, learn from, and improve on what they observe, but their verticality, their upright posture, which lets them rise up from the horizontal earth, raise their eyes up from the supporting ground and "gaze upon the splendor of the starry firmament."[248] Did the sublime spectacle of the starry sky awaken the spirit sleeping in Vitruvius' proto-humans, somewhat as the snake's promise, "you will be like God," opened the eyes of Adam and Eve? Did it awaken them at the same time to their own time-bound existence, to their mortality, even as eye and spirit, open to the firmament's apparently unchanging order, let them dream of a more perfect, more genuinely humane dwelling, not subject to the terror of time?

In the introduction to Book II, Vitruvius disclaims originality for his account of the origin of building, acknowledging, without naming, his debt to "those writers who have devoted treatises to the origins of civilization and the investigation of inventions."[249] The most important of these would appear to have been Cicero's teacher, the Stoic Posidonius.[250] Vitruvius' description of the human being as the being who looks up to the firmament is at any rate quite in keeping with the Greek understanding of the human being as *zoon lógon échon*, which becomes the Latin *animal rationale*. As the animal that possesses

---

[247] Hans Blumenberg, *Das Lachen der Thrakerin: Eine Urgeschichte der Theorie*, (Frankfurt am Main: Suhrkamp 1987).
[248] Vitruvius, *The Ten Books of Architecture*, Morris Hickey Morgan (Trans.), (New York: Dover, 1960), book 2, chap. 1, 1, p. 38.
[249] Vitruvius, *The Ten Books of Architecture*, Morris Hickey Morgan (Trans.), (New York: Dover, 1960), book 2, chap. 1, 1, p. 37.
[250] Wilhelm Poppe, *Vitruvs Quellen zum zweiten Buche 'de architectura.'* Dissertation, Kiel, 1909.

reason, the human being is the intersection of horizontal temporality and a vertical linking time to eternity: the *erecti homines*, the upright human beings, are not bound to their particular place, as are the *prona animalia*, the prone animals. Standing up and gazing at the firmament, admiring its order, the human being transcends his or her natural place. In the *Phaedrus* Plato thus attributes wings to the soul. Our winged soul lets us dream of flying, dream of leaving behind this terrestrial prison. Think once more of Daedalus and Icarus and their waxen wings. Balloons, airplanes, and now spaceships have offered themselves as more potent figures of liberation to us moderns, symbols of "a freedom that always had meant not being fettered to the earthly, even if that was thought as transmigration of souls or ascent to heaven."[251]

Related to the Greek *zoon lógon échon* is the Biblical understanding of human beings as beings who, created in the image of God, look up to God and thus transcend themselves as earth-bound creatures, measuring themselves by the idea of a timeless, eternal logos. As I have tried to show, every attempt to speak the truth is witness to such self-transcendence, for when I claim truth for what I have to say, I claim more than that this is how I now happen to see some matter: the truth I claim is in principle open to all. When I claim, correctly let us assume, that right now, at this specific time, there are seventeen people in this room, I also claim that what I assert, will never become false. It will never be the case that at this particular time there were not seventeen people in this room. All claims to truth are made *sub specie aeternitatis*.

To be sure, from the very beginning the pursuit of truth has been shadowed by that warning of Simonides, cited already by Aristotle, that the truth about reality will ever elude us human knowers. But even if Simonides should prove right and absolute truth should prove to be the property of God alone—such mundane truths as in my example presumably do not count as the kind of knowledge in question—the mere attempt to speak the truth is sufficient to show that we do indeed look up to and measure ourselves by a timeless, placeless logos, belonging to no one or to all.

The question remains, however, is that theoretical impulse that attempts to seize the truth about reality just because we want to know, one that deflects us from our true vocation, or is it one that fulfills it? The question is whether that theoretical curiosity in which philosophy has its origin is legitimate. Once again Aristotle set the stage for subsequent discussion:

---

251 Hans Blumenberg, *Die Vollzähligkeit der Sterne*, 2nd ed. (Frankfurt am Main: Suhrkamp, 1997), p. 110.

> Hence also the possession of it (genuine knowledge, absolute truth) might be justly regarded as beyond human power; for in many ways human knowledge is in bondage, so that according to Simonides, 'God alone can have this privilege', and it is unfitting that man should not be content to seek the knowledge that is suited to him. If then there is something in what the poets say, and jealousy is natural to the divine power, it would probably occur in this case above all, and all who excelled in this knowledge would be unfortunate.[252]

It is easy to imagine a Christian theologian reading this with approval. Man's present condition is subject to the fall and its consequences. Among these consequences are also epistemological ones: our sight and intellect are no longer those of Adam in paradise. And was it not even in Adam's case a presumption that let him listen to the snake's promise, *eritis sicut Deus*, to think that human beings might know as only God knows?

But Aristotle is of a different mind. He raises the question of the legitimacy of theory only to dismiss it:

> But the divine power cannot be jealous (nay, according to the proverb, 'bards tell many a lie'), nor should any other science be thought more honorable than one of this sort. For the most divine science is also the most honorable; and this science alone must be, in two ways, most divine. For the science which it would be most meet for God to have is a divine science; and so is any science that deals with divine subjects....[253]

In late Antiquity we meet more and more often with voices that see in the desire for such knowledge just another desire that must meet with disappointment. Epicurus and Lucretius would rid us of such an exaggerated demand for knowledge. Cognitive resignation is seen as a precondition of happiness. But more important for us is Augustine's critique of the desire to know. A key text is Book X of the *Confessions*. Recall that the authors of the *Condemnation of 1277* followed Augustine.

> To this is added another form of temptation more manifoldly dangerous. For besides the concupiscence of the flesh which consisteth of the delight of all the senses and pleasures, wherein its slaves, who go far from Thee, waste and perish, the soul hath, through the same senses of the body a certain vain and curious desire, veiled under the title of knowledge and learning, not of delighting the flesh, but of making experiments through the flesh. The seat

---

[252] Aristotle, *The Complete Works of Aristotle, The Revised Oxford Translation*, Jonathan Barnes (Ed.), 2 vols, (Princeton: Princeton University Press, 1984), *Metaphysics*, I, 982b28–683a1.
[253] Ibid., 983a13–6.

whereof being in the appetite of knowledge, and sight being the sense chiefly used for attaining knowledge, it is in Divine language called lust of the eyes.[254]

Here we have the Christian counter-position to the Aristotelian: all men by nature desire to know. We are curious creatures. Augustine might add, perhaps, but if so, then only because nature has been corrupted by the fall, by sin. "From this disease of curiosity are all those strange sights exhibited in the theater. Hence men go out to search out the hidden powers of nature (which is besides our end), which to know profits not, and wherein men desire nothing but to know."[255]

Such sentiments lead easily to a celebration of the person who remains simple, free of the false learning of the philosophers, content with the knowledge suited to our earth-bound condition. The claim to truth was thus understood again and again as the illegitimate appropriation of something that belongs to God. It is in this context that we have to understand Descartes' attempt to interpret his method as a divine gift and that what he has to teach is a practical, not a theoretical science.

But if the fall has to be thought of only negatively, why is paradise regained placed above paradise lost? Why do Augustine and Thomas Aquinas speak of *felix culpa*, of the fortunate fall? The Christian understanding of the fall is thus profoundly ambiguous.

The Christian suspicion of theory could and often did claim Socrates for a pagan precursor. Had not Socrates renounced his youthful excursions into the philosophy of nature and regretted such thinking that neglected the needs of the soul. When the 15th century cardinal Cusanus celebrates learned ignorance and calls the Socratic main figure of several of his dialogues an *idiota*, an untutored, unread person, but of sound common sense, he follows that theme. Cusanus certainly is suspicious of the tradition-bound learning that too often prevented openness to what needed to be thought. But the suspicion of theory as pursued in the universities is only one theme with him. More important is another, which, following Aristotle, makes the desire to know constitutive of our humanity and then goes on to legitimate that desire by saying that since God instilled in us this desire it cannot be vain. It must be capable of finding the knowledge appropriate to it, which includes importantly a knowledge of the limits of our reason. We need to become learned about our ignorance. The gulf that

---

[254] Augustine, *Confessions*, Edward B. Pusey (Trans.), (New York: Modern Library, 1949), Book X, pp. 231–232.
[255] Ibid., p. 232.

separates our finite understanding from God and his infinite creation will not be bridged. Not that we human beings should therefore renounce scientific inquiry, even though it can only approximate and never seize divine truth.

With Cusanus we find ourselves on the threshold of Renaissance humanism. Although looking back, one might also say that Cusanus is attempting to reconcile Augustine and Thomas Aquinas, according to whom, translating Aristotle into a Christian context, *omnis scientia bona est*, all science is good.

I pointed to the Bible, which teaches us to understand the human being as created in the image of God. But the Bible accompanies this account with a warning: did the promise of the snake's *eritis sicut deus* not mislead Adam and Eve and lead to their expulsion from that paradise that had assigned them their proper pace. Once man had been expelled from paradise, he sought to compensate himself in different ways for what he had lost. This led Cain to build the first city and his descendants to become the inventors of all sorts of arts and crafts. The snake's seductive promise invites us to ponder the danger slumbering in human verticality, to consider whether, as already Simonides feared, the self-elevation of the human being that is inseparable from the search for truth will not cost us our earthly home and lead to our destruction. Think once more of Icarus, who seduced by the splendor of the light of the sun flew higher and higher until the heat melted the wax of his wings and sent him plunging into the sea. The story of the tower of Babel varies what is at bottom the same theme.

5 The Disenchanted World

As pointed out, the progress of science, more especially the progress of astronomy, invites us to consider our earth a spaceship, floating through endless space, resembling ever less a house raised on firm foundations in which everything has its proper place. Objectively looked at, we are just an insignificant speck in the universe. We encountered this changed understanding of the world already in Kant's *Critique of Practical Reason:* "The first sight, of a countless multitude of worlds, annihilates, as it were, my importance as an *animal creature* that, after having for a short time been provided (one knows not how) with vital force, must give back again to the planet (a mere dot in the universe) the matter from which it came."[256] Schopenhauer begins the second volume of *The World as Will and Representation* with essentially the same reflection: "In endless space

---

[256] Immanuel Kant, *Kritik der praktischen Vernunft*, A288; *The Critique of Practical Reason*, Werner S. Pluhar (Trans.), (Indianapolis: Hackett, 2002), p. 203.

countless luminous spheres, round each of which some dozen smaller illuminated ones revolve, hot at the core and covered with a hard cold crust; on this crust a moldy film has produced living and knowing beings; this is empirical truth, the real, the world.[257] In "On Truth and Lie" Nietzsche, as we saw, was to appropriate that sentiment: "Once upon a time, in some out of the way corner of that universe which is dispersed into numberless twinkling solar systems, there was a star upon which clever beasts invented knowing. That was the most arrogant and mendacious minute of 'world history,' but nevertheless, it was only a minute. After nature had drawn a few breaths, the star cooled and congealed, and the clever beasts had to die" (TL 79).

And can the substance of this empirical truth be challenged? The world that our science has uncovered does not care for us. These heavens do not declare the glory of God. Researchers such as Drew McDermott are right: of values, God, or freedom science can have no knowledge. For such things there is no room in its logical space. And it is not just science that threatens to strip reality of meaning. As Friedrich Heinrich Jacobi already knew, every attempt to fully comprehend all that is has to lead to nihilism, where this nihilism may well lead in turn to also typically modern attempts to reoccupy the now vacant center with some human construction, where I am thinking especially of attempts to endow art with a religious significance, but also of that second religiosity, as Oswald Spengler called it, which today is making attempts to give new life to a religion increasingly left behind by the progress of science.[258] And in this connection we should not forget the quasi-religious appeal of totalitarian ideologies. It is impossible to understand the success of National Socialism if one fails to consider its exploitation of the death of God.

A very different response to nihilism is given by the existentialist or postmodern affirmations of this loss of the center: does this loss not promise us human beings an altogether new freedom? Are we human beings, possessing reason, not able and permitted to be the center of our concerns, in the face of the scientifically conditioned and again and again repeated loss of all sorts of different centers? Hasn't man been said to be the measure of all things. The rediscovery of the profundity of this saying by Protagoras by Alberti and Cusanus helps mark the beginning of a distinctly modern humanism.[259] To be sure, a

---

[257] Arthur Schopenhauer, *The World as Will and Representation*, vol. 2, E. F. J. Payne (Trans.), (New York: Dover, 1966), p. 3.
[258] Oswald Spengler, *Der Untergang des Abendlandes*, 2 vols, (München: Beck, 1923), vol. 2, pp. 280–281.
[259] See Karsten Harries, *Infinity and Perspective* (Cambridge, MA: MIT Press, 2001), pp. 184–199.

whole series of Copernican revolutions has called the place of man near the center into question. I am thinking not so much of Kant's Copernican revolution, which, while it denied the human knower a knowledge of things in themselves, yet placed him at the very center of the world of phenomena. Bertrand Russell had good reason to suggest that Kant would have been more nearly right, had he spoken of a Ptolemaic counter-revolution, since he attempted to restore the human knower to that central place from which Copernicus had dethroned him.[260] As a matter of fact, Kant himself does not use the expression "Copernican revolution," although what he says, certainly invites talk of his having effected a Copernican revolution. But we cannot dismiss Russell's objection. Not that talk of a Ptolemaic counter-revolution quite fits. But Kant did attribute to the human subject a central part in the constitution of the world of phenomena that invites talk of a distinctly modern anthropocentrism. This is even more true of Kant's ethics.

But when I spoke of Copernican revolutions that entailed a loss of the center, I was thinking not so much of Kant as of the Darwinian revolution, which invites us to understand ourselves in the image of the ape rather than that of God; or of that of Freud, which would have us understand our proud consciousness as a plaything of unconscious drives that prevent us from being master in our own home; or of a materialist approach such as that endorsed by McDermott, which has no place for a self at all. But as did already the Copernican revolution, as did Kant, all these revolutions presuppose a faith in the ability of human reason to take the measure of reality. In this sense they all invite talk of a modern anthropocentrism.

And have these revolutions really robbed us of our earthly home? Admittedly, there is a sense in which not only astronautics, but more fundamentally our whole science has left the human being behind, so far behind that at times the person seems to have become all but invisible. But our life-world, even if increasingly shaped by technology, cannot be understood as the technical world-picture that Heidegger likes to invoke. "The Age of the World Picture" remains a caricature that seizes on much that is essential; but fortunately it remains a caricature. And in this spirit we can say of astronautics and our science that, while they may have left us behind, they left us still at home, have left us our home, even if that home may no longer be able to shelter us quite as effectively—or should we say suffocatingly?—as in former times. That we find ourselves still at home on this endangered earth may disappoint dreamers of journeys to some sublime realm

---

[260] Bertrand Russell, *Human Knowledge, Its Scope and Limits* (New York: Simon and Schuster, 1948), p. 9.

somewhere beyond the earth or those who hope that some technological utopia will finally fulfill the promise of paradise.

The progress of astronomy and astronautics has indeed contributed to the disenchantment of the world. Looking up the stars, Vitruvius's original human beings felt themselves to be looking up to the manifestation of a timeless logos that provided their building here on earth with a measure. Not so very different was the way the medievals still experienced the sky above. Do we today still have a similar experience when we look up to the stars? What do the stars, rendered ever less visible by air- and light-pollution, still have to tell us? Is the artificial light that allows us to transform night into day not light enough? And must something similar not be said of the light of our human reason, that *lumen naturale* that our science would have us understand not so much as a gift, but as a product of a mindless necessity? What need is there for God?

Still, the need not to feel alone in the universe, to experience at least traces of some other intelligence out there, has outlived the destruction of the geocentric world picture, outlived also the death of God effected by science. And does our science not demand that there be intelligent extraterrestrial beings? As old as the modern world picture, which would have us look at the earth as a by no means unique star, is the expectation that sooner or later we would encounter intelligent extraterrestrials. Thus Nicolaus Cusanus, who already in the 15th century envisioned an infinite universe and denied the earth its central position, thus denying the cosmos its house-like character, also played with the thought of intelligent inhabitants of other heavenly bodies, e.g., the moon, a thought that kept returning again and again, so with Bruno and Kepler; and even the so enlightened Kant thought higher beings, perhaps reborn, more spiritual humans, inhabited the outer planets.[261] And even if such expectations have been disappointed over and over, are they not justified by our science, which would have us understand intelligent life as the product of natural processes, beginning with the big bang, even if the details remain unknown for the time being? From the very beginning, it would seem, nature had to give birth to spirit. Given this vast universe, is it not just another anthropocentric prejudice to think that intelligent life should have evolved just once, just on this earth? Science has no place for what is unique. Whatever it comprehends must be in principle reproducible.

Unfortunately, this planetary system has proved extremely inhospitable, with the one exception of our earth. That we recently should have discovered

---

[261] Immanuel Kant, *Allgemeine Naturgeschichte und Theorie des Himmels oder Versuch von der Verfassung und dem mechanischen Ursprunge des ganzen Weltgebäudes nach Newtonischen Grundsätzen abgehandelt*, A185.

traces of water on the moon and on Mars even a lake submerged under the ice is only mildly reassuring: no trace of any inhabitants! And even if our astronomers with their telescopes are looking deeper and deeper into and that means also back into the history of the universe, the hoped for or perhaps feared extraterrestrial beings have still not made a peep. And with every astronomical und astronautic progress the conviction grows that for all practical purposes we are alone. Even if somewhere out there, there should be intelligent beings, curious or compassionate enough, or perhaps just stupid enough, to seek to make contact with us, the cosmic distances make it ever more improbable that we shall ever be in a position to engage in a conversation with these unknown beings, whom we dread and yet somehow desire. We don't have the necessary time. And thus it is not at all surprising that the valentine that we sent on August 20, 1977 with the space craft Voyager 2 into space, with an unknown address, including a gold-plated audio-visual disk, crammed with representative music, information about life on this earth, greetings in 60 languages, including Latin, including also a playing device and easy to follow instructions, despite all that effort, remained without an answer. 1989 it passed Neptune.[262] Today it is in the outermost layer of the heliosphere, about to enter interstellar space. It still is sending us valuable information about the extremities of our solar system. But still no answer. We seem to be alone. Was all the effort worth it?

Why did we visit the moon? Just because it has for so long been such a striking presence and suddenly it became possible to pay our nightly companion a visit? Because of that curiosity, that desire to know that Augustine condemned as lust of the eyes, as *concupiscentia*? This desire to know just in order to know is indeed part of the human essence. Again and again our curiosity will lead us beyond what is familiar and its perspectives, let us journey away from home to distant parts, to what fascinates just because it is unfamiliar, even if it may threaten shipwreck and disaster. But is not the possibility of disaster part of the fascination?

Human curiosity will repeat the loss of paradise over and over. The pursuit of truth demands objectivity. Objectivity again demands that we transform our world, this world that still provides us first of all and most of the time with something like a home, into a world that does not know anything like home and whose time lets the time of our life shrink to almost nothing. Nihilism is the price to be paid for the pursuit of objective truth.

---

262 See Hans Blumenberg, *Die Vollzähligkeit der Sterne*, 2nd ed. (Frankfurt am Main: Suhrkamp, 1997), pp. 501–504.

XII Astronoetics

1 What is Astronoetics?

In the preceding chapter I mentioned "astronoetics" – What did I mean by that word? What is "astronoetics?" An explanation is needed. I found the word in Hans Blumenberg's *Die Vollzähligkeit der Sterne*,[263] a posthumously published collection of reflections written down in the course of three decades that all circle around the concept of theory, more precisely in its last section, which bears the title: *Was ist Astronoetik?* "What is astronoetics?" Blumenberg begins that section by telling us that, had he not lacked the taste for dedications, he would have dedicated this book to Wolfgang Bargmann, a well-known brain anatomist, good at writing grant proposals, who urged his colleagues at the university of Kiel to do likewise. That was in 1958. As I mentioned in the preceding chapter, the first sputnik had been launched the year before and was generating widespread consternation that Russian astronautics had left the West behind. Bargmann did his best to encourage his colleagues to take advantage of this situation and help eliminate this intolerable *Forschungsrückstand*, this research lag, by formulating and submitting grant proposals. Blumenberg knew of course that pure thinking is a breadless art, notwithstanding the story about Thales cornering the olive market, a story meant no doubt to show that philosophers, too, can be quite practical and worldly, should they only wish to be so. Blumenberg did not quite respond this way when pressured to make his contribution to the effort to help the West catch up with the Russians. But he decided to do his bit by at least simulating his colleague's concern. And so he, too, wrote a grant proposal, requesting unspecified financial support for an investigation of the then still invisible backside of the moon by pure thought alone—also a comment on quite a bit of philosophy, The results were to be published in a journal to be called *Current Topics in Astronoetics*. Thus astronoetics received its name. As Blumenberg no doubt expected, his proposal did not receive the requested funding. The prehistory of astronoetics, to be sure, goes back at least to Thales. Philosophy and astronoetics have indeed the same origin.

In 1958 few suspected that it would not be so very long until the backside of the moon would be photographed and astronauts actually land on the moon. Astronautics would seem to have left astronoetics behind, just as the progress of science would seem to have left much philosophy behind. Has philosophy not

---

[263] Hans Blumenberg, *Die Vollzähligkeit der Sterne*, 2nd ed. (Frankfurt am Main: Suhrkamp, 1997).

long claimed as its own the white spots left on the maps we are furnished by science, their whiteness an irresistible invitation to pure thinking and imagining to take flight? The number of such spots, however, is shrinking.

But, as Blumenberg reminds us, "'Astronoetics' is called so not just as an alternative to 'astronautics'—to think of instead of actually travelling somewhere. 'Astronoetics' also names the thoughtful consideration of whether, and if so, just what sense it would make to travel there. It could be that even after a successful roundtrip, the question whether the effort had been worthwhile could not be decided."[264] Astronoetics, so understood, does not just precede, but also follows astronautics. In Blumenberg's astronoetics centrifugal curiosity is balanced by centripetal care for the earth. And so understood astronoetics may well deserve funding after all. By occasionally pouring cold water on projects that might take many billions to realize, billions perhaps better spent in other ways, astronoetics might make an important contribution to human welfare.

2 Loss of the Center

In the age of astronautics, is there really a need for this questionable discipline, astronoetics? Astronautics here can also serve as a metaphor for technology. Closely related thus is the question: in the age of technology and the science that supports it, is there still a need for philosophy? Confronted with the serious work of the scientist, is insistence on the breadless and all too often seemingly pointless activity of pure thinking not difficult to defend?

Blumenberg understood himself and invites us late moderns to understand ourselves as those left at home by astronautics and just because of this in need of astronoetics. Left at home!—That may suggest regret at having been left behind by those more venturesome and daring. The wondrous discoveries that awaited the astronauts are denied to us who remained stuck here on earth. And have the practitioners of astronoetics not been left in speculative dust by the progress of astronautics? But more needs to be said: despite repeated trips to the moon, in a fundamental sense astronautics has left all of us, and that includes Neil Armstrong and his fellow astronauts, at home here on earth, perhaps to wonder whether the effort to leave it was worth it.

To point out that astronautics has left us at home is more than a trivial platitude. The observation may be tinged by regret, for dreams of leaving home, that

---

[264] Hans Blumenberg, *Die Vollzähligkeit der Sterne*, 2nd ed. (Frankfurt am Main: Suhrkamp, 1997), p. 320.

2 Loss of the Center — 201

place assigned us by our nature and history, for some much more wonderful future, have long been part of dreams of freedom, gnostic dreams that invite us to look at this world into which we have been cast as a world that withholds what we deeply desire, not really a home at all, but more like a prison. And is science not finally allowing us to escape this prison? Think of the concept artist Mireille Suzanne Francette Porte, who called herself herself Sainte Orlan: With the help of plastic surgery and psychoanalysis she wanted to make herself into a new person. Orlan called her work "a struggle against the innate, the inexorable, the programmed, Nature, DNA (which is our direct rival as far as artists of representation are concerned), and God!"[265] A gnostic discontent with the place we are assigned by nature here finds particularly striking expression. The project of making oneself into another person is of course self-contradictory and doomed to fail. But it does raise a serious question: What limits are set to human self-manipulation? And here I am interested not so much in in the factual limits imposed by the current state of medical technology, as in what finally is a problem of ethics: If this were possible, should any person be able to make him- or herself into whatever person they might choose to be? If not, what are the constraints?

And there is that other, but related question: What limits are set to our manipulation of the earth? Is our earth more than a reservoir of materials to be used by us as we see fit? The other side of the gnostic understanding of our body and of this earth as prisons are dreams of escaping such prisons, of a homecoming to an altogether different, freer form of existence that our technology will open up for us. Blumenberg warns us not be seduced by such dreams.

Long before astronautics became a reality, when it was still no more than a dream of astronoetics, the progress of astronomy, and more generally of science, had already made this earth seem ever less homelike—as Blumenberg put it, *dieses Dasein wollte nicht gemütlicher werden*[266]— inadequately translated as "our being in this world did not want to become more comfortable" —where this *wollte nicht, "did not want to,"* is somewhat ambiguous in that it suggests both a progress in which we find ourselves caught up and something we ourselves will and for which we bear responsibility. This growing *Ungemütlichkeit*[267] finds expression in Nietzsche's earlier cited lament that since Copernicus we seem to be slipping ever faster away from every center into nothingness?[268] As

---

265 "Orlan", From *Wikipedia*, the free encyclopedia.
266 Ibid.
267 If *Gemütlichkeit* could be translated as "coziness," "comfortableness" or "hominess," *Ungemütlichkeit* suggessts the opposite.
268 Friedrich Nietzsche, *On the Genealogy of Morals and Ecce Homo*, Walter Kaufmann and R. J. Hollingdale (Trans.), (New York: Vintage, 1989), p. 155.

Nietzsche understands it, the modern world is shadowed by what the conservative art historian Hans Sedlmayr lamented as the *Verlust der Mitte*,[269] the loss of the center, of a measure able to provide our lives with the needed orientation; or, we can say, shadowed by the death of humanism. But is this loss, like the loss of paradise, not a price that we have to pay to become truly of age, to realize the promise of our freedom? Is it not constitutive of humanity come of age, as the Biblical story of the fall hints?

As Heidegger points out, our understanding of what makes a person a person is indebted to the Greek and Christian conception. Even when efforts are made to think beyond it, such efforts nevertheless remain tied to it. What then is this conception? The human being is understood as:

(1) *zoon lógon échon* (GA2, 65; SZ, 48),

(2) created in God's image (GA2, 65; SZ 48)

The second formulation especially recognizes that human being is constituted by transcendence: thinking of himself as created in the image of God, man transcends himself. Quoting Calvin and Zwingli, Heidegger remarks:

> The idea of transcendence, according to which man is more than a mere something endowed with intelligence, has worked itself out with different variations. The following quotations will illustrate how these have originated; '*His praeclaris dotibus excelluit prima hominis conditio, ut ratio, intelligentia, prudentia, judicium non modo ad terrenae vitae gubernationem suppeterent, sed quibus transcenderet usque ad Deum et aeternam felicitatem.*' ['Man's first condition was excellent because of these outstanding endowments: that reason, intelligence, prudence, judgment should suffice not only for the government of this earthly life, but that by them he might *ascend beyond* even unto God and to eternal felicity.'] *Denn dass der mensch sin ufsehen hat uf Gott und sin wort, zeigt er klarlich an, dass er nach siner natur etwas Gott näher anerborn, etwas mee nachschlägt, etwas zuzugs zu jm hat, das alles on zwyfel darus flüsst, dass er nach dem bildnus Gottes geschaffen ist.* ['Because man looks up to God and his Word, he indicates clearly that in his very Nature he is born somewhat closer to God, is something more *after his stamp*, that he has something that *draws him to God* — all this comes beyond a doubt from his having been created in God's image.'] (GA2, 66; SZ, 49. Translations by the translators of SZ in brackets).

Just as Vitruvius understands man as the animal that looks up to the timeless firmament, Calvin and Zwingli understand man as drawn to God. Created in the image of God, man is here said to transcend himself.

But we do not need to posit the existence of God to account for the human power of self-transcendence. Even if we hold with Nietzsche that God is a fiction,

---

269 Hans Sedlmayr, *Der Verlust der Mitte* (Munich: Ullstein, 1959).

that man created God in his own image, that fiction testifies to the human power of self-transcendence, implicit in the Greek understanding of man as the animal that possesses logos. That very possession made Adam and Eve susceptible to the snake's promise and let them lose paradise, a loss human beings have repeated over and over again. And, to return to Nietzsche's lament, is our modern world not especially shadowed by this loss of the center?

3 Postmodern Levity

But to repeat the counter-question: should this loss of the center be understood just as a loss? Is it not rather something that raises us above our animal desires? Recall Ortega y Gasset's characterization of the human being as the being that has fallen out of and lost its place in nature, ever discontented, seeking things it had never had. And this restlessness Ortega called what is highest in the human being. Technology is said to have its origin in this discontent, which has us press ever forward, seeking to satisfy ever new, emerging needs.

Ortega celebrates this restlessness. We do not meet here with the kind of longing for lost plenitude that we meet with in Heidegger. Jean-François Lyotard might thus have opposed Heidegger's modernism to Ortega's postmodernism. Like Ortega, Lyotard challenged the nostalgic longing for some lost center or plenitude, which he associated with modernism, opposing to modernist nostalgia postmodernism's joyful embrace of endless innovation.[270] What homecoming could satisfy our freedom?

According to Lyotard, modernism, and he is thinking here first of all of artistic modernism, is born of a longing for lost reality. "Modernity, whenever it appears, does not occur without a shattering of belief, without a discovery of the lack of reality in reality, – a discovery linked to the invention of other realities."[271] The artist's fictions are to compensate us for a reality experienced as somehow less weighty, less real than it should be.

Lyotard's talk of reality's lack of reality presupposes that in an important sense reality has not been lost. And how could it have been lost? First of all and most of the time we do not doubt our body's reality, the reality of those we live with, of the things we encounter. How then are we to understand reality's

---

[270] Jean-François Lyotard, "Answer to the Question: What is the Postmodern," in *The Postmodern Explained* (Minneapolis: University of Minnesota Press, 1993), p. 13.
[271] Ibid., p. 9.

"lack of reality," this background condition of what Lyotard takes to be a modernist sensibility.

Lyotard hints at the answer when he claims that modern art longs for "the all and the one, for a reconciliation of the concept and the sensible, for a transparent and communicable experience,"[272] longs for the incarnation of what can be thought and dreamed of in what can be seen and experienced, an incarnation so complete it would absorb us in a way that would leave no room for questions such as: What is this work about? What does it mean? Absorption and presence have thus become key words in discussions of modernist painting. Much here recalls Schopenhauer. Modern art appears here as just one expression of modernity's unhappy consciousness, unhappy precisely because never quite at home in the world, with things, which it projects against a background of a dream of plenitude that renders whatever happens to be the case arbitrary and contingent. Full presence would defeat arbitrariness and contingency. Nostalgia for lost plenitude, lost presence, is on this view the dominant mood of modern art. Consider Hofmannsthal's Lord Chandos, or Wittgenstein's *Tractatus*. In related fashion the painter Frank Stella dreamed of an art so lean, accurate, and right that it would allow us just to look at it.[273] This would allow the observer to become a pure eye, would let us experience the artwork as a presence no longer haunted by unfulfilled possibilities, by absent meaning. "Presentness is grace," Michael Fried wrote of such art, finding in the grace offered us by the modern artist the secular *Ersatz* for the sacred denied to us.[274] But Fried's hope for such *Ersatz* grace is vain: never will the painting be lean enough. It will always still mean something, even if it means only to present itself as simply being. Thus we experience the painting as a presentation of a finally unpresentable presence. To use Lyotard's language: the artwork seeks to show "that there is something we can conceive of, which we can neither see nor show."[275] Just this, according to Lyotard, "is at stake in modern painting." This formulation is close to Kant's characterization of the sublime which is said to present itself to the eye in such a way that reason is forced to think of the infinite as given in its entirety.[276] But this remains a mere idea that haunts

---

[272] Ibid., p. 16.
[273] "Questions to Stella and Judd," Interview with Bruce Glaser, edited by Lucy R. Lippard, *Minimal Art. A Critical Anthology*, Gregory Battcock (Ed.), (New York: Dutton, 1968), pp. 157-158.
[274] Michael Fried, "Art and Objecthood," *Minimal Art: A Critical Anthology*, Gregory Battcock (Ed.), (New York: E. P. Dutton, 1968), p. 147.
[275] Lyotard, "Answer to the Question: What is the Postmodern," p. 11.
[276] Immanuel Kant, *Critique of Judgment*, Werner Pluhar (Trans.), (Indianapolis: Hackett, 1987), p. 111.

the presentation. The presentness that would mean grace according to Fried remains absent.

That Lyotard should invoke the Kantian category of the sublime to characterize the vain pursuit of the presentation of a reality that remains unpresentable is not surprising. But we should note that the pursuit of presence demanded by Fried of a truly modern art had long been associated with the term beauty. Consider once more Frank Stella's statement of his goals as a painter, a statement quite in keeping with the self-sufficiency demanded of the beautiful at least since Alexander Gottlieb Baumgarten.[277]

> I always get into arguments with people who want to retain the old values in painting, the humanistic values that they always find on the canvas. If you pin them down, they always end up asserting that there is something there besides the paint on the canvas. My painting is based on the fact that only what can be seen is there. It really is an object. Any painting is an object and anyone who gets involved enough in this finally has to face up to the objectness of whatever he's doing. He is making a thing. All that should be taken for granted. If the painting were lean enough, accurate enough, or right enough, you would just be able to look at it. All I want anyone to get out of my paintings, and all that I ever get out of them, is the fact that you can see the whole idea without confusion.... What you see is what you see.[278]

Stella does not seem at all concerned to show "that there is something we can conceive of, which we can neither see nor show." Quite the opposite. He means to create works that are experienced as simply present. Such a painting is not meant to point beyond itself, is not meant to be taken as either symbol or allegory. Its point is not to say something. It can therefore be neither true nor false. What matters here is not that the work point us towards a higher reality, but that it provide an occasion for a distinctive sort of enjoyment that does not require any justification outside itself. Supported by the central strand of philosophical aesthetics and art history, by Baumgarten, Kant, and Schopenhauer, by Panofsky and Fried, we can call such an approach to works of art as first of all occasions for pleasure, albeit pleasure of a quite distinctive kind, aesthetic. On this aesthetic understanding of beauty, the point of art is to provide us with experiences that bear their *telos* within themselves and are thus set off from the rest of life, which has been bracketed, distanced. The autotelic character of aesthetic experience thus understood is reflected in the understanding of the

---

[277] See Karsten Harries, *Art Matters: A Critical Commentary on Heidegger's The Origin of the Work of Art* (New York: Springer, 2009), pp. 1–2.
[278] "Questions to Stella and Judd," Interview with Bruce Glaser, edited by Lucy R. Lippard, *Minimal Art. A Critical Anthology*, Gregory Battcock (Ed.), (New York: Dutton, 1968), pp. 157–158.

work of art, which is to be a self-sufficient aesthetic object, a whole possessing the necessary closure.[279] So understood aesthetic experience is the experience of a plenitude lacking in our everyday dealings with reality, somewhat like an oasis in the desert of the world.

But Lyotard can point out that the beautiful work of art so understood is a fiction that may have haunted an artist such as Frank Stella or a critic such as Michael Fried,[280] but that resists realization. Modernist beauty does indeed invite us to understand it as a modification of the sublime. Here Lyotard's characterization of the aesthetics of sublime painting: "As painting, it will evidently 'present' something, but negatively. It will therefore avoid figuration or representation; it will be 'blank' [*blanche*] like one of Malevich's squares; it will make one see only by prohibiting one from seeing; it will give pleasure only by giving pain."[281] Modernist sensibility refuses representation and figuration because it senses in all that art might represent a lack of reality, an arbitrariness, an absence of what might make things weighty enough to be worthy of the artist's celebrating representation. But the weightiness it pursues must necessarily elude it.

But what has been called a lack of reality need not be understood as a lack at all. It may be considered an opportunity. This change in mood is said to characterize postmodernism, as Lyotard understands it. Postmodern art is understood as modern art that has shed the modernist nostalgia for plenitude and weightiness, for absorption and presence, for God and reality.

> If it is true that modernity unfolds in the retreat of the real and according to the sublime relationship of the presentable with the conceivable, we can (to use a musical idiom) distinguish two essential modes in this relationship. The accent can fall on the inadequacy of the faculty of presentation, on the nostalgia for presence experienced by the human subject and the obscure and futile will that animates it in spite of everything.[282]

But such nostalgia can also be shed:

> Or else the accent can fall on the power of the faculty to conceive, on what one might call its 'inhumanity' (a quality Apollinaire insists on in modern artists), since it is of no concern to the understanding whether or not the human sensibility or imagination accords with

---

[279] See Karsten Harries, *The Broken Frame. Three Lectures* (Washington: Catholic University Press, 1989).
[280] Cf. Michael Fried, "Art and Objecthood," *Minimal Art: A Critical Anthology*, Gregory Battcock (Ed.), (New York: E. P. Dutton, 1968), p.147: "Presenteness is grace."
[281] Lyotard, "Answer to the Question: What is the Postmodern," p. 11.
[282] Ibid., p. 13.

what it conceives—and on the extension of being and jubilation that come from inventing new rules of the game, whether pictorial, artistic, or something else."[283]

Within modern art Lyotard thus distinguishes two strands, one ruled by *melancholia,* melancholy, the other committed to *novatio,* innovation. Thus he opposes the German expressionists to Braque and Picasso, Malevich to the later Lissitzky, de Chirico to Duchamp. And thus we may want to oppose Stella to Rauschenberg or Anselm Kiefer to Gerhard Richter.

Postmodern art, and more generally, postmodernism, is said by Lyotard to have rid itself of that nostalgia for the lost center that governs modernism, nostalgia that still dreams of Mediterranean landscapes, of temples and Roman fountains, of laurel, roses, and oranges, of ruins haunted by the now absent gods. Turning its back on such nostalgia, postmodernism is glad to play, eager to explore whatever is new and unexpected, celebrating a freedom that refuses to recognize whatever boundaries are supposed to hold it as an increase in being and joy. Recall St. Orlan who called her work "a struggle against the innate, the inexorable, the programmed, Nature, DNA (which is our direct rival as far as artists of representation are concerned), and God!"

4 Icarus

A tendency towards self-displacement, a certain self-de-centering is, I have suggested, inseparably bound up with human freedom. I referred to the Biblical understanding of human being as created in the image of God. But this reference implies a warning: the snake's promise suggests that human verticality carries with it the danger that, by claiming a higher place, a permanence and plenitude denied to them, human beings, like the proud, globular protohumans of Aristophanes in Plato's *Symposium,* will only lose their proper perfection and place and instead of rising above their mortal condition become less than they were. It is in the splitting of these more perfect globular protohumans that Aristophanes locates the origin of our humanity, which precisely because the result of a splitting, is constituted by love, by a desire for a plenitude denied to us. But we mortals can gain whatever plenitude is granted to us only by discovering and embracing spirit without. Were we to pursue a godlike self-sufficiency we would lose whatever happiness is granted to us mortals. We think once more of Icarus, who, lured by the splendor of the sun, flew high above the earth only to fall and

---

283 Ibid., p. 13.

perish. *Cadet impostor dum super astra vehit* is the inscription above Alciatus' Icarus emblem, which bears the title *In Astrologos, Wider die Sterngucker*, against the star-gazers.[284] This Icarus emblem would have made a good cover image for Blumenberg's projected journal *Current Topics in Astronoetics?*[285]

Could we add as another possible translation of *In Astrologos: Wider die Astronoetiker*, against the practitioners of astronoetics? But the *Astronoetiker* is not someone who actually seeks to fly high above the earth, although he does delight in thinking about and in reading accounts of such flights, even when they end in disaster. Such flights do not tempt him to leave the earth, they rather let this earth appear more precious, a bit more homelike, just as a winter storm raging outside may make the warmth within seem even more comfortable.

5 Our Unique Earth

Recall once more the beginning of Nietzsche's early fragment *On Truth and Lie in an Extra-Moral Sense*, so popular with postmodern critics weary of all centers:

> Once upon a time, in some out of the way corner of that universe which is dispersed into numberless twinkling solar systems, there was a star upon which clever beasts invented knowing. That was the most arrogant and mendacious minute of "world history," but nevertheless, it was only a minute. After nature had drawn a few breaths, the star cooled and congealed, and the clever beasts had to die (TL 79).

The universe does not present itself to us as made for us humans, nor as made to be known by us. It is this thought of cosmic indifference that readily leads to nihilism.

But with what right can one deduce from the various decenterings effected by science that human beings could or should no longer be the center of their own world? As Blumenberg has pointed out, there is no logical connection between geocentrism and anthropocentrism, no logical connection between scientific decenterings on the one hand, and existential decenterings, on the other. That this is so is one important lesson of Blumenberg's astronoetics. There is a sense in which not just astronautics, but science has left us behind, so far behind that it has lost sight of the whole human being; but to say it has left us behind is to say also that it has both left us at home and left us our home. In this

---

[284] See Andreas Alciatus, *In Astrologos* (Icarus), *Emblematum libellus* (Paris, 1542).
[285] Cf. Hans Blumenberg, *Die Vollzähligkeit der Sterne*, 2nd ed. (Frankfurt am Main: Suhrkamp, 1997), pp. 49–51.

double sense Blumenberg helps us to understand and affirm ourselves as those left at home by astronautics.

What is needed to let us feel at home in the world? I would suggest that as long as we do not experience in our world incarnations of spirit we cannot feel at home in it. That may sound like an expression of a hopeless longing for something denied to us who are truly of today. But such experiences are familiar to all of us. They begin with the experience of other human beings: spirit without here responds to spirit within. We need not stop there. Think of experiences of beautiful nature, or of the admiration and reverence Kant experienced looking at the starry sky above him, or of Vitruvius, who, as we saw, had his primitive builders gaze at the starry firmament and build their houses in the image of the unchanging order they perceived to make them more homelike. The firmament was experienced by them as an incarnation of some divine spirit. Spirit above seemed to answer to spirit below.

Many of us still experience at least a pale echo of such correspondence when we look up at the stars. Such an experience finds expression in some verses by the poet Hans Carossa that Hans Blumenberg cites in the beginning of *Die Vollzähligkeit der Sterne:*

> Finsternisse fallen dichter
> Auf Gebirge, Stadt und Tal.
> Doch schon flimmmern kleine Lichter
> Tief aus Fenstern ohne Zahl.
> Immer klarer, immer milder,
> Längs des Stroms gebognen Lauf,
> Blinken irdische Sternenbilder
> Nun zu himmlischen herauf. [286]

> Ever denser darkness falls
> Over moutains, city, valley.
> But small lights already glitter
> From countless windows.
> Ever clearer, ever milder,
> Following the river's curve,
> Human constellations
> Now look up to those in heaven.

The constellations formed, as darkness falls over mountain, city, and valley, by the artificial lights of human habitations seem to answer to the constellations above. But what are the latter still to those of us living in a modern metropolis

---

[286] Ibid., p. 33. My translation.

with its over-presence of artificial light? "In what province," asks Blumenberg, "will those live, who can relate Hans Carossa's verses to their own experiences?" "Perhaps the poet wanted to speak of something that already then was no longer self-explanatory, because it gave expression to a trust in the world, that made it for the belated reader a dark text, let it become something no longer understood, under suspicion of a no longer permitted *Behaglichkeit*"—ill translated as comfort, here perhaps better as homelike comfort. "But," Blumenberg continues, "this, too, must be kept in mind: that the poet did not know and did not expect the consolation that was granted to those who came only a little later by seeing the earth from space, our own planet before the black darkness of the sky,"[287] "this cosmic oasis on which the human being lives," as he had described it in *Die Genesis der kopernikanischen Welt*. "This miracle of an exception... in the midst of the celestial desert is no longer 'also a star,' but the only one that seems to deserve this name."[288]

Left behind by astronautics! We admire the great discoverers of new worlds, like to see ourselves, like Nietzsche, in the image of a Columbus.

But, as it says in Hölderlin's poem "Die Wanderung," "The Journey," and with this quotation Heidegger concludes his essay "The Origin of the Work of Art":

> "*Schwer verlässt/ Was nahe dem Ursprung wohnt den Ort.*
>
> Only with difficulty does what dwells near the origin leave the place. [My translation]"

Between the two experiences, that of the poet Hölderlin and the philosopher Blumenberg lies astronautics, lies its promise or hope to discover somewhere out there, some time in the future, at least a trace of life, even intelligent life, and for the founder of astronoetics Blumenberg of even greater interest, the disappointment not to have found anything of the sort, the further disenchantment of the cosmos that astronautics has brought us. The successes of astronomy and astronautics and the disenchantment that followed them go together. They have led to an ever clearer awareness of the uniqueness and the fragility of this earth, to the knowledge that we human beings, as far as we can see, will remain bound to this home, that there is no even remotely realistic alternative. From this awareness will or rather should grow a new responsibility: "Only as the experience of a return will it come to be accepted that for us human beings

---

[287] Ibid.
[288] Hans Blumenberg, *Die Genesis der kopernikanischen Welt* (Frankfurt am Main: Suhrkamp, 1975). Robert M. Wallace (Trans.), *The Genesis of the Copernican World* (Cambridge, MA: MIT Press, 1987), pp. 793–794.

there is no alternative to the earth, just as there is no alternative to our human reason."[289] And this home astronomy and astronautics have left us.

Blumenberg seems to me right when he insists that there is no alternative to the earth, also right to insist that there is no alternative to human reason. But how would a philosophy look that really appropriated this twofold claim of this practitioner of astronoetics? It would be unnecessary to claim that there is no alternative to human reason if human beings, like the young Wittgenstein, had not long dreamed and are still dreaming of a reason that surpasses our everyday human reason and lays hold of the objects as they are in themselves, a reason that is not contaminated by our language and its metaphors, perspectives and prejudices, but lays hold of things as they really are. The hope that such a purified reason would render us the masters and possessors of nature, including our own nature, feeds this dream, where such mastery also promises a return to our true self. And this is no empty dream. Blumenberg knew very well that Descartes' promise of a practical philosophy that would render us the masters and possessors of nature was anything but idle. This promise and the scientific and technological progress that it brought us shows that our reason is indeed capable of a self-elevation that lets us oppose to that body-dependent understanding of space that makes the earth the center of my world an infinite cosmos; to my limited life-time limitless world-time. It also lets us oppose to that language in which we express our thoughts the idea of a pure language, a language that no human being ever spoke; to the embodied self that casts a shadow, inescapably bound to a particular place and time, the idea of a pure subject, an ideal observer, bound by neither time nor space, who would understand things as they really are, as they are in themselves. Every attempt to realize the promise of this self-elevation has to leave behind or beneath our life-world, that reality in which most of the time we are still at home.

But does the pursuit of truth not demand just such a self-elevation? As the *zoon lógon échon*, the animal rationale, isn't the human being the animal that to become human has to elevate itself above the animal. And does this self-elevation not also promise more adequate access to things as they really are? More adequate access to the truth?

---

[289] Hans Blumenberg, *Die Genesis der kopernikanischen Welt* (Frankfurt am Main: Suhrkamp, 1975). Robert M. Wallace (Trans.), *The Genesis of the Copernican World* (Cambridge, MA: MIT Press, 1987), p. 794.

6 Post-postmodern Geocentrism

Francis Bacon and Descartes both played with the thought that the new science would restore to us that paradise that Adam's bite into the apple that Eve offered him is said to have cost us. And they were not alone with this thought, the hope that our reason would lead us out of the cave in which we presently find ourselves to our true home, to some variant of the Platonic land of truth. But how are we to think this home? The hope for such a homecoming founders on the Antinomy of Being.

It has always been easier to find metaphors for the lack thought to be inseparable from the human condition than for a state of plenitude. One such metaphor for the former condition, which Blumenberg discusses in detail, is that of a ship at sea, uncertain of its origin, uncertain of its goal. In the absence of firm land, the ship here becomes a kind of substitute home.

In this connection Blumenberg cites Paul Lorenzen, who compares our everyday language with such a ship.

> If there is no *terra firma*, the ship must have been built at high sea, not by us, but by our ancestors. They therefore must have been able to swim and—perhaps making use of some floating wood—may have built themselves first a raft, which they then improved again and again until it became such a comfortable ship that today we no longer have the courage to leap into the water and to begin all over.[290]

Does Lorenzen mean to criticize us for lacking such courage? Or is the ship, even if inadequate in many ways, yet so comfortable that it suffices us or at least should suffice us? Comfortable enough to make it seem stupid to dare the leap? As Blumenberg remarks, Lorenzen's parable makes it somewhat difficult to understand why human beings, who have gotten used to the comfortable life on their ship, should even want to leave it and to start all over again, perhaps on a better newly built ship, perhaps even on *terra firma*. But we are denied the prospect of *terra firma* by the Antinomy of Being and for the building of a new ship we lack the necessary material. Blumenberg speaks for himself when he remarks that the metaphor

> strengthens the inclination to become in that comfortable ship once again the spectators of those who have the courage and would spread it to leap into the water and to begin all over

---

[290] Paul Lorenzen, *Methodisches Denken*. Frankfurt/M. 1968. Cited in Hans Blumenberg, *Schiffbruch mit Zuschauer*. (Suhrkamp: Frankfurt/M. 1979), pp. 73–74.

—perhaps trusting that they will be able to return to the still intact ship as the preserve of a despised history.[291]

We sense here what separates Blumenberg, the founder of astronoetics, from thinkers who, following the example of Descartes, would replace the ship on which we happen to find ourselves with a better ship that our reason is to build us. To be sure, Descartes warns us, not to let our demiurgic fervor to build a new world tear down the old house, in which after all one was able to live quite comfortably, before the new house has been built. It is advice that Blumenberg underscores.

Reading Blumenberg we sense something of that postmodern resistance to the Cartesian thought architectures that our reason would raise. But we also sense the distance that separates him from a thinker such as Heidegger, who does not expect reason to furnish us with an architecture that will allow us to dwell, but nevertheless invites us to leave our, if less than perfect, yet quite comfortable ship, calling for another kind of thinking, *ein anderes Denken*, but without a clear understanding of where such thought is to lead us.

But Blumenberg's reading of the parable also shows what separates him from those postmodern thinkers who with good reason sense a certain affinity. The sublimity of the ocean does not lead Blumenberg to forget the modest beauty of the ship. And thus he does not heed their call to leap into the water, not in order to build a new ship, but in order to enjoy the freedom of swimming, to be sure, only as thinkers, well aware that the modest security offered by the ship remains for them as human beings, to which when tired of their thinking swimming, they can return. Blumenberg is no such swimmer.

What is it that tempts us human beings to leave our after all quite comfortable ship? To repeat a question I asked earlier: why did we visit the moon? Is it sufficient to point to that desire to know that according to Aristotle determines the essence of human being? Again and again that desire will repeat the loss of paradise, for truth demands objectivity. Such objectivity, as Blumenberg, following Nietzsche and Wittgenstein remarks, has to bracket everything that makes our world meaningful and lets us take an interest in persons and things, has to transform our familiar world into *the* word and thus into "a sphere of indifference towards all."[292] The knowing subject's loss of individuality, its disembodiment, the loss of its shadow, are the other side of this indifference of the

---

[291] Hans Blumenberg, *Schiffbruch mit Zuschauer.* (Suhrkamp: Frankfurt/M. 1979), p. 74.
[292] Hans Blumenberg, *Lebenszeit und Weltzeit* (Frankfurt /M.: Suhrkamp, 1986), p. 306.

world. Both have their ground in the possibility of a self-elevation that is inseparable from our humanity.

> The mundane subject perfects itself, by making the most difficult of all concessions one might ask of it: to let its world become the world, to see its life-time joined to other life-times transformed into world-time, and thus strange to itself. Nothing is happening here that could be avoided because it is painful, that we are allowed to avoid in order to preserve for the subject its undisturbed subjectivity.
>
> It is the renunciation of the claim to be the measure of all things that lets the subject discover the meaning of its existence: in its contingency to have been left in the lurch and disregarded by the world, but yet to know and discover this world as what could not be without its renunciation and the renunciation by all of their subjectivities.[293]

It is difficult to understand this passage. The human being is said to perfect itself by pursuing truth. But that pursuit has to deny the world whatever once made it homelike. The reality now discovered is indifferent to human needs, including the human need to know. To discover the meaning of our existence, Blumenberg suggests, we have to renounce the Protagorean "man is the measure of all things." But when Blumenberg asserts that the world could not be without the renunciation of the claim that man is the measure of all things, he makes the being of the world dependent on the human subject after all. One again we run into the Antinomy of Being.

To the extent that this transformation of the world that once offered us shelter into the world penetrates our life-world, shapes and transforms it, it has to become increasingly uncomfortable, a reason why just today we need Blumenberg's astronoetics, which juxtaposes to the centrifugal desire of the astronaut the centripetal desire to return home, a desire that knows about the value of being comfortably at home.

In this connection Blumenberg reminds us once more of something that Kant, Schopenhauer, and Nietzsche already knew, that our earth, that once, as the supposed center of a well-ordered divine world-architecture, assigned us our place near the cosmic center, lost its uniqueness and has become just one star among countless others. But this is not the last word about the earth and its uniqueness.

> One simply has to forget when engaged in such considerations the names and dates of existing bodies and their relations in order to attend to the strange contingency that this earth, so discriminated by its position in the universe—which once, before Copernicus had been considered an excellent place for a *theoria* of the world, a place where 'nothing

---

[293] Hans Blumenberg, *Lebenszeit und Weltzeit* (Frankfurt /M.: Suhrkamp, 1986), p. 306.

could escape' one—as a result of the technology of space travel quite unexpectedly has "shown" us a property that suggests something like grace: the possibility of a possible return to it, once one has been so curious or vainglorious to leave it. Odysseus—once more and dressed in the space suit of a human paradigm: To return to Ithaca, this has not changed, demands and rewards the widest detour.[294]

In the age of astronautics astronoetics opens a path to a new, post-Copernican, post-postmodern geocentrism.

---

294 Hans Blumenberg, *Die Vollzähligkeit der Sterne*, 2nd ed. (Frankfurt am Main: Suhrkamp, 1997), p. 383.

XIII Conclusion: The Snake's Promise

1 An Old Story[295]

I would like to begin this concluding chapter with a story from the Old Testament that, now almost forty years ago, I heard Professor Friedrich Weinreb, this questionable, but unforgettable commentator on the Jewish stories surrounding the Book of Genesis, tell a group of us that had gathered in Zurich for a conversation on the topic "Technology and Reality."

Professor Weinreb spoke of Adam; he spoke of Cain, said to have built the first city, to which he is supposed to have given the name of his son Henoch, where one has to wonder where the inhabitants of this first city are supposed to have come from. And Weinreb spoke of Cain's inventive descendants; he spoke of Lamech, said to have sung the first song, and of his two wives, Adah, who was to bear him children, and Zillah, who, in order to preserve her beauty, was supposed to remain childless and yet bore him a son, Tubal-cain, said to have been the first to work iron and copper into tools and weapons. Tubal-cain is said to have accompanied the blind Lamech when he went hunting, telling him where the game was hiding. One day, glimpsing some horned creature, the son told his blind father where to direct his arrow. The horned quarry turned out to be their ancestor Cain, who had thus been marked by God. And the blind Lamech, aware of the prophecy that Abel's murder was to be avenged in the seventh generation, beside himself in his grief, inadvertently killed Tubal-cain who had directed the fateful arrow. Thus the race of Cain completed itself in the seventh generation.

But what does this story from the Old Testament have to do with the topic of this seminar, the Antinomy of Being? The point of that antinomy is to show that reality will finally elude the reach of our reason, that all attempts to comprehend it will inevitably replace reality with more or less inadequate human constructions. In that sense it seeks to open us to an awareness of what I have called the material transcendence of reality.[296] And openness to that transcendence, I argued further, is a condition of living a meaningful life, where I am thinking first of all, but not only, of openness to others, and not just to those close to us, but also to those whose lives do not intersect with our own and especially

---

[295] The substance of this concluding chapter was first presented on September 4, 2001 at University College Dublin as "The Snake's Promise: Technology and Art on the Threshold of the Third Millennium."

[296] See note 79.

to those who will come after us. But what does all that have to do with the story I just told you?

I am not a scholar of the stories that surround the book of Genesis and it even seems inappropriate to attempt to force such narratives, which invite ever different retellings and interpretations, exploring countless different directions, unto the Procrustes bed of univocal explanation. But I do want to respond to something in the story that spoke to me. That my response misses what once mattered to those who first told it seems all but certain, for what I heard into the story is something that has become a problem especially in our modern world, a problem that has long occupied me. But then, does it not belong to the essence of such stories that again and again they furnish metaphors that invite us to decipher promise or threat, blessing or curse of our own situation, to reflect on the path we have taken and where it might lead us?

It should not surprise you that I should want to link Cain to the architect Daedalus, he, too, a murderer, not of his brother, but of his more gifted nephew Perdix with whose education he had been entrusted. In both cases the murder is the result of an inability to accept that the other has been graced in a way denied to the murderer. Condemned for his murder, Daedalus, too, becomes a fugitive and a wanderer on the earth.

The loss of home lets both Cain and Daedalus become builders. Cain is thus said in *Genesis* to have built the first city. And it is to the race of Cain that we are said to owe both art and technology. To both we restless moderns look in pursuit of something that might compensate us for what we find lacking in the world that is our lot. The work of the tools and weapons forging Tubal-cain may be understood as the potentiation and completion of the work his ancestor Cain had begun when he built the first city.

2 Return to Myth in the Age of Technology?

But what is such a story to teach us? Does it not only dress up in mythological garb what we already know? Part of our spiritual situation is a proud self-assertion, a claim to autonomy, shadowed by a restless discontent that has called into question many of the convictions that once supported the cultural edifice in which we still live, if not really dwell. With what Nietzsche called the death of God, that edifice would seem to have lost both founder and foundation, developing now all sorts of cracks and fissures. There is a widespread sense that we have lost our way and direction and are now drifting, carried into a new millennium by a technology that seems ever less an instrument firmly in our control. Carried where? Towards a destruction of the earth? Towards a destruction of self? The still growing power that technology and science have given us presents us with ever more intractable problems and questions.

As the tale of Cain shows, from its very beginning technology has been shadowed by the suspicion that it is somehow cursed, supported by an exaggerated self-assertion that must end in the destruction of the world it helped create. Many have thus challenged the hegemony of science and technology, have attempted to oppose to objectifying reason a more meditative thinking, have dreamed of a return to myth, of narratives and images strong enough to found a new ethos. Nietzsche's *Birth of Tragedy* is an example. So is Heidegger's essay on *The Origin of the Work of Art*. But such talk has not really touched the power it would challenge. All too often such perhaps beautiful and edifying reflections have turned out to be little more than at times stimulating, entertaining, but finally inconsequential game-playing. Hermann Hesse spoke in this connection of a *Glasperlenspiel*, a playing with glass beads.[297] I fear that Hesse's prophecy for the third millennium of an aesthetic-intellectual play with inherited cultural values that will take the place of art, philosophy, and religion may stand up very well. Much of the theorizing in the arts and humanities today invites interpretation as just such a game. But Hesse also insisted that, despite its beauty, such play remains impotent, barren. How is this barrenness to be understood?

Such questioning caused me to perk up my ears when I heard Weinreb tell the story of Zillah, who, pretty as a picture, in order to preserve her beauty, was supposed to remain childless. And yet she embraced Lamech and bore him Tubal-cain and this embrace was to destroy the race of Cain in its origin: helping his blind father to aim his arrow at some horned creature, Tubal-cain became responsible for the death of the horned Cain.

My preoccupation with art and technology let me hear the story as follows: Zillah, who to preserve her beauty is supposed to keeps her distance from the cursed technological world represented by Cain and his descendants, yet embraces that world. And this embrace of technology by a beauty supposed to remain barren leads to a potentiation of the evil destiny that shadowed the race of Cain from the very beginning.

But how are we to think that embrace? How do technology and beauty belong together? Part of the modern understanding of the aesthetic has been an insistence on the distance supposed to separate the aesthetic sphere, the realm of beauty, from reality. Insistence on such distance, however, is inevitably

---

[297] See Karsten Harries, *Change and Permanence. A Study of Structure, Symbol, and Idea in Eight Major Prose Works by Hermann Hesse*, Scholars of the House Program, Yale University, 1958.

shadowed by widespread discontent with just this distance, which bids the artist to content himself with beautiful illusion, with mere fiction. Should art not be more than that? Should it not return beauty to reality and thus regain something of the world- building power once possessed by myth? Should art not transform reality instead of keeping its distance from it? And is this not especially true today when a fast growing computer and video technology present artists with ever new challenges? Instead of turning their back on that technology, should artists not embrace it? Part of our modern world is the seductive if dangerous dream of an embrace of technology by beauty: dream of a return of myth in the age of technology. The following reflections consider this dream.

3 Our Discontent with Technology

I spoke of a widespread discontent with the rule of technology over our life-world. Such discontent finds characteristic expression in Heidegger's rhetorical question: "Is there still that quiet dwelling of man between earth and sky? Does the meditative spirit still preside over the land? Is there still home that nourishes roots, in whose soil the human being ever stands, i.e., is rooted?"[298] In ever different forms such a questioning lament, here on the verge of degenerating into mere kitsch, has become part of our spiritual situation.

We may want to object: should there even be such rootedness? Must we not call into question Heidegger's nostalgic longing for Black Forest farm-house, field-path, and bell-tower? Do we not all know what we owe to a technology that has come to define our life-world? To be sure, I, too, find it difficult at times not to lament the way things and the earth have been neglected or, worse, violated by technology and, connected with it, the rootlessness of modern man. I understand Heidegger's lament that "All the things, with which modern communications technology constantly stimulates, assaults, and presses human beings, are today already much closer to us than the field surrounding the farm, the sky over the land, the hourly passage of night and day, closer than habit and custom in the village, closer than the tradition of our native world."[299] But I also know that today such sentences sound quite dated: who of us still lives, who would want to live on a farm, surrounded by its field? Our life-world has been shaped by technology. Computer and television, car and airplane are much closer to most of us than "the field surrounding the

---

[298] Martin Heidegger, GA16, p. 521.
[299] Martin Heidegger, GA16, p. 521.

farm, the sky over the land." Such proximity has granted us a freedom not known to Heidegger's village-dwelling peasant. And who today would want to let go of such freedom? Do we not know that we would become homeless in our world, were we to attempt to keep our distance from technology? Do we not have to embrace technology if we are to find our own ground and soil to stand on? Is it not precisely the nostalgia for reservations beyond the reach of technology that today lets us become homeless?

To be sure, Heidegger, too, would have us understand what he calls *Gelassenheit*, a term he borrowed from Meister Eckhart, not simply as a turn away from technology, but as a simultaneous yes and no to the technological world,[300] a world that will continue to shape our lives in ways impossible to foresee. Heidegger's fear is that technology may so bewitch and blind us that someday calculating reason alone will be considered valid.[301] Think of the *Tractatus!* Given such an understanding of responsible discourse, my talk of an Antinomy of Being would have to be dismissed as mere idle talk. Objectifying reason here is taken to circumscribe reality. Committed to such an understanding of reality, human beings would indeed have denied and cast away what makes them truly human: would have lost the openness to what is higher and alone can render our lives meaningful.

I understand what lets Heidegger plead for a life that keeps its distance from technology. And many of us not only dream now and then of such a mode of existence, but take steps to escape, at least for a time, say when on a vacation, to such a way of life. But most of us also know better than to let such dreams and escapes rule our lives. And it is not only the way of life we have chosen for ourselves, the freedom that technology has brought us, that forbids us such a step, but also, and more importantly, our responsibility for others. Just think of all that technology has accomplished and still needs to accomplish: of agriculture or medicine; of the way our rapidly evolving communications technology has challenged the way earlier generations were bound by place. What are we, having entered a new millennium, to make of Heidegger's assertion that technology today threatens "the rootedness of man in its innermost essence?"[302] Can technology not offer us a new home, an altogether new kind of rootedness? Think of the many people today who have grown up with the computer. Will they not simply dismiss Heidegger's claim "that here, by means of technology, an attack on the

---

[300] Martin Heidegger, GA16, p. 527.
[301] Martin Heidegger, GA16, p. 527.
[302] Martin Heidegger, GA16, p. 522.

life and the essence of the human being prepares itself, compared with which the explosion of the hydrogen bomb means little?"[303]

Do we even need roots? Are human beings like turnips, stuck in the ground? Heidegger would have us tie what deserves to be called "dwelling" to a saving of the earth that neither wants to master, nor to exploit it, to a receiving of the sky that lets day be day, night be night—I share such unhappiness with the still rising flood of artificial light that makes it ever more difficult for today's city dweller to see the stars.[304] But the progress of technology has to bring with it a loss of roots. The better human beings succeed in asserting themselves as the masters and possessors of nature, the less will they be able to experience nature as a power that assigns them their place. And does the gain in freedom not more than compensate us for the loss of place?

More questionable is our attempt to assert ourselves as masters and possessors of our own nature, an attempt that has been furnished by modern medicine with means that make remaking yourself much more than just an idle dream. Think once more of St. Orlan! Understood as material for the progress of technology, neither nature, nor our own nature, can furnish us with a measure. Unless we ourselves establish the limits or boundaries of that progress, it has to lose its way in what knows neither limit nor measure. But where is such a limitation of the progress of technology to find its measure?

If in such questioning our technological civilization's discontent finds voice, it all too often also betrays something like an enjoyment of the elicited dark mood, an aestheticizing of the lamented loss. One distances oneself from the power said to threaten "the rootedness of man in its innermost essence," but one makes no attempt to effectively challenge that power. One laments the rootlessness of our existing, the growing uniformity of a world ever more tightly embraced by the new technology, conjures up visions of past, supposedly more humane times, hopes to discover in the wisdom of other cultures impulses that may open some new path. The suspicion that we have lost our way and direction shadows our technological age. The young Nietzsche spoke in *The Birth of Tragedy* of "the disaster slumbering in the womb of theoretic culture."[305] Today we may even find some consolation in such talk: the slumbering disaster still leaves us some time—enough time perhaps to find the means to avert the disaster that has been prophesied. But we find it difficult to believe in the effectiveness of

---

303 Martin Heidegger, GA16,.p. 525.
304 Cf. Hans Blumenberg, *Die Vollzähligkeit der Sterne*, 2nd ed. (Frankfurt am Main: Suhrkamp, 1997), p. 33.
305 Friedrich Nietzsche, *"The Birth of Tragedy" and "The Case of Wagner,"* Walter Kaufmann (Trans.), (New York: Vintage, 1967), p. 112.

such means. Heidegger's attempt to oppose to instrumental reason meditative thinking seems to offer us little more than an intellectual vacation from the reality in which we live. It invites a kind of inner emigration that takes its leave from the technological world, teleologically suspends it, Kierkegaard might have said, even as it allows that world to enter our everyday, gladly accepts the many ways in which it has made our lives easier, but yet keeps its distance in order to thus save the essence of human being. The question is whether we can afford such a salvation: does Heidegger's broken "yes" and "no" not led into a barren, because only aesthetic, refusal of reality?

We hear today of the illegitimate hegemony of scientific, objectifying reason. But do we know how to distinguish between false hegemony and legitimate rule? Many today seek to oppose to the objectifying reason that rules in science the power of the poetic imagination communicating itself in stories and images, supposed to give us access to long buried but vital dimensions of reality. But can we take the imagination that seriously? Does our understanding of reality not deny us this? To be sure, we must take care not to allow technology to circumscribe our lives, have to learn how to limit its rule. But we must take care that such attempts not lead us to trade the only reality we know for a merely imagined reality. Does the power that we have granted the reason that rules our science and technology not also mean the impotence of a thinking that seeks refuge in images and stories? If we are to effectively challenge objectifying, calculating reason, we first have to recognize the ground of its legitimacy. Only then can we attempt to determine the boundaries of the realm in which it rightly rules and perhaps open up a space beyond that realm that may allow narratives and pictures to regain something of their lost mythical power. Here Kant continues to challenge us.

4 The Objectification of Reality

It would be a mistake to understand that modern rootlessness lamented by Heidegger simply as a function or a result of our technology. The progress of technology only carries an uprooting into our everyday that is a presupposition of the understanding of reality that rules our science. This understanding of reality rests on a twofold reduction of the world in which we find ourselves caught up first of all and most of the time. A first reduction—I have spoken of a pictorialization of reality—turns the world into a picture, the human being into a mere observer. Science has its origin in the conviction that reality will uncover its secrets only to those who are able to bracket their all too human interests and cares. Such bracketing transforms what is into the object of a pure sight. At the origin of philosophy, and that is to say also at the origin of science, we find thus the pleasure in just observing the starry sky above, a spectacle that would seem to have little to do with our daily concerns. Heidegger thus understands curiosity as the governing mood of scientific research. "Curiosity" lets one think of sin, of the Augustinian *concupiscentia*. Was it not curiosity, the demand to see as God sees, which led to the loss of paradise? And does such curiosity not rule all science? The scientist wants to see, wants to understand, often forgetting in the process himself and his place in the world. Was it not this lust of seeing that caused already Thales to tumble into his well?

But is it necessary to thus connect curiosity and sin? The Greeks, at any rate, thought differently: do we human beings not become truly human precisely when we free ourselves from our all too human everyday cares and concerns and in such godlike self-elevation enjoy the spectacle nature offers us? The God of Aristotle thus, as we saw, does not know anything of envy and our attempts to approach such divinity remain free from sin.

The understanding of reality that rules our science presupposes also a second reduction. Instead of a pictorialization of reality, we can now speak of its objectification. Let me recapitulate: our first access to reality is always bound to particular perspectives. How things present themselves depends on our situation, on the place that nature and society, body and language, space and time have assigned us. Often we remain so caught up in these perspectives that they remain unquestioned. But as soon as we understand a perspective as such, in thought at least we are already beyond the limits it would impose. To reiterate: our thoughts are free. This freedom will not allow itself to be bound to particular points of view. It knows no roots, leaps beyond every barrier one would erect, and leads to the ever repeated demand for a less situation-bound access to things, for an ever less perspectival form of representation, that is to say, for an ever more objective representation of things. What allows us to rank our science above its Aristotelian predecessor is first of all the fact that it answers more fully to these demands. This higher rank has to bring with it the devaluation of imaginative thought and the elevation of calculative thinking. To see things perspectivally is to not see them as they are. Such reflection on perspective and point of view leads inevitably to the idea of a subject that, free of all perspectives, sees things as they really are. This idea reduces the reality that gives itself to our eyes, and more generally to our senses, to the mere appearance of an objective reality that no eye can see, no sense can sense, that only a rational thinking can reconstruct. The understanding of reality on which our science and technology rest has its ground in this idea of a pure subject, made into a regulative ideal.

It has been suggested, e.g. by Heidegger, that this idea rests on an uncritical secularization of the Christian concept of God. Heidegger thus would have us understand this idealized subject as a remainder of Christian theology within philosophy of which philosophy should have rid itself long ago (GA2, 303; SZ 229). That there is in fact a historical connection is, as I pointed out,[306] easily shown. The theology of the Middle Ages belongs to the prehistory of modern science. But such undeniable dependence cannot delegitimate the idea of a pure subject and the correlative idea of an objectified reality. We should ask rather: how was it even possible for human beings to think God's sight as not bound by any perspective? Such thinking presupposes a power of self-transcendence, of self-elevation, that is inseparable from human freedom.

Inextricably bound up with such an objectification of reality is the gulf that now opens up between what comes to be understood as the real and the visible. Nietzsche had good reason to call Copernicus and Boscovich "the greatest and most victorious opponents of visual appearance."[307] Not only does such objectifying reflection force us to understand what presents itself to our senses as appearance of a reality that remains invisible; but what can appear to us at all is only the tiniest fragment of the whole of reality. The finite speed of light alone is sufficient to establish this. The essential invisibility of reality so understood lets us understand Hegel's pronouncement that art, from the side of its highest vocation, is for us moderns a thing of the past. That highest vocation, as Hegel understood it, was to disclose reality. The understanding of reality that I have sketched here has to deny art that vocation. Measured by it, the truth claims of poetic or imaginative thinking today can no longer be taken seriously. They require another sort of legitimation.

The other side of this objectification of reality is our so often lamented rootlessness. So understood reality presupposes the idea of a pure, and that is to say placeless subject. In the thinking of this idea, the human being transcends that situation which binds him to a particular place, a particular time, becomes the Cartesian thinking subject. Such a thinking subject can know no roots. Descartes' meditations interpreting the human essence as *res cogitans* help us to understand the essential homelessness of modern man. Not that the concretely existing human being ever experiences him- or herself as such a *res cogitans*. But again and again we measure our concrete being in the world by the idea of a subject that would understand things as they are. This idea lets us understand

---

[306] See chapter II, 4 above.
[307] Friedrich Nietzsche, *Beyond Good and Evil* (1886), *Jenseits von Gut und Böse*, I, 12. *Sämtliche Werke: Kritische Studienausgabe*, ed. by G. Colli und M. Montinari. 5, p. 26.

our own existing as only possible, as an accident. We moderns live on earth *sub specie possibilitatis,* restless, without a permanent home.[308] And that restlessness, that awareness of our contingency has its foundation in a self-assertion that would have us see as God sees.

We may not forget one thing in this connection: the idea of an absolute subject may furnish our understanding with a measure, but we possess no intuition that corresponds to that measure. We do not see like God. All our experiencing remains bound to particular situations, particular perspectives. This means that our intuition will never satisfy what truth so understood demands, that our experience of reality does not yet give us insight into it, that we have to work for such insight. Only in the re-constructions of our own spirit does nature yield us her secrets.

Some have objected that reality so understood is confused with a merely human construction. Must that twofold reduction I have sketched not deny us access to the life-world and thus contact with what alone deserves to be called reality? And can we not break the hegemony of natural science by revealing its art character? Thus Nietzsche dared, raising and by the same stroke undermining Kant's *Critique of Pure Reason,* "*to look at science in the perspective of the artist, but at art in that of life.*"[309] So understood, the scientist, too, is an artist, even if he has to forget this if he is to understand himself as the servant of truth. With his concepts he would imprison the imagination. But the imagination refuses to be thus imprisoned. The human urge to metaphor formation now turns to other realms, to myth and to art. In "On Truth and Lie in an Extra-Moral Sense" Nietzsche demands thus the liberation of the poetic intuition. His critique of science and of its claim to truth would serve such liberation.

But we must not make things too easy for ourselves. Appealing to what not long ago was called the new philosophy of science, many today seek to console themselves with a relativizing of science that would blur the fundamental opposition between science and myth, science and art. Faced with a technology that would seem to recognize no limits, that threatens to crush humanity in its embrace, it may seem comforting to hear that science does not really represent nature as it is, that it too traffics only with models, conjectures, abstract metaphors that can claim no necessity and permit countless others. Does the reflection on science and its special point of view not deny any absolutization of that point of

---

[308] Martin Heidegger, *Gelassenheit, GA*16, p. 527.
[309] Friedrich Nietzsche, *"The Birth of Tragedy" and "The Case of Wagner,"* Walter Kaufmann (Trans.), (New York: Vintage, 1967), p. 19.

view? Must such considerations not call into question the faith that the twofold reduction of reality that I sketched above offers us the key to nature's secrets?

And yet this faith, supported by experience, continues to determine our understanding of reality. Nietzsche's critique was unable to shake that faith. And equally impotent has been the critique of his many successors. We don't do justice to science when we understand it as just another intellectual game, subject to the indicated twofold reduction. Descartes' promise of a practical philosophy that would let us understand the power and ways of nature just as we understand the different techniques employed by our craftsmen was much more than just a promise. To understand something here means to be able to make it. Only in technology does science so understood complete itself. The modern understanding of nature does not rest content with that twofold distancing from the life world I have indicated. As technology, it reenters the life world. Modern science is not the pleasurable contemplation of the world, but work. Its model here is not the idle God of Aristotle, but the active creator God of the Bible.

5 "We Have Art So We May Not Perish From The Truth"

I have tried to show that the understanding of reality presupposed by our science rests on a twofold reduction of the life-world. Only the second reduction, its objectification, leads to that separation of reality and visibility that threatens to render all image-bound thinking impotent. The first reduction on the other hand distances the observer from reality, places him before it as before a picture.

Such pictorialization is presupposed by Alberti's perspective construction and by an art ruled by it. Alberti's method promises to render the painter the master and possessor, not of nature, but of its visual appearance. To be sure, as Plato already insisted, appearance should not be confused with reality. To lay claim to truth, the thinker has to leave such superficiality behind, has to try to seize the reality that here appears. The second reduction of which I spoke responds to this seemingly obvious insufficiency of all mere pictures. But the appeal of Alberti's art demands more thought.

Already the first reduction distances us from the things that first of all and most of the time always already in countless ways move and speak to us. They are transformed into pictorial objects. To this pictorialized world corresponds the modern subject. With good reason Heidegger could thus call modernity the age of the world picture.

But with Alberti this subject remains first of all a seeing subject, an eye, and as such bound to a particular body, to a particular here and now. The position of this eye, its point of view, determines the way in which reality can appear to it. This form of representation rules the painter's work as Alberti understands it.

The attempt to master this form of representation led to the discovery of the art of perspective. The theory of perspectival seeing and, more fundamentally, of perspectival experience, is a logic of appearance, in this sense phenomenology and this is precisely the meaning that Kant's great contemporary Johann Heinrich Lambert gave to that word. So understood, phenomenology lets the human subject understand itself as the measure of the experienced world, which now has become pictorial appearance.

Think once more of Alberti's *On Painting!* With this book already we stand on the threshold of modernity. The way that art here is given a new direction is a consequence of a reflection on the way the human subject measures whatever appears to it. Like his contemporary Nicolaus Cusanus, Alberti, too, in this connection appeals to the famous proposition of Protagoras, condemned by both Plato and Aristotle, that man is the measure of all things.[310] That measure is present in every perspectivally correct representation. Mastery of this form of representation enables the painter not only to represent nature so convincingly that we may wonder at times where reality leaves off and illusion begins, but also to create altogether new worlds. The painter's mastery of perspective renders him, according to Alberti, a second God. The snake's promise, thou shalt be as God, here seems to have found its realization.

To be sure, the price of the painter's success, so understood, is a loss of reality. Alberti is not concerned about this. He is too impressed by the magical power of his art to understand this loss as indeed a loss. And yet the reader is made to wonder by the way Alberti connects his understanding of the artwork as a second creation with the story of Narcissus.[311] Narcissus, so Alberti likes to tell his friends, where we, his readers, are included in this seemingly intimate circle, was the inventor of the art of painting. We all know the story: in love with his own beauty mirrored in the water, Narcissus loses both reality and life. Is it here that we should seek the origin of the work of art? Or does this story cast light only on a characteristically modern understanding of art that links it to a loss both of reality and of life?

By subjecting art in this way to the human being and his perspective, Alberti lets art lose what Friedrich Ohly has called the "spiritual perspective" of medi-

---

[310] Leon Battista Alberti, *On Painting*, John R. Spencer (Trans. and Intro.), (New Haven and London: Yale University Press,1956), p. 55.
[311] Alberti, *On Painting*, p. 64. See Karsten Harries, "Narcissus and Pygmalion," *Philosophy and Art. Studies in Philosophy and the History of Philosophy*, Daniel O. Dahlstrom (Ed.), (Washington: The Catholic University of America Press, 1991), pp. 53–72.

eval art. This spiritual perspective had its measure not in the human being, but in God. "It does not relativize by means of a this-worldly point of view, but is oriented towards the absolute, makes the created transparent towards the eternal."[312] The Middle Ages thus understood the artwork as a sign of transcendence. Ohly speaks of "perspective in the truest sense, in that it looks through the visible to the invisible, through the *significans* to the *significatum*." Alberti's *On Painting* gives voice to an altogether different understanding of art. Subjected to our human perspective, paintings no longer point to a higher reality, no longer are they metaphors of transcendence. The progressive loss of transcendence is part of the progress of post-medieval art, which compensates us for this loss by aestheticizing painting and more generally art.

To aestheticize something is to subject it to a measure thematized by aesthetics. By "aesthetics" I do not mean here simply the philosophy of beauty or of art. "Aesthetics," as I am using the term, presupposes a particular approach to art. A passage from Baumgarten's *Reflections on Poetry* of 1735[313] helps to clarify this approach – it is to this dissertation that we owe not just the word "aesthetic"; it also can be considered the first rigorously worked out philosophical aesthetics. Baumgarten, too, calls the artist, here the poet, a second God. This analogy leads him to claim that a poem should be like God's creation. What a philosopher like Leibniz said of the world, can therefore also be said -- so Baumgarten – of the work of art: like the divinely created cosmos, so the art-work should be a perfectly ordered whole, sufficient unto itself. So understood the work of art should not mean something else, but be just as it is. That painting, so understood, should lose, first its symbolic or allegorical, then its representational character, and finally should take its leave from all meaning, is only to be expected.

To the self-sufficiency of the art work so understood corresponds the self-sufficiency of the aesthetic experience. Such art does not serve some other purpose, does not help prepare a better future, cannot be justified along these lines, but also is not in need of such a justification. The aesthetic experience justifies itself and because it does, delivers us from the demand for meaning and content. Art allows us to forget the cares and business of the everyday. *Ars gratia artis*. So understood art offers us no window to reality, but rather keeps its distance from it, must keep its distance, for it is just this distance that gives it its seductive magic. Art so understood offers us a substitute for the paradise we have lost. Its beauty is the barren beauty of Zillah in the story with which I began this final chapter.

---

[312] Friedrich Ohly, *Schriften zur mittelalterlichen Bedeutungsforschung* (Darmstadt: Wissenschaftliche Buchgesellschaft, 1977), pp. 15, 35–37.

[313] Alexander Gottlieb Baumgarten, *Reflections on Poetry*, Karl Aschenbrenner and William B. Holther (Trans.), (Berkeley: University of California Press, 1964), par. 68, p. 63.

6 The Art-Work of the Future

In *The Will to Power* Nietzsche writes that we have art so that we would not perish over the truth[314] and already in *The Birth of Tragedy* we find the assertion that without beautiful illusion human beings would not be able to bear reality. Art, as it is here understood, delivers us from the feeling that our existence lacks meaning. I said the same about the aestheticizing art I just described. But deliverance in that case meant a flight from reality. Nietzsche on the other hand demands an art that embraces reality and with this embrace endows it with sense. Only when thus transformed into an aesthetic phenomenon by the subject does our reality, does our existence appear forever justified. Only the artist, as Nietzsche understands him, is said to give dignity and meaning to our existing.

Nietzsche is well aware that our enlightened technological age has no place for such an art, an art strong enough to found an ethos. Just because of this, this is said to be the age of an ever growing nihilism. As we have seen, the very power over the world that our science and technology have granted us presupposes an understanding of reality, if you wish an ontology, that while leaving art its beauty, yet cuts it off from reality so understood. The artistic treasures we have inherited have been reduced to objects of a merely aesthetic interest. If, as Nietzsche demands and hopes, art is to turn once again into myth, if pictures and stories are to regain their ethical power, must the hegemony of rational thinking not be challenged and broken? In order to break this hegemony Nietzsche sought to unmask the faith in the power of reason that supports such hegemony as without foundation. What kind of truth is it that science claims? To return to the young Nietzsche's previously considered answer:

> What then is truth? A movable host of metaphors, metonymies, and anthropomorphisms: in short, a sum of human relations which have been poetically and rhetorically intensified, transferred, and embellished, and which, after long usage, seem to a people, to be fixed, canonical, and binding. Truths are illusions which we have forgotten are illusions; they are metaphors that have become worn out and have been drained of sensuous force, coins which have lost their embossing and are now considered as metal and no longer as coins (TL 84).

How good this sounds to those who would break the hegemony of objectifying reason. Science is here moved in the neighborhood of art, only that it is poorer in that it has to dissolve pictures with sensuous power into pale concepts; also

---

[314] Friedrich Nietzsche, *The Will to Power.* Walter Kaufmann and R.J. Hollingdale (Trans.), (Random House: New York, 1967).

less honest, more ignorant, in that the scientist forgets that his reality is the product of his artistic doing. Humanists, disturbed by the hegemony of science, may find consolation in such considerations that would raise the Copernican reflection that geocentrism rests on no more than an anthropocentric illusion that lets us place this earth that we happen to find ourselves on at the center, to a yet higher level, by showing that post-Copernican science remains itself caught in an anthropocentric illusion. Should insight into the self-deception that supports science not free us from its power? Postmodern thinkers have thus liked to claim Nietzsche as one of their own. But this is false consolation, unable to limit the ever progressing power of science and technology because origin and essence of this power remain ill understood. The young Nietzsche sought the origin of this power in the Socratic faith "that thought, using the thread of causality, can penetrate the deepest abysses of being, and that thought is capable not only of knowing being, but even of correcting it."[315] The step back to the mythic art of Greek tragedy and its understanding of reality was to become the step that would return to art that ethical function Plato had denied to it, and would thus become a step forward, to the saving, healing art-work of the future, which would replace the ghostly reality of our science with a reality that would once again be full of color and life, an intoxicating Dionysian reality that would mean a new health.

But as Nietzsche was all too soon forced to recognize, such Wagnerian talk of the art-work of the future can only provide the neediness that gave rise to it with an aesthetic cover. An impatient hope here leads to too easy, precipitous formulations that cannot change a reality that is experienced as profoundly deficient. To be sure, just that deficiency endows such thinking with a seductive power. We appreciate *The Birth of Tragedy* today much as we appreciate a poem or a musical performance, say of Wagner's *Ring*. But like everything aesthetic, such enjoyment remains barren as Zillah was supposed to remain. Nietzsche's later self-critical postscript to *The Birth of Tragedy* today has more to teach us as than that book itself. In that book an aestheticizing thinking attempts to embrace science in order to deny it its power. But what presents itself as an attack turns out to be, like all aestheticizing, in fact a flight.

I am not concerned here with *The Birth of Tragedy* but with the type is represents. Again and again such dreams of an embrace of reality by art have proven just that: mere dreams.

---

[315] Friedrich Nietzsche,*"The Birth of Tragedy" and "The Case of Wagner,"* Walter Kaufmann (Trans.), (New York: Vintage, 1967), p. 95.

7 The Artist as Leader?

But is this necessary? Did not Lamech know the beautiful Zillah after all and she bore him Tubal-cain? Is it not possible to conceive an aestheticizing of this technological world that will allow human beings to feel truly at home in it? To be sure, we should not expect poets, musicians, or philosophers to bring about such a transformation of reality. Architects and especially and most disturbingly politicians are better candidates. To give just one example—and once again it is not the particular example that matters here, but the type it represents—Gropius founded the Bauhaus in order to return to architecture its ethical function.

> What is architecture: The crystalline expression of man's noblest sentiments, his ardor, his humanity, his religion! That is what it once was! But who living in our age that is cursed with practicality still comprehends its all-embracing, soul-giving nature? We walk through our streets and cities and do not howl with shame at such deserts of ugliness! Let us be quite clear: the grey, hollow, spiritless mockups in which we live and work will be shameful evidence for posterity of the spiritual descent into hell of our generation, which forgot that great, unique art: architecture.[316]

Once again building was to become edification. Feininger's woodcut on the title page of the Bauhaus's first program shows thus a Gothic cathedral in modern cubist forms. Architecture was to lead the different arts away from their "self-sufficient distinctiveness" back to a unity that would once again embrace them all and at the same time would overcome the separation of art from reality. Once again art would embrace and transfigure reality. The architect would shape the space and time of everyday experience in such a way that individuals are recalled from the dispersal into which they are led by the modern world to an order in which they would be able to recognize once again their place and vocation. "Structures created by practical requirements and necessity do not satisfy the longing for a world of beauty built anew from the bottom up, for the rebirth of that spiritual unity which ascended to the miracle of the Gothic cathedrals."[317] This vision of a no longer just aesthetic, but community building unity recalls the expectations that once bound Nietzsche to Wagner. In both cases what was hoped for remained unrealized, I want so say, fortunately could not be realized. For should it become reality, such a work would have to assign the individual his place in such a way that he would himself become part of an aesthetic

---

[316] [Walter] Gropius, [Bruno] Taut, and [Adolf] Behne. "New Ideas on Architecture." In Programs and Manifestoes in 20th Century Architecture, Ulrich Conrads (Ed.), Michael Bullock (Trans.), (Cambridge: MIT Press, 1978), p. 31.
[317] Ibid., p. 46.

whole and thus receive his meaning. But to become such a part, the individual must give up the better part of his freedom and thus his essence. What makes this vision a nightmare is the power of a technology that suggests possibilities of manipulating human material that would make it impossible to still speak of an autonomous subject. Human beings would here have themselves been degraded into mere human material. We can imagine an artist who finds in the new communications technology a far more encompassing and effective medium than Gropius ever found in architecture, an artist who would use for his media human beings and technology. In such an art technology and aesthetics would truly embrace one another.

The attempt to aestheticize the life-world is thus likely to let the artist become a politician. Thus Heidegger, taking his cues from Plato and Aristotle, once understood the state as a work of art and sought the "inner truth and greatness"[318] of National Socialism in the attempt to repeat the art-work of the Greek polis in a form in keeping with this age of technology. Here, too, the artist become statesman is to master reality in such a way that it will once again present itself as an order in which each individual can find his proper place. Once again chaos is to become cosmos.[319]

To do justice to Heidegger we would have to distinguish the reality that he so fatally misunderstood from what he read into that reality, would have to consider carefully the distinction Heidegger draws between our modern aestheticizing art and what he takes to be true art. We would have to address the question whether our modern understanding of reality and the aestheticizing of art do not belong together. Must the modern artist not understand himself with Alberti as a second God, creating an ideally self-sufficient object that takes its leave from reality? So understood art can lay no claim to truth. What could truth still mean? To the extent that it allows itself to be ruled by the aesthetic approach so understood, the art-work is unreal in its very essence. We, especially the artists among us, may want to challenge this distance between art and reality, but should art succeed, as Wagner, Nietzsche, and Heidegger dreamed, in overcoming this distance, would our reality not have to lose its reality, become unreal, become its own simulacrum?

"You shall be as God." Modern science and modern art both answer to this promise, each in its own way. Both threaten to cover up reality with a second,

---

318 Martin Heidegger, *Einführung in die Metaphysik*, GA 40, p. 208.
319 See Karsten Harries, "Heidegger as a Political Thinker," *The Review of Metaphysics*, vol. 29, no. 4, 1976, pp. 644–669.

man-made reality. Both invite us to understand the creator of this second reality as a second God.

8 The Snake's Promise

Science seeks to understand reality in order to master it. This, it turns out, is an infinite task. Never will our desire for mastery be satisfied. Never will the human subject become its own foundation. Just because of this the progress of technology knows no limits. By their very nature, science and technology thus remain related to a reality always still to be mastered. Their covering up of reality can therefore never be complete.

Aestheticizing art is more successful in covering up reality, even, perhaps especially when it draws its themes from reality. For reality is now only material for the artist that in the art-work loses its independence. Thus transformed it no longer demands anything of us, presents itself as no more than occasions for aesthetic enjoyment. Reality has been left behind.

Less innocent is the aestheticizing, today so prevalent, of thinking, the transformation of humanistic scholarship into an often very ingenious intellectual game. For as we enter a new millennium, as technology has opened up altogether new possibilities of mastering and manipulating nature, including human nature, the task of reflecting on place and way, on where we have come from and where we should be going, on the place technology should have in our lives has become more urgent than ever. The aestheticizing of thinking betrays this task.

Still more dangerous is the attempt to aestheticize reality, to transform our own life and the world in which we live into a work of art, especially dangerous when that attempt uses technology as a means to achieve its ends. Should that attempt succeed it would indeed have to destroy our technological culture in its very origin. For technology seeks to master reality and as such remains in its very essence related to reality. The aestheticizing of reality means its derealization, means the loss of reality.

What lets human beings listen to the snake's promise is the terror of time. Again and again this terror lets human beings distort reality, including their own reality, for reality and time cannot be divorced. The terror of time means also a fear of reality. Never will reality satisfy our demands for security. In this sense one could speak of the essential lack of reality. What I have called the Antinomy of Being is an expression of that lack. For every attempt to overcome that lack, be it by means of science, be it by means of art, makes us deaf to its claims, denies us access to its transcendence in which all meaning finally has its ground, a ground that by its very essence will not be mastered. To open windows to that reality we must find the strength to abandon the hope to take charge of reality, the hope to be in this sense like God. Only such strength will allow us to be genuinely open to the claims persons and things place on us, will let us understand that we do not belong to ourselves, that we cannot invent or imagine what will give our lives measure and direction, but have to receive and discover it. There was and there still is art born of such response-ability. And there was and still is thinking born of the same ability to respond. The main task both the arts and the humanities face today is not to deconstruct, but to open windows in the house reason has built: windows to transcendence. Nietzsche had good reason to be suspicious of the claim that our science gives us somehow a more adequate access to reality than the access that we are provided by our eyes, or more generally by our embodied selves, to be suspicious of the pursuit of objective truth. To be sure, if we understand truth with Kant as the adequacy of knowledge with its object, we readily arrive at an understanding of reality as the totality of objects. But with his antinomies Kant sought to call such an understanding of reality into question. This book thus circled around the question: what do we mean by reality? Related is Heidegger's question of Being. It is a question that I have tried to show has no good answer. And the fact that it has no good answer, I tried to show further, is not something grudgingly to be admitted, but a condition of a life worth living. The Antinomy of Being helps us to appreciate the wisdom of Nietzsche's words:

> Oh, those Greeks! They knew how to live. What is required for that is to stop courageously at the surface, the fold, the skin, to adore appearance, to believe in forms, tones, words, in the whole Olympus of appearance. Those Greeks were superficial—*out of profundity.*[320]

The key to what makes our lives meaningful, I am convinced, is to be found in what Nietzsche here calls superficiality.

---

[320] Friedrich Nietzsche, *The Gay Science*, Walter Kaufmann (Trans.), (Random House, 1974). Second Preface, p. 38. Cf. *Nietzsche contra Wagner* Conclusion.

Bibliography

Alberti, Leon Battista, *On Painting*, John R. Spencer (Trans. and Intro.), (New Haven and London: Yale University Press,1956).
Alciatus, Andreas, *In Astrologos* (Icarus), *Emblematum libellus* (Paris, 1542)
Apel, Karl-Otto, *Transformation der Philosophie*, 2 vols. (Frankfurt: Suhrkamp Taschenbuch Verlag, 1976).
Aquinas,Thomas, *Basic Writings of Saint Thomas Aquinas*, 2 vols., Anton C. Pegis (Ed.), (New York: Random House, 1945).
Aristotle, *The Complete Works of Aristotle, The Revised Oxford Translation*, Jonathan Barnes (Ed.), 2 vols., (Princeton: Princeton University Press, 1984).
Augustine, *Confessions*, Edward B. Pusey (Trans.), (New York: Modern Library, 1949).
Bartning, Otto, (Ed.), *2. Darmstädter Gespräch 1951. Mensch und Raum* (Darmstadt: Neue Darmstädter Verlags-Anstalt, 1952).
Battcock, Gregory (Ed.), *Minimal Art: A Critical Anthology* (New York: E. P. Dutton, 1968).
Baumgarten, Alexander Gottlieb, *Reflections on Poetry*, Karl Aschenbrenner and William B. Holther (Trans.), (Berkeley: University of California Press, 1964).
Beissner, Friedrich, *Hölderlins Übersetzungen aus dem Griechischen* (Stuttgart; Metzler, 1933).
Blumenberg, Hans, *Die Legitimität der Neuzeit* (Frankfurt am Main: Suhrkamp, 1966). Robert M. Wallace (Trans.), *The Legitimacy of the Modern Age* (Cambridge, MA: MIT Press, 1983).
Blumenberg, Hans, *Die Genesis der kopernikanischen Welt* (Frankfurt am Main: Suhrkamp, 1975). Robert M. Wallace (Trans.), *The Genesis of the Copernican World* (Cambridge, MA: MIT Press, 1987).
Blumenberg, Hans, *Schiffbruch mit Zuschauer* (Suhrkamp: Frankfurt am Main, 1979).
Blumenberg, Hans, *Lebenszeit und Weltzeit* (Frankfurt am Main: Suhrkamp, 1986).
Blumenberg, Hans, *Das Lachen der Thrakerin: Eine Urgeschichte der Theorie* (Frankfurt am Main: Suhrkamp, 1987).
Blumenberg, Hans, *Die Vollzähligkeit der Sterne*, 2nd ed. (Frankfurt am Main: Suhrkamp, 1997).
Blumenberg, Hans, *Theorie der Unbegrifflichkeit*, Anselm Haverkamp (Ed.) (Frankfurt am Main: Suhrkamp, 2007).
Boehm, Omri, *Kant's Critique of Spinoza* (New York: Oxford University Press, 2014).
Borges, Jorge Luis, "The Fearful Sphere of Pascal," *Labyrinths, Selected Stories and Other Writings* (New York: New Directions, 1964).
Bruno, Giordano, *The Ash Wednesday Supper*, Edward A. Gosselin and Lawrence S. Lerner (Ed. and Trans.), (Hamden: Archon, 1977).
Casey, Edward S., *The Fate of Place. A Philosophical History* (Berkeley: University of California Press, 1997).
Chamisso, Adelbert von, "Faust. Eine Tragödie in einem Akt. Ein Versuch", *Musenalmanach auf das Jahr 1804*, L. A. v. Chamisso and E. A. Varnhagen (Eds.). (Leipzig: Carl Gottlob Schmidt, 1804), pp. 193–215. *Sämtliche Werke*. vol 1, (München: Winkler, 1975), pp. 500–511.
Chamisso, Adelbert von, *Peter Schlemihl's wundersame Geschichte* (Leipzig: Reclam, 1834).

Chamisso, Adelbert von, *Peter Schlemihl*, John Bowring (Trans.), The Project Gutenberg EBook. Transcribed from the 1889 Cassell & Company edition by David Price.

Chamisso, Adelbert von, *Reise um die Welt mit der Romanzoffischen Entdeckungs-Expedition in den Jahren 1815–1818 auf der Brigg Rurik, Kapitain Otto von Kotzebue*, (Leipzig: Reclam, 1836).

Cicero, Marcus Tullius, *Pro Milone* – The Latin Library, www.thelatinlibrary.com/cicero/milo.shtml

Cohn, Norman, *The Pursuit of the Millennium*, 2nd edition (New York: Harper Torchbooks, 1961).

"Condemnation of 219 Propositions" in Arthur Hyman and James J. Walsh (Eds.) *Philosophy in the Middle Ages* (Indianapolis: Hackett, 1973).

Conrads, Ulrich, (Ed.), Programs and Manifestoes in 20th Century Architecture, Michael Bullock (Trans.), (Cambridge: MIT Press, 1978).

Copernicus, Nicolaus, *De revolutionibus orbium coelestium* (Nürnberg: Johannes Petreius, 1543). Translated in *The Portable Renaissance Reader*, James Bruce Ross and Mary Martin McLaughlin (Eds.) (New York: Viking, 1953).

Cusanus, Nicolaus, *Nicholas of Cusa on Learned Ignorance. A translation and appraisal of* De docta ignorantia (Minneapolis: Banning Press, 1981).

Cusanus, Nicolaus, *On God as Not-Other. A translation and an Appraisal of De li non aliud* by Jasper Hopkins (Minneapolis: Banning, 1987).

Dahlstrom, Daniel O., *Heidegger's Concept of Truth* (Cambridge: Cambridge University Press, 2001).

Dante Alighieri, *The Divine Comedy*, Carlyle Wicksteed (Trans.), (New York: Random House, 1950).

Descartes, René, *The Philosophical Writings of Descartes*, 2 vols., John Cottingham, Robert Stoothoff and Dugald Murdoch (Trans.), (Cambridge: Cambridge University Press, 1985).

Dostoevsky, Fyodor, *The Best Short Stories*, D. Magarshack (Trans.), (New York: Random House, 1955).

Eckhart, Meister, *Predigten*, Josef Quint (Ed. and Trans.), 3 vols. (Stuttgart: Kohlhammer, 1936–1976).

Eckhart, Meister, *Meister Eckhart*. Raymond B. Blakney (Ed. and Trans.), (New York: Harper, 1957).

Faruqee, Anoka, *Search Versus Re-Search: Recollections of Josef Albers at Yale*, a film by Anoka Faruqee, Published July 1, 2016. https://www.youtube.com/watch?v=cC7671N76_Q

Johann Gottlieb Fichte, *The Vocation of Man*, Roderick M., Chisholm (Ed. and Intro), (New York, Liberal Arts Press, 1956).

Fichte, Johann Gottlieb, *Grundlage der gesamten Wissenschaftslehre* (1794). (Hamburg: Meiner, 1956).

Frege, Gottlob, *Begriffsschrift, eine der arithmetischen nachgebildete Formelsprache des reinen Denkens* (Halle: Louis Nebert, 1879), S. Bauer-Mengelberg (Trans.), *Concept Script, a formal language of pure thought modelled upon that of arithmetic*, in J. van Heijenoort (Ed.), *From Frege to Gödel: A Source Book in Mathematical Logic, 1879–1931* (Cambridge, MA: Harvard University Press, 1967).

Frege, Gottlob, "*Der Gedanke*," in *Logische Untersuchungen*, Günther Patzig (Ed. and Intro.), (Göttingen: Vandenhoeck und Ruprecht, 1966).

Friedländer, Paul, "Aletheia" in *Plato: An Introduction* (New York: Pantheon Books, 1958), pp. 221–229.
Hamann, Johann Georg, *Metakritik über den Purismus der reinen Vernunft* (1785) in *Hamanns Schriften*, Friedrich Roth (Ed.), vol.7, (Berlin: Riemer, 1825).
Harries, Karsten, *Change and Permanence. A Study of Structure, Symbol, and Idea in Eight Major Prose Works by Hermann Hesse*, Scholars of the House Program, Yale University, 1954.
Harries, Karsten, *In a Strange Land. An Exploration of Nihilism*, PhD dissertation, Yale University, 1961.
Harries, Karsten, *The Meaning of Modern Art: A Philosophical Interpretation* (Evanston: Northwestern University Press, 1968).
Harries, Karsten, "Heidegger as a Political Thinker," *The Review of Metaphysics*, vol. 29, no. 4, 1976, pp. 644–669.
Harries, Karsten, *The Bavarian Rococo Church: Between Faith and Aestheticism* (New Haven: Yale University Press, 1983).
Harries, Karsten, "Truth and Freedom," *Edmund Husserl and the Phenomenological Tradition*, Robert Sokolowski (Ed.), (Washington: Catholic University Press, 1988), pp.131–155.
Harries, Karsten, *The Broken Frame. Three Lectures* (Washington: Catholic University Press, 1989).
Harries, Karsten, "Narcissus and Pygmalion," *Philosophy and Art. Studies in Philosophy and the History of Philosophy*, Daniel O. Dahlstrom (Ed.), (Washington: The Catholic University of America Press, 1991).
Harries, Karsten, *The Ethical Function of Architecture* (Cambridge, MA: MIT Press, 1997).
Harries, Karsten, *Infinity and Perspective* (Cambridge, MA: MIT Press, 2001).
Harries, Karsten, "On the Power and Limit of Transcendental Reflection," *From Kant to Davidson. Philosophy and the Idea of the Transcendental*, Jeff Malpas (Ed.), (London and New York: Routledge, 2002), pp. 139–161.
Harries, Karsten, "World-Picture and World-Theater: Wonder, Vision, Knowledge," *Laboratory, Theater. Scenes of Knowledge in the 17th Century*, Helmar Schramm, Ludger Schwarte, Jan Lazardzig (Eds.), (Berlin, New York: de Gruyter, 2005), pp. 507–525.
Harries, Karsten, *Art Matters: A Critical Commentary on Heidegger's "The Origin of the Work of Art"* (New York: Springer, 2009).
Harries, Karsten, "Architecture and Anarchitecture: The Antinomy of Building," *Aesthetic Pathways*, vol. 1, nr. 1, December 2010, pp. 59–78.
Harries, Karsten, *Die Bayerische Rokokokirche. Das Irrationale und das Sakrale* (Dorfen: Hawel Verlag, 2009).
Harries, Karsten, *Between Nihilism and Faith: A Commentary on Either/Or* (Berlin and New York: DeGruyter, March 2010).
Harries, Karsten, "What Need is There for an Environmental Aesthetics," *The Nordic Journal of Aesthetics*, no. 40–41, 2010–2011, pp. 7–22.
Harries, Karsten, "Vom Widerwillen gegen Architektur oder die Antinomie des Seins"/ "On the Ill Will Against Architecture or The Antinomy of Being," *Displaced Fractures. Über die Bruchlinien in Architekturen und ihren Körpern*, Thomas Trummer und Heike Munder (Eds.), Migros Museum für Gegenwartskunst, Zürich, 2011.
Harries, Karsten, *Wahrheit: Die Architektur der Welt* (Paderborn: Wilhelm Fink, 2012).

Harries, Karsten, "The Theory of Double Truth Revisited," *Politics of Practical Reasoning. Integrating Action, Discourse, and Argument*, Ricca Edmondson and Karlheinz Hülser (Eds.) (Plymouth: Lexington Books, 2012), pp. 205–225.

Harries, Karsten, "The Antinomy of Being: Heidegger's Critique of Humanism," *The Cambridge Companion to Existentialism*, Steven Crowell (Ed.), (Cambridge: Cambridge University Press, 2012), pp. 178–198.

Harries, Karsten, "Longing for Ithaca: On the Need for a Post-Copernican Geocentrism," *From the Things Themselves, Architecture and Phenomenology*, Benoit Jacquet and Vincent Giraud (Eds.), (Kyoto: Kyoto University Press. École francaise d'Extrême-Orient, 2012), pp. 495–522.

Harries, Karsten, "The Antinomy of Being and the End of Philosophy," *Division III of Being and Time: Heidegger's Unanswered Question of Being*, Lee Braver (Ed.), (Cambridge, MA: MIT Press, 2015), pp. 133–148.

Hartmann, Geoffrey. "Literary Criticism and its Discontents," *Critical Inquiry*, vol. 3, no, 2.

Headley, John M. *Tommaso Campanella and the Transformation of the World* (Princeton: Princeton University Press, 1997).

Heer, Friedrich, *Europäische Geistesgeschichte* (Stuttgart: Kohlhammer, 1953).

Martin Heidegger *Gesamtausgabe* (Frankfurt am Main: published by Vittorio Klostermann, 1977–).

Heidegger, Martin, *Sein und Zeit (1927)*, *Gesamtausgabe*, vol. 2 (Frankfurt am Main: Klostermann, 1977). *Being and Time.* John Macquarrie and Edward Robinson (Trans.), (New York and Evanston: Harper, 1962).

Heidegger, Martin, *Kant und das Problem der Metaphysik* (1929), *Gesamtausgabe*, vol. 3 (1991).

Heidegger, Martin, *Erläuterungen zu Hölderlins Dichtung*, *Gesamtausgabe*, vol. 4 (1981).

Heidegger, Martin, *Holzwege (1935–1946)*, *Gesamtausgabe*, vol. 5 (1977).

Heidegger, Martin, *Vorträge und Aufsätze (1936–1953)*, *Gesamtausgabe*, vol. 7 (2000).

Heidegger, Martin, *Wegmarken* (1919–1958), *Gesamtausgabe*, vol., 9 (1976).

Heidegger, Martin, *Unterwegs zur Sprache*, *Gesamtausgabe*, vol. 12, (1985).

Heidegger, Martin, *Aus der Erfahrung des Denkens* (1910–1976), *Gesamtausgabe*, vol. 13 (1983).

Heidegger, Martin, *Zur Sache des Denkens (1962–1964)*, *Gesamtausgabe*, vol. 14, (2007). D. F. Krell, (Ed. and Trans.), *Basic Writings* (New York: Harper Collins, 1993).

Heidegger, Martin, *Reden und andere Zeugnisse eines Lebensweges (1910–1976)*. *Gesamtausgabe*, vol. 16 (2000).

Heidegger, Martin, *Einführung in die phänomenologische Forschung, (WS 1923/24) Gesamtausgabe*, vol. 17 (1994).

Heidegger, Martin, *Die Grundprobleme der Phänomenologie* (1927), *Gesamtausgabe*, vol. 24 (1975). Translated in *The Basic Problems of Phenomenology*, revised Edition, Albert Hofstadter (Trans.), (Bloomington: University of Indiana Press, 1988).

Heidegger, Martin, *Hölderlins Hymne "Andenken" (Wintersemester 1941/42)*, *Gesamtausgabe*, vol. 52 (1982).

Heidegger, Martin, *Hölderlins Hymne "Der Ister" (Sommersemester 1942)*, *Gesamtausgabe*, vol. 53 (1984).

Heidegger, Martin, *Beiträge zur Philosophie (Vom Ereignis)* (1936–1938), F.-W. von Herrmann (Ed.), 1989, 2nd ed. 1994. *Gesamtausgabe*, vol. 65 (1989).

Heidegger, Martin, *The Question Concerning Technology and other Essays*, William Lovitt (Trans. und Info.) (New York: Harper Torchbooks, 1977).
Herder, Johann Gottfried, "Eine Metakritik zur Kritik der reinen Vernunft," aus "Verstand und Erfahrung," *Sprachphilosophische Schriften*, Erich Heintel (Ed.), (Hamburg: Meiner, 1960).
Hertz, Heinrich, *Die Prinzipien der Mechanik in neuem Zusammenhange dargestellt. Unveränderter fotomechanischer Nachdruck der Ausgabe*, Leipzig 1894 (= Gesammelte Werke, Band III). Darmstadt: Wissenschaftliche Buchgesellschaft, 1963. *Principles of Mechanics*, D. E. Jones and J. T. Walley (Trans.), (London: Macmillan, 1899).
Hickey, Lance, "Kant's concept of the transcendental object," *Manuscrito* 24, 1, 2001, pp. 103–139.
Hofmannsthal, Hugo von, "Ein Brief". *Ausgewählte Werke in zwei Bänden* (Frankfurt am Main: Fischer, 1957), vol. 1.
Hofmannsthal, Hugo von, "The Letter of Lord Chandos," *Selected Prose*, Mary Hottinger and Tania and James Stern (Trans.), (New York: Pantheon, 1952).
Hopkins, Jasper, *Nicholas of Cusa on Learned Ignorance. A translation and appraisal of* De docta ignorantia (Minneapolis: Banning Press, 1981).
Humboldt, Wilhelm von, *On Language, On the Diversity of Human Language Construction and its Influence on the Mental Development of the Human Species*, Michael Losonsky (Ed.), Peter Heath (Trans.), (Cambridge: Cambridge University Press, 1999).
Hyman, Arthur and James J. Walsh (Eds.), *Philosophy in the Middle Ages* (Indianapolis: Hackett, 1973).
Jacobi, Friedrich Heinrich, *Jacobi an Fichte* (Hamburg: Perthes, 1799).
Jacobi, Friedrich Heinrich, "Beylage. Ueber den transcendentalen Idealismus," *Friedrich Heinrich Jacobis Werke*, vol. 2 (Leipzig: Fleischer, 1815).
Jacobi, Friedrich Heinrich, *Jacobis Spinoza Büchlein nebst Replik und Duplik* (München: G. Müller, 1912).
Jacobi, Friedrich Heinrich *Über die Lehre des Spinoza in Briefen an den Herrn Moses Mendelssohn* (Breslau: Löwe, 1785)
Jacobi, Friedrich Heinrich, *Allwill*, J. U. Terpstra (Ed. and Intro.), (Groningen: J.B. Wolters, 1957).
Jordan, Pascual, "Kosmogonische Anschauungen der modernen Physik," *Naturwissenschft – Religion – Weltanschauung. Clausthaler Gespräch 1948* (Clausthal-Zellerfeld, 1949), pp. 25–33.
Kant, Immanuel, *Werke in sechs Bänden*, Wilhelm Weischedel (Ed.), (Darmstadt: Wissenschaftliche Buchgesellschaft, 1966).
Kant, Immanuel, *The Critique of Judgment*, Werner S. Pluhar (Trans.), (Indianapolis: Hackett, 1987).
Kant, Immanuel, *The Critique of Pure Reason*, Paul Guyer, Allen W. Wood (Eds. and Trans.) (Cambridge: Cambridge University Press, 1999).
Kant, Immanuel, *The Critique of Practical Reason*, Werner S. Pluhar (Trans.), (Indianapolis: Hackett, 2002).
Kant, Immanuel, *Metaphysische Anfangsgründe der Naturwissenschaft*, (Riga: Hartknoch, 1786), Ernest Belfort Bax (Trans.), *The Metaphysical Foundations of Natural Science*, CreateSpace Independent Publishing Platform (June 12, 2015).

Kierkegaard, Søren, *Concluding Unscientific Postscript*, David F. Swenson and Walter Lowrie (Trans.), (Princeton: Princeton University Press, 1974).

Koyré, Alexandre, *From the Closed World to the Infinite Universe* (New York: Harper Torchbook, 1958).

Kožnjak, Boris, "Who let the demon out? Laplace and Boscovich on determinism," *Studies in History and Philosophy of Science* (2015), Part A 51, pp. 42–52.

Lambert, Johann Heinrich, *Neues Organon Oder Gedanken Über Die Erforschung Und Bezeichnung des Wahren Und Dessen Unterscheidung Vom Irrtum Und Schein* (Leipzig: Wendler, 1764).

Laplace, Pierre-Simon, Marquis de, *A Philosophical Essay on Probabilities*, Frederick Wilson Truscott and Frederick Lincoln Emory (Trans.), (New York: Wiley, 1902).

Leibniz, Gottfried Wilhelm, *New Essays on Human Understanding*, Peter Remnant and Jonathan Bennett (Eds.), (Cambridge: Cambridge University Press 1981).

Litt, Theodor, *Mensch und Welt. Grundlinien einer Philosophie des Geistes* (München: Federmann, 1948).

Lorenzen, Paul, *Methodisches Denken* (Frankfurt am Main: Suhrkamp, 1968).

Lyotard, Jean-François, *The Postmodern Explained* (Minneapolis: U. of Minnesota Press, 1993).

Mackie, John Leslie, *Ethics, Inventing Right and Wrong* (New York City, Viking, 1977)

Manchester, Paula, "Kant's Conception of Architectonic in its Philosophical Context," *Kant Studien*. Volume 99, Issue 2, June, 2008.

McDermott, Drew, "How Moral Absolutism Can Be True and False at the Same Time; Or: Non-Phenomenological Existentialism," draft.

McLaughlin, Eleanor, "The Heresy of the Free Spirit and Late Medieval Mysticism," *Medievalia et Humanistica*, n. s. 4 (1973).

Moore G. E., "The Refutation of Idealism," Originally published in *Mind*, n. s. 12 (1903), pp. 433–53. Reprinted in *Selected Writings*, Thomas Baldwin (Ed.), (London: Routledge, 2013).

Musk, Elon, "Making Humans a Multi-Planetary Species," *New Space*, Vol. 5, No. 2, Commentary, Published Online:1 Jun 2017https://doi.org/10.1089/space.2017.29009.emu

Nagel, Thomas, *The View From Nowhere* (New York: Oxford University Press, 1986).

Newton, Isaac, *Philosophiae Naturalis Principia Mathematica*, Book. 1 (1689); Andrew Motte (Trans.), (1729), rev. Florian Cajori, (Berkeley: University of California Press, 1934).

Nietzsche, Friedrich, *Thus Spoke Zarathustra, The Portable Nietzsche*, Walter Kaufmann (Trans.), (New York: Penguin Books, 1954)

Nietzsche, Friedrich, *"The Birth of Tragedy" and "The Case of Wagner,"* Walter Kaufmann (Trans.), (New York: Vintage, 1967).

Nietzsche, Friedrich, *The Will to Power*. Walter Kaufmann and R.J. Hollingdale (Trans.), (Random House: New York, 1967).

Nietzsche, Friedrich, *The Gay Science*, Walter Kaufmann (Trans.), (Random House, 1974).

The Portable Nietzsche, Walter Kaufmann (Ed. and Trans.), (Hamondsworth: Penguin, 1976).

Nietzsche, Friedrich, *Philosophy and Truth: Selections From Nietzsche's Notebooks of the Early 1970's*, Daniel Breazeale (Ed. and Trans.), (Atlantic Highlands: Humanities Press, 1979).

Nietzsche, Friedrich, *On the Genealogy of Morals and Ecce Homo*, Walter Kaufmann and R. J. Hollingdale (Trans.), (New York: Vintage, 1989).

Nietzsche, Friedrich, Sämtliche Werke, *Kritische Studienausgabe* in 15 vols. G. Colli and M. Montinari (Eds.), (München/ Berlin/ New York: Deutscher Taschenbuch Verlag and de Gruyter, 1980).
Ohly, Friedrich, *Schriften zur mittelalterlichen Bedeutungsforschung* (Darmstadt: Wissenschaftliche Buchgesellschaft, 1977).
Plantinga, Alvin, "Methodological Naturalism?" *Origins & Design*, Winter 1997.
Plato, *Collected Dialogues*, Edith Hamilton and Huntington Cairns (Eds.), (Princeton: Princeton University Press, 1961).
Poppe, Wilhelm, *Vitruvs Quellen zum zweiten Buche 'de architectura.'* Dissertation, Kiel, 1909.
Preger, Wilhelm, *Beiträge zur Geschichte der religiösen Bewegung in den Niederlanden in der zweiten Hälfte des vierzehnten Jarhunderts, Abhandlungen der königlich bayerischen Akademie der Wissenschaften* (Historische Classe), vol. XXI, Part 1 (Munich, 1984).
Reinicke, Helmut, *Aufstieg und Revolution. Über die Beförderung irdischer Freiheitsneigungen durch Ballonfahrt und Luftschwimmkunst* (Berlin: Transit, 1988).
Riccardi, Mattia, "Nietzsche's critique of Kant's thing in itself," *Nietzsche-Studien* 39, 2010, 3.
Richter, Jean Paul, *Vorschule der Ästhetik, Jean Paul's sämmtliche Werke* (Berlin: G. Reimer, 1827), vol. 41.
Rickert, Heinrich, *Fichtes Atheismusstreit und die Kantische Philosophie. Eine Säkülarbetrachtung,* Sonderdruck aus den *Kantstudien.* (Berlin: Reuther &. Reichard, 1899).
Rilke, Rainer Maria, *Die Aufzeichnungen des Malte Laurids Brigge, Werke in 3 Bänden*, (Frankfurt am Main: Insel 1966), vol. 3. pp. 107–346. English translation by William Needham: https://archive.org/stream/TheNotebooksOfMalteLauridsBrigge/TheNotebooksOfMalteLauridsBrigge_djvu.txt.
Russell, Bertrand, *Human Knowledge, Its Scope and Limits* (New York: Simon and Schuster, 1948).
Sartre, Jean-Paul, *Being and Nothingness*, Hazel E. Barnes (Trans. and Intro.), (New York: Philosophical Library, 1956).
Schopenhauer, Arthur, *Die Welt als Wille und Vorstellung*, 2 vols. (Wiesbaden: Brockhaus, 1965). E. F. J. Payne (Trans.), *The World as Will and Representation*, 2 vols. (New York: Dover, 1966).
Schrader, George A., "Basic Problems of Philosophical Ethics. On Lewis White Beck: *A Commentary on Kant's Critique of Practical Reason* [Zur Diskussion]", in: *Archiv für Geschichte der Philosophie* 46, 1964.
Sedlmayr, Hans, *Die Revolution der modernen Kunst* (Hamburg: Rowohlt, 1955).
Sedlmayr, Hans, *Der Tod des Lichtes* (Salzburg: O. Müller, 1964).
Sedlmayr, Hans, *Der Verlust der Mitte* (München: Ullstein, 1959).
Seuse, Heinrich, *Das Buch der Wahrheit, Daz buechli der warheit*, Loris Sturlese and Rüdiger Blumrich (Eds.), Loris Sturlese (Intro.), Rüdiger Blumrich (Trans.), Mittelhochdeutsch – Deutsch (Hamburg: Meiner, 1993).
Spampanato, V.,*Vita di Giordano Bruno, Con documenti edite e inedite*, vol. 1 (Messina: Principato, 1921).
Spengler, Oswald, *Der Untergang des Abendlandes*, 2 vols. (München: Beck, 1923).

Swift, Jonathan, *Gulliver's Travels Into Several Remote Nations of the World*, The Project Gutenberg eBook, Release Date: June 15, 2009 [eBook #829] Transcribed from the 1892 George Bell and Sons edition by David Price.

Szabó, László V., "Zu Hugo von Hofmannsthals Nietzsche-Rezeption," *Jahrbuch der ungarischen Germanistik* 2006, pp. 69–93.

Tugendhat, Ernst, *Der Wahrheitsbegriff bei Husserl und Heidegger*, 2nd. ed. (Berlin: de Gruyter, 1970).

Vitruvius, *The Ten Books of Architecture*, Morris Hickey Morgan (Trans.), (New York: Dover, 1960).

Wittgenstein, Ludwig, *Tractatus Logico Philosphicus*, C. K. Ogden (Trans.), (London: Routledge and Kegan Paul, 1922).

Wittgenstein, Ludwig, *Philosophical Investigations*, G. E. M. Anscombe (Trans.), (New York: Macmillan, 1959).

Wittgenstein, Ludwig, *Zettel, 40th Anniversary Edition. G. E. M. Anscombe, G. H. von Wright* (Eds.), (Oakland: University of California Press, 2007).

Yates, Frances A. *Giordano Bruno and the Hermetic Tradition* (Chicago and London: The University of Chicago Press, 1979).

Index

Abel 216
Abraham 140
Adah 216
Adam 125, 190, 192, 194, 203, 212, 216
Albers, Josef 3–5
Alberti, Leon Battista 115, 195, 226–228, 232
Alciatus, Andreas 208
Aldrin, Buzz 184
Apel, Karl-Otto 40–41, 42, 51
Apollinaire, Guillaume 206
Aquinas, Thomas 13–14, 28–30, 36, 140, 160, 162–163, 193–194
Aristophanes 119–120, 182, 207
Aristotle 3, 9, 19, 32, 90, 103, 125, 128, 131, 142, 147, 160–161, 176–177, 179, 181, 191–194, 213, 223, 226–227, 232
Armstrong, Neil 184, 200
Augustine 22, 125–126, 147, 160, 163, 177, 192–194, 198
Averroes 160
Avicenna 136, 160

Bacon, Francis 24, 212
Bargmann, Wolfgang 199
Baumgarten, Alexander Gottlieb 8, 205, 228
Berkeley, George 13, 19
Blumenberg, Hans 5, 11, 119, 130, 132, 182–183, 189–191, 198–201, 208–215, 221
Boehm, Omri 165, 166
Bolyai, János 105
Borges, Jorge Luis 133
Boscovich, Roger Joseph 33, 35, 94, 150–151, 224
Bourdin, Père 48
Braque, Georges 207
Brumbaugh, Robert S. 6
Bruno, Giordano 128–134, 140, 197, 231
Burke, Edmund 172

Cain 126, 194, 216–218
Calvin, John 202
Campanella, Tommaso 128, 130–131

Camus, Albert 71
Carossa, Hans 209–210
Carson, Rachel 184
Casey, Edward S. 142
Cassirer, Ernst 36
Chamisso, Adelbert von 64–66, 73–74., 76, 78–80, 81, 115, 117
Charles, Jacques 185
Chirico, Giorgio de 207
Cicero, Marcus Tullius 135
Columbus, Christopher 130. 184, 210
Cohn, Norman 131, 136–139
Copernicus, Nicolaus 11, 32, 35, 94, 128–130, 132, 134, 150, 181–182, 189, 196, 201, 214, 224
Coutelle, Marie-Joaseph 186
Cusanus (Nicholas of Cusa) 6, 32, 90, 133–134., 166–169, 193–195, 197, 227

Daedalus 186, 188, 191, 217
Dahlstrom, Daniel 35, 40, 227
D'Arlandes, François Laurent 185
Darwin, Charles 196
Descartes, René 5–6 , 21–22, 48–49, 66, 70, 75, 79, 86, 115–117, 120, 121, 131, 142, 149–150., 165–166., 193, 211–213, 224, 226
Dietmar von Aist 135
Dostoevsky, Fyodor 140, 148
Duchamp, Marcel 207

Eckhart, Meister 22–23, 136–139, 220
Elizabeth, Queen of England 132, 133
Epicurus 192
Euclid 105–196, 141–142
Eve 125, 190, 194, 203, 212

Feininger, Lyonel 231
Fichte, Johann Gottlieb 33, 64–71, 75–78, 81, 89, 96, 111–112, 114, 148–154
Franklin, Benjamin 186
Frege, Gottlob 22, 36, 100
Freidank 135

Freud, Sigmund 196
Fried, Michael 204–206
Friedländer, Paul 43

Gagarin, Juri 184
Galileo, Galilei 5, 128–130, 150
Gauss, Carl Friedrich 105
George, Stefan 17, 20, 23, 24
Glenn, John 184
Goethe, Johann Wolfgang von 4, 64, 103
Gore, Al 182–184
Gropius, Walter 231–232
Guzzoni, Alfredo 87

Habermas, Jürgen 41
Hall, Asaph 121
Hamann, Johann Georg 51
Hartmann, Geoffrey 63
Hartmann, Nicolai 81
Headley, John M. 128, 130
Hegel, Georg Friedrich Wilhelm 46, 64, 131, 224
Heidegger, Martin 1–2, 4–6, 13–25, 28–30, 35–45, 66, 70, 81–88, 92, 95, 111, 114–115, 126–127, 142–147, 172–175, 177–178., 188, 196, 202, 203, 205, 210, 213, 218–226, 232, 234
Henoch 216
Henry III, King of France 132–133
Henry IV, King of France 133
Herder, Johann Gottfried 21, 51, 57
Herrmann, Friedrich Wilhelm von 83
Hertz, Heinrich 100–102, 105, 112
Hesse, Hermann 6, 218
Hickey, Lance 34, 44
Hoelzel, Adolf 4
Hofmannsthal, Hugo von 24–27, 41, 44, 66, 79, 97, 204
Hölderlin, Friedrich 16, 127, 188, 210
Homer 43
Humboldt, Wilhelm von 51, 57
Hume, David 90
Husserl, Edmund 6, 35, 40, 43, 82, 111

Icarus 186, 191, 194, 207–208.
Isaac 140
Itten, Johannes 4

Jacobi, Friedrich Heinrich 34, 71, 74–77, 96, 112, 148, 195
Joachim of Fiore 130, 131
John XXII, Pope 139
Johnson, Samuel 19
Jordan, Pascual 3

Kandinsky, Wassily 4
Kant, Immanuel 1–3, 6, 8, 10, 13, 19, 28–36, 38–42, 44, 46–48, 50–52, 54, 56–60, 66, 68, 74–77, 81, 84, 89–90, 92, 94, 96, 103–111, 113, 121, 128, 140–142, 148–149., 151, 153–160, 162–172, 175, 183, 194, 196–197., 204–205, 209, 214, 222, 225, 227, 234
Kaufmann, Walter 25, 56,
Kiefer, Anselm 207
Kierkegaard, Søren 6, 70, 71, 76, 88–89, 136, 140, 222
Koyré, Alexandre 128, 134
Kožnjak, Boris 151
Kubrick, Stanley 185

Lambert, Johann Heinrich 39, 99, 227
Lamech 216, 218, 231
Laplace, Pierre-Simon, Marquis de 150–151.
Leibniz, Gottfried Wilhelm 97, 110, 160, 165–166, 228
Lessing, Gotthold Dphfraim 54, 74, 131
Lindbeck, George 14
Linnaeus, Carolus 103
Lissitzky, El 207
Litt, Theodor 22, 43
Lobachevsky, Nicolai 105
Loos, Adolf 122
Lorenzen, Paul 212
Lovejoy, Arthur 128
Lucretius 192
Lyotard, Jean-François 203–207

Mackie, John Leslie 93
Malevich, Kasimir 206–207
Manchester, Paula 75
Marx, Karl 131
McDermott, Drew 88–96, 102, 111, 113–114, 148, 152, 155, 158, 195, 196

McLaughlin, Eleanor 136
McMullin, Ernan 108
Mendelssohn, Moses 74
Montgolfier, Jacques Étienne 185
Montgolfier, Joseph Michel 185
Moore, G. E. 67, 70
Musk, Elon 187–189

Nagel, Thomas 43
Napoleon Bonaparte 135
Narcissus 227
Neurath, Otto 90–92, 94, 107
Newton, Isaac 14, 15, 98, 142, 164, 172, 177
Nietzsche, Friedrich 4, 8, 10, 11, 19, 25, 27–30, 32–33, 35, 38, 46–63, 64, 66, 71, 81, 90, 94, 96, 113–114, 119, 120, 122, 124, 134, 150, 182, 189, 195, 201–203, 208, 210, 213, 214, 217, 218, 221, 224–226, 229–232, 234

Ohly, Friedrich 227–228
Orlan, Sainte (Mireille Suzanne Francette Porte) 201, 207, 221
Ortega y Gasset, José 126–127, 203

Panofsky, Erwin 205
Pascal, Blaise 133
Pelagius 163
Perdix 217
Picasso, Pablo 207
Pilâtre de Rozier, Jean François 185–186
Plantinga, Alvin 108
Plato 5, 6, 8, 10, 22–24, 32, 43, 54, 98, 119, 141, 163, 177, 179, 183, 191, 207, 226, 227, 230, 232
Poppe, Wilhelm 190
Posidonius 190
Protagoras 195, 214, 227
Ptolemy 32

Rauschenberg, Robert 207
Reinicke, Helmut 186
Riccardi, Mattia 30
Richter, Gerhard 207
Richter, Jean Paul 71
Rickert, Heinrich 76

Rilke, Rainer Maria 178–182
Robert, Nicolas 185
Romain, Pierre 185
Rousseau, Jean-Jacques 103
Russell, Bertrand 22, 100, 196
Ruysbroeck, John 137

Sartre, Jean-Paul 7, 64, 71, 165
Schiller, Friedrich 10
Schopenhauer, Arthur 4, 19–20, 47, 52, 54, 56, 57, 61, 63, 96, 102, 105, 120–122, 138, 173, 194, 195, 204, 205, 214
Schrader, George A. 6, 183
Sedlmayr, Hans 115, 123, 202
Seeger, Pete 134–135
Sellars, Wilfrid 6
Seuse, Heinrich (Suso) 139
Siger of Brabant 89–90, 160
Simonides 191–192, 194
Socrates 119, 120, 182–183, 193
Spengler, Oswald 195
Spinoza, Baruch 64, 74–76, 81, 97, 148, 152, 165
Stella, Frank 204–207
Stifter, Adalbert 115
Strauss, Richard 79
Sturlese, Loris 139
Szabó, László V 27

Thales 73, 119, 120, 125, 190, 199, 223
Tubal-cain 216–218, 231
Tugendhat, Ernst 35, 40, 42, 43
Turgenev, Ivan 71

Vaucanson, Jacques de 159
Virgil 32, 133
Voltaire 110

Wagner, Richard 230–232
Walther von der Vogelweide 135
Weinreb, Friedrich 216, 218
Whorf, Benjamin 59
Wittgenstein, Ludwig 5, 6, 9, 12, 18, 21, 22, 24, 45, 86, 94, 96–100, 102–105, 108–110, 116, 155, 204, 211, 213

Yates, Frances 130, 131, 133

Zeno 6, 141
Zeus 119

Zillah 216, 218, 228, 230, 231
Zwingli, Huldrych 202

www.ingramcontent.com/pod-product-compliance
Lightning Source LLC
Chambersburg PA
CBHW020644230426

43665CB00008B/313